PENGUIN BOOKS

THE ISLAMIST

Ed Husain was an Islamist radical for five years in his late teens and early twenties. Having rejected extremism he traveled widely in the Middle East and worked for the British Council in Syria and Saudi Arabia. Husain received wide and various acclaim for *The Islamist*, which was shortlisted for the Orwell Prize for political writing and the PEN / Ackerley Prize for literary autobiography, among others. He is a co-founder of the Quillium Foundation, Britain's first Muslim counter-extremism think tank. He lives in London with his wife and daughter.

Praise for *The Islamist*

'*The Islamist* could not be more timely... Husain's is a disturbing picture... In a wake-up call to monocultural Britain, it takes you into the mind of young fundamentalists'   *Observer*

'A courageous memoir... explosive'   *Evening Standard*

'*The Islamist* should be prescribed like medicine. Whatever your prejudices, it will eat into them like acid'   *Daily Telegraph*

'A revealing and alarming account'   *Guardian*

'Gripping... far more than just an arresting testimony of a mind freeing itself from the shackles of extremism. It is an extraordinarily written memoir of growing up in the Eighties and Nineties, with moving family vignettes and lyrical passages... compelling'   *Mail on Sunday*

'The penetrating insight of a former insider . . . A uniquely well-informed guide to the netherworld of British Islamism... a riveting personal narrative'   John Gray, *Literary Review*

'Unique... openly and frankly discusses life inside radical Islamic organizations and crucially reveals important warnings about the future of Islam... It is also a call to ordinary Muslims to reclaim their faith'
Asian Leader

'Explains the appeal of extremism for an intelligent young mind and is an intensely personal protest against political Islam'   *Guardian*

'A shocking exposé of life inside London's spreading Islamist groups'
London Paper

'An impassioned plea for tolerance . . . Anyone interested in how extremist Islam has established its grip on this country should read this insider account from a former radical'   *Metro*

'Provides telling insight'   *Daily Express*

The Islamist

*Why I Became an Islamic Fundamentalist,
What I Saw Inside, and Why I Left*

ED HUSAIN

PENGUIN BOOKS

PENGUIN BOOKS

Published by the Penguin Group

Penguin Group (USA) Inc., 375 Hudson Street, New York, New York 10014, U.S.A.

Penguin Group (Canada), 90 Eglinton Avenue East, Suite 700, Toronto,
Ontario, Canada M4P 2Y3 (a division of Pearson Penguin Canada Inc.)

Penguin Books Ltd, 80 Strand, London WC2R 0RL, England

Penguin Ireland, 25 St Stephen's Green, Dublin 2, Ireland (a division of Penguin Books Ltd)

Penguin Group (Australia), 250 Camberwell Road, Camberwell,
Victoria 3124, Australia (a division of Pearson Australia Group Pty Ltd)

Penguin Books India Pvt Ltd, 11 Community Centre,
Panchsheel Park, New Delhi – 110 017, India

Penguin Group (NZ), 67 Apollo Drive, Rosedale, North Shore 0632,
New Zealand (a division of Pearson New Zealand Ltd)

Penguin Books (South Africa) (Pty) Ltd, 24 Sturdee Avenue,
Rosebank, Johannesburg 2196, South Africa

Penguin Books Ltd, Registered Offices:
80 Strand, London WC2R 0RL, England

First published in Penguin Books (UK) 2007
This edition with a new afterword first published in Penguin Books (USA) 2009

1 3 5 7 9 10 8 6 4 2

All quotations of Rumi are taken from *Rumi: A Spiritual Treasury*,
copyright © Oneworld Publications.

LIBRARY OF CONGRESS CATALOGING IN PUBLICATION DATA
Husain, Ed.
The Islamist : why I became an Islamic fundamentalist, what I saw inside,
and why I left / Ed Husain.—2009 ed., with a new afterword
p. cm.
ISBN 978-0-14-311598-4
1. Husain, Ed. 2. Muslims—Great Britain—Biography.
3. Islamic fundamentalism—Great Britain. 4. Radicalism—Great Britain.
5. Extremists—Great Britain—Biography. I. Title.
BP65.G7H87 2009
320.5′57092—dc22   [B]   2009004575

Printed in the United States of America

for
al–Rasul al–Karim
The Generous Prophet

Contents

Preface   xv

1. Made in England   1

2. Teenage Rebellion   19

3. The Ultimatum   36

4. Islam Is the Solution   48

5. We Will Rule the World   67

6. Inside Hizb ut-Tahrir   83

7. Targeting Communities   111

8. Inferior Others   129

9. Farewell Fanaticism   154

10. Entering the World: Which Life?   165

11. Metamorphosis   185

12. 9/11   200

13. The Road to Damascus   214

14. Saudi Arabia: Where is Islam?   234

15. Return to England   269

    Afterword: What About America?   287

    Acknowledgements   299

Beware of extremism in religion; for it was extremism in religion that destroyed those who went before you.

The Prophet Mohammed (570–632)

The Islamist

Preface

During the course of our lives we all change our views and direction; some of us do so more radically than others. For me, the alteration of my worldview is a troubling tale. The person I now am finds it difficult to recognize the person I once was. Yet, with time and experience, I evolved. As John Maynard Keynes famously quipped, 'When the facts change, I change my mind.'

At times we are victims of our own milieu. Pope Benedict XVI, for a host of reasons, found himself a member of the Hitler Youth. St Paul, a Pharisaic persecutor of Christians, became a believer in Christ and spread the faith into Rome and beyond. Tony Blair, once an ardent activist in the Campaign for Nuclear Disarmament, ended up with his finger on Britain's nuclear trigger.

This book is a protest against political Islam, based on my own experience as a British Muslim who grew up in London, became an extremist – an Islamist – and saw the error of his ways. Having undertaken this journey, I feel it is my human duty to speak out against what I see masquerading in Britain as 'Islam'. The Koran commands Muslims to 'speak the truth, even if it be against your own selves'. It is my hope that this book will fulfil this obligation.

This is the story of my journey from the *inside*, in the fullest sense of the word: inside today's Islam, inside Britain's Muslim communities, inside my own heart.

Mohamed M. Husain
London, 2007

1. Made in England

It is a mark of self-confidence: the English have not spent a great deal of time defining themselves because they haven't needed to. Is it necessary to do so now?

   Jeremy Paxman, British author and broadcaster

My earliest memories are fond recollections of school trips to the green, serene English countryside. I remember the uninhibited joy of walking along the coast in Upnor, being invited aboard cheerful anglers' small boats, and devouring fish and soggy chips together. I recall a visit to the New Forest, removing mud from our Wellington boots at streams, swimming in rivers, and drinking hot chocolate together at night around the hearth of an old, creaky floor-boarded hut. Our teachers would read from Roald Dahl's *Big Friendly Giant* or Kipling's *Jungle Book* and then send us off to sleep for the night in rows of bunk beds inside large wooden dormitories set in a forest clearing. Often Susie Powlesland, our elegant head teacher complete with a disciplinarian streak and half-moon reading glasses, would come to tuck us in, dispensing goodnight kisses as required.

   Sir William Burrough primary school in Limehouse was almost an extension of my home. The teachers would often visit my parents and I remember going to Ms Powlesland's house to pick cherries in her garden. She loved her pupils so much that even her social life revolved around us. At weekends she often took us to theatres in the West End, where many of the stories we read in class came alive on stage. My particular favourite was *Peter Pan*. I liked his ability to do the undoable: to fly.

Growing up in Britain in the 1980s was not easy. Looking back, I think Ms Powlesland was trying to create her own little world of goodwill and kindness for the children in her care. We grew up oblivious of the fact that large numbers of us were somehow different – we were 'Asian'. The warmth of the English fishermen in Upnor did not exist in the streets of east London.

'Pakis! Pakis! F— off back home!' the hoodlums would shout. The National Front was at its peak in the 1980s. I can still see a gang of shaven-headed tattooed thugs standing tall above us, hurling abuse as we walked to the local library to return our books. Ms Powlesland and the other teachers raced to us, held our hands firmly, and roared at the hate-filled bigots.

'Go away! Leave us alone,' they would bellow to taunts of 'Paki lovers' from the thugs. Little did I know then that one day I, too, would be filled with abhorrence of others.

The colour-blind humanity of most of my teachers, strength in the face of tyranny, taught us lessons for the rest of our lives. Britain was our home, we were children of this soil, and no amount of intimidation would change that – we belonged here. And yet, lurking in the background were forces that were preparing to seize the hearts and minds of Britain's Muslim children.

I was the eldest of four, with a younger brother and twin sisters. My father was born in British India, my mother in East Pakistan,* and we children in Mile End. My father arrived in England as a young man in 1961 and spent his early days as a restaurateur in Chertsey, Surrey. In ethnic terms I consider myself Indian, lamenting the hasty post-colonial blunder of creating two Pakistans. Somewhere in my family line there is also Arab ancestry; some say from Yemen and others the Hijaz, a mountainous tract of land along the Red Sea coast in Arabia.

---

*Now Bangladesh.

This mixed heritage of being British by birth, Asian by descent, and Muslim by conviction was set to tear me apart in later life.

I remember my father used to buy us fresh cakes from a Jewish baker in Brick Lane. Our Koran school building had inherited mezuzahs on the door panels, which our Muslim teachers forbade us from removing out of respect for Judaism. My birthday, a family event at our home, is on Christmas Day. My mother would take us to see Santa Claus every year after the school Christmas party. We made a snowman in our garden, lending it my mother's scarf. Opposite our childhood home in Limehouse, a three-storey Victorian terrace, stood Our Lady Immaculate Catholic church with a convent attached. We were friends of the sisters; our car was parked beside the nunnery every night. We helped out in the church's annual jumble sale. There was never any question of religious tension, no animosity between people of differing faiths. My mother still speaks fondly of her own childhood friends, many of whom were Hindu. But as I grew older, all that changed. The live-and-let-live world of my childhood was snatched away.

School was the centre of my life. Our days were filled with painting, drawing, reading, writing practice, physical exercise, mathematics, setting the tables for lunch, playing. To instil confidence in us to stand up to the National Front bullies Ms Powlesland had even organized martial arts classes three evenings a week.

Personally, I did not particularly enjoy sparring with others, nor was I particularly good at making hum-hoo noises before landing a punch on my opponent's hardened stomach. Still, every two months we entered karate competitions in Soho, where masters from Japan tested our combat skills against other, mostly British, candidates. Thanks to Ms Powlesland and my parents' insistence, I progressed through the ranks and obtained a brown belt.

The Sir William Burrough was a magnet for middle-class

liberals who wanted to teach in London's East End. They came to give us a helping hand in life and, judging by the enthusiasm they exhibited, I think they rather enjoyed being with us. But all was not well all of the time.

There was Mr Fowler, the school caretaker, who clearly loved his on-site accommodation but loathed the increasing number of Asian children who were filling his school. And there was Mr Coppin.

It was a school rule that each term we were divided into dining groups of six; we lunched together and laid the table on a rota system. One day I forgot that it was my turn to help set the cutlery. Mr Coppin, moustachioed and blue-eyed, came into the dining hall and grabbed me by the arm. Taking me aside, he lowered his face to mine and yelled, 'Why didn't you set the table?'

'I forgot, Mr Coppin,' I whimpered.

'Forgot? How dare you forget?' he shouted, his hands resting on his knees. 'You're in trouble, young man! Do you understand?'

'Yes, Mr Coppin,' I said.

Then he said something that I have never forgotten. Of me, a nine-year-old, he asked, 'Where is your Allah now then, eh? Where is he? Can't he help you?'

What was he talking about? I wondered. What did Allah have to do with it? Besides, I did not even know precisely who Allah was. I knew Allah was something to do with Islam, but then I also wondered if Islam and Aslan from *The Lion, the Witch, and the Wardrobe* were in any way linked. After Mr Coppin's outburst, I thought it wiser not to ask.

Months before I left Sir William Burrough I had an accident on the school playground. I fell off a bike and cut my chin. Immediately Cherie, a teacher in whose classroom proudly hung a photo of her standing beside a waxwork of Margaret Thatcher at Madame Tussauds, rushed to help me. She drove me to hospital and held my hand throughout the entire ordeal of stitches and aftercare. As we stepped out of the hospital building she asked me if I wanted a piggy back. Thinking it was some sort of boiled sweet, I happily agreed.

Then, to my bewilderment, she went down on all fours and told me to climb on. I still remember her straightening her dungaree straps, and pushing back her glasses before taking off with me, an eleven-year-old Asian boy with a huge plaster on his chin, clinging on for dear life. Cherie drove me home and showered me with love and care in the days that followed.

That experience with Cherie, a white, non-Muslim teacher, and the commitment of Ms Powlesland and her staff to me and other pupils at Sir William Burrough stayed in my mind. It helped me form a belief in Britain, an unspoken appreciation of its values of fairness and equality. It would take me more than a decade to understand what drove Ms Powlesland and Cherie. I was fortunate to have such marvellous teachers at such a young age. For later in life, when I doubted my affinity with Britain, those memories came rushing back.

My parents were strong believers in single-sex education; Ms Powlesland was adamantly opposed to it. She spent hours trying to explain to my parents that I should be sent to a co-educational secondary school. She visited us at home one evening and tried to persuade my parents that attending Stepney Green, the nearest boys' school, was not right for me.

'He's an intelligent boy,' she said. 'Send him to a better school.'

'Stepney Green is a boys-only school. He will be able to study without distractions. The other schools are mixed and I don't think that is a conducive environment for education,' my father responded.

They spoke for a long time, and the more Ms Powlesland tried to prevail on my parents, the deeper they dug in their heels.

Stepney Green school was a twenty-minute walk from my home in Limehouse. In the summer of 1987 my father taught me how to tie a knot for my smart school tie, polish my shoes well, and walk upright in a blazer. He drove me to the school and we went inside the large assembly hall. The sizeable space was filled with hundreds of chairs in straight rows, occupied by young Asian boys in elegant uniforms. I had never seen so many Asian adolescents together in one place.

The white teachers, mostly men, were huddled in a corner waiting to welcome the new intake. Looking around me, I wished I was back at Sir William's. At Sir William's my classmates included Jane, Lisa, Andrew, Mark, Alia, Zak. Here everyone was Bangladeshi, Muslim, and male.

A few weeks into term I realized I was hopeless at taking notes from a blackboard. Soon it was discovered that I was short sighted and needed glasses.

I went with my mother to a local optician and she ensured I got a pair I liked and felt confident wearing. I was fond of my new specs, they reminded me of Professor Calculus from the *Adventures of Tintin*. My self-admiration did not last long.

At school, the boys shouted 'Glass Man' at me, and soon, 'Boffin'. My first year at school was the worst year of my life. Unhappy and with hardly any friends, I became withdrawn and very introverted. I would talk quietly to myself most of the time. When I discovered Kevin Arnold from *The Wonder Years*, I drew comfort from the fact that here was another kid who always stood out from the crowd and talked to himself. Nevertheless I hated going to school.

As time went by, things got worse. Many of my fellow pupils were new arrivals from Bangladesh who spent their entire weekends watching melodramatic Indian films, filling their minds with tales of Bollywood romance and heroism. On Monday mornings they would talk noisily about actors and actresses whose names I had never heard. They would sing love songs in Hindi. Many of the boys spoke about their experiences in Bangladesh before they arrived in Britain. They lived in council flats and many were neighbours. In contrast, I was tucked away with news-watching parents in a Victorian terrace in Limehouse. I could not relate to the boys and they knew I did not fit in.

I tried to do well at school. My mother helped me with my homework and was as supportive as possible. At school, how-ever, chaos soon reigned. Discipline became a real issue both in and out of class.

The new head sacked an African teacher from Kenya, only to see the teacher hold demonstrations in the playground with his tutorial group demanding that he be reinstated. He held after-school protest meetings outside the school gates which led to mounted police patrols designed to keep him and his students out.

In a nasty but unrelated turn of events the school annexe was torched one weekend. All the boys knew who had burnt down our classroom but no one dared speak. The local youth gangs in Stepney would 'knife us'. Gang warfare between Asian youths in Stepney and those in other areas increased. Stabbings became widespread. Tabloid newspapers, I remember, dubbed Stepney Green the 'worst school in Britain'. Teachers were embarrassed to say they worked there.

I stopped wearing my glasses, which meant I was useless in class as well as at football and rugby. I developed a loathing for sports. But at least I was no longer 'Glass Man' or 'Boffin'. I moved between different circles of 'friends', never quite settling down with any one group. The emerging Asian gangs in the East End had an impact on our school. Many of the boys had an affiliation of sorts to the Brick Lane Mafia or the rival Cannon Street Posse, the Stepney Green Posse or the Bow Massive. I had to choose among these, but how could I?

Gang involvement meant playing truant regularly, meeting

up after school, hanging out together at the weekends, wearing leather jackets, smoking cigarettes, growing your hair long, and being on standby to back up a fellow gang member if attacked. None of these things was possible for me: my parents would not have accepted such behaviour. Besides, I lived in Limehouse – what business did I have in Brick Lane? Or Bow? How would I explain such excursions to my father?

Uncommitted, I continued to be a loner at school, occasionally bullied, frequently sworn at, and regularly ignored in most classes. How I yearned to be back at Sir William Burrough.

My parents ran a very tight ship at home. We were an extremely close family, not particularly wealthy, nor especially poor. Like most families in Britain in the 1980s, we could not afford foreign holidays.

I think my parents eventually realized that choosing Stepney Green had been a mistake. And they were keen to compensate. Every summer my father took us to visit family and friends in Birmingham and Manchester. Occasionally he gave us tours of London, explaining the historical significance of the Tower of London, the Palace of Westminster, St Paul's Cathedral. But a place of pride for my father was the residence of Mahatma Gandhi in Bromley-by-Bow. Whenever we passed Kingsley Hall, about two miles from where we lived, my father would point to the blue plaque which marked Gandhi's stay in London, where he trained to become a barrister.

My father's second favourite was Winston Churchill's statue on the green across from the House of Commons. Although Gandhi and Churchill were bitterly opposed in their vision for India, my father admired both men's tenacity and leadership skills. In our car the radio was permanently tuned to Radio 4. On the hour, every hour, Dad would listen to the news. His concern with current affairs left an indelible mark on me.

My father's intellectual preoccupations were not limited to

history and politics. A key part of his life, from a very young age, had been religion. He often told me that his family, particularly on his mother's side, were pious, saintly individuals. His maternal uncle had been a disciple of a famous sage from Badrpur, a district in the Indian province of Assam. Following in his footsteps, my father had met and committed himself to a famous *pir*, or spiritual master, from the India–Bangladesh border region of Sylhet. This *pir*, Shaikh Abd al-Latif, was also a theologian and had studied the Koran in Mecca. He was famed in the Indian subcontinent not by his own name, but by the designation of his home village, Fultholy. Out of veneration, his followers did not call him by his name but, in the Indian tradition, Fultholy Saheb.

Once a year since 1976 the shaikh from Fultholy had been visiting Britain. The shaikh was a master of five Muslim mystical orders, as well as the founder of over 400 religious seminaries in India and Bangladesh. My father was a fervent disciple and had learnt much from his spiritual guide.

In many ways he was like a father figure to my parents. He was softly spoken and always looked down when he walked, treading gently on the earth. He had a sturdy frame, light-brown skin, and a grey beard. He was in his seventies when I first met him as a child. He had blessed me by putting food in my mouth while my mother stood by and said, 'This is your Grandpa.'

I liked Grandpa. Most of all, I used to delight in watching him slowly tie his turban, wrapping his head with a long piece of cloth, as befitted a humble Muslim, though he also seemed like a Mogul monarch. (Muslim scholars and kings both wore the turban in veneration of the Prophet Mohammed.)

Whenever Grandpa visited Britain to teach Muslims about spirituality, my father accompanied him to as many places as he was able. My father believed that spiritual seekers did not gain knowledge from books alone, but learnt from what he called *suhbah*, or companionship. True mastery of spirituality required being at the service, or at least in the presence, of a noble guide. Grandpa was one such guide. I often asked if I could join my father, but he said no; he wanted me to stay in school.

He had been to see my head of year and returned home, trying to persuade me to concentrate on my studies. I tried, but failed. In morning assemblies we sat in rows while others ran past us out of the school, off for a day's shoplifting in Oxford Street. Merchandise was on offer the following day at unfeasibly low prices. Our teachers stood and watched, uninterested and unable to do anything. How could I learn? What was I to learn?

During the summer holidays of 1989 I joined Grandpa and his entourage of disciples on a week-long trip to Birmingham. His visits to us at home had been brief, but now I was able to observe him closely during long motorway journeys and on trips between mosques or to visit the sick. Grandpa was a tranquil, sombre, even serious man. He was not given to excessive talk or loud laughter. Ceaselessly he would read books on religion, poetry, history, mysticism, biographies of the Prophet in Urdu and Arabic. Occasionally he would come across a riveting point and then share it with those who were travelling with him.

He often read aloud in Urdu, and explained his points in intricate Bengali, engaging the minds of others while I looked on bewildered. As they compared notes on abstract subjects in impenetrable languages, I buried myself in *Inspector Morse* or a Judy Blume. I heard names such as 'Mawdudi' being severely criticized, an organization named Jamat-e-Islami being re-futed and invalidated on theological grounds. All of it was beyond me.

In Birmingham Grandpa gave me his books to carry. Others smiled at me. To carry Grandpa's books was considered an honour, a blessing. There were more such blessings to come. More than anybody, my parents were proud that I now carried books for their *pir*.

His days were full. He was invited by Muslims for breakfast, lunch, tea, and dinner. I carried his books and went with him. Occasionally he would look back, smile, and ask for a book, which I would gladly pass, using both my hands as a mark of respect.

One evening, during a quiet moment, he looked at me and asked me to recite from the Koran. I looked back at him nonplussed. I had attended Koran classes at weekends, and studied with my mother at home, but not with any particular intention to recite in public. But the Koran is not a mere reading text; it is to be recited, and this requires honing all sorts of verbal skills and an understanding of *tajwid*, the art of Koranic recital.

I mustered up my energy and read three very short verses. Grandpa listened patiently and smiled.

'Whenever you visit me,' he said, 'please recite to me and I will help you improve.'

Throughout the rest of our trip I often recited the Koran to Grandpa. I sat before him with an Arabic Koran, skullcap on my head, cross-legged on the floor. I would read aloud and he would close his eyes meditatively. Occasionally he would open them and correct my pronunciation, elongation, word stress, or intonation. Then, he would allocate new readings to me by reciting first with perfect *tajwid*, which he had learnt in Mecca, and I would read after him.

I learnt much from his silence, his focus, respect, and love for the Koran. More than anything else I loved being the centre of this holy man's attention for even half an hour a day.

I grew to love him, and he me. My mother had told me stories of the Prophet Mohammed and how he loved his two grandsons, Hasan and Husain, and they in turn loved him to the extent that they would climb onto his shoulders, kissing and hugging him while he led the believers in prayer. I experienced something of the Prophet's love for his grandchildren, as taught me by my mother, in the way Grandpa treated me.

Back in London, I visited Grandpa as often as possible. Now, in addition to undisturbed private Koran classes, I joined him and his large group of disciples on Thursday evenings in what they called *dhikr*. A group of people would sit on the floor and chant Arabic names of God repeatedly for up to an hour, often with the lights switched off. In the dark they sat and concentrated on God in the presence of their spiritual master. These gatherings were often in the Brick Lane mosque. But though I was there because of Grandpa, I often sneaked away. I was fourteen. I had no understanding of what was going on except that there were echoes of 'A-l-l-a-h' 'A-l-l-a-h' in a pitch-dark prayer hall in Brick Lane.

In those days the Brick Lane mosque still had pews on the first floor, a remnant of its 1740s construction as a chapel by French Huguenots, an earlier immigrant community. Then it became a synagogue for east European Jews in the nineteenth century and, finally, a mosque for recently arrived Muslims from Southeast Asia.

Grandpa had a large following around Brick Lane. Many of the mosque leaders, imams, and members of the congregation were his *murids*, or disciples. While he led his students in remembrance of God, I wandered around upstairs scribbling 'I woz ere' in the grime on the unused pews. Towards the end of the *dhikr*, the imam of the mosque, or another one of Grandpa's students, would recite from memory in Arabic the life of the Prophet Mohammed. This was known as a *mawlid*, a recalling of the miracles prior to and on the day of the Prophet's birth in seventh-century Mecca. At the end of the *mawlid* the entire gathering would stand and sing greetings to the Prophet, hoping to invoke his spiritual presence. This standing and singing in Arabic was something I enjoyed; I would run down and sing to my heart's content. I relished the tune and melody, although understanding very little. At the *mawlid* there was always an ambience that made most of us feel as one, united in purpose, standing and singing in praise of the Prophet.

My father would organize an annual *mawlid* gathering in our home, invite his friends and Koran reciters who would sing songs of praise, chant biographical details, then rise to their feet and to the most melodious, heart-warming tune sing the chorus of:

> *Ya Nabi Salam 'Alayka* (O Prophet, Peace unto You)
> *Ya Rasul Salam 'Alayka* (O Apostle, Peace unto You)
> *Ya Habeeb Salam 'Alayka* (O Beloved, Peace unto You)
> *Salawathu Allah 'Alayka* (The Prayers of God upon You)

Often frankincense would be burning and the fragrance would fill the air. Many would close their eyes in deep contemplation. I recall peeping at the standing adults and pondering. Their humility and tears of joy were unbounded. I later learnt that the lovers of the Prophet expected, indeed often experienced, the Prophet's spiritual presence in these gatherings.

The *dhikr* and *mawlid* gatherings I attended were organized for Grandpa by his students. Afterwards they served dinner. Grandpa was invited by all sorts of people, rich and poor: imams, businessmen, teachers, doctors, restaurateurs, cab drivers. He always started his meal with a prayer and shared his food with others. He never ate alone, always with a group. I had no inkling that his conduct was based wholly on the lifestyle and teachings of his beloved, the Arabian Apostle of God, Mohammed.

In the summer of 1989, and again in 1990, I joined Grandpa touring cities where he had large groups of devotees. He tirelessly visited people's homes, helping the sick, comforting the bereaved, praying for the broken-hearted, and writing amulets for those who sought them for blessings. I continued studying with him and my recitation of the Koran improved. My pronunciation of difficult Arabic was perfected by Grandpa. In later life this was to hold me in excellent stead among Arabs in the Middle East.

Grandpa now thrust me into the public realm. In mosques across Britain, before he addressed large crowds of first-generation immigrant Muslims from the Indian subcontinent, mainly Bangladesh, he asked me to recite from the Koran.

The first time he called on me to recite, at a mosque in Cardiff, my legs went weak as I took the microphone. But as Grandpa smiled and patted my back in encouragement I felt an inner strength to continue and conjured up courage – I wanted to show Grandpa that his patience and hard work had yielded results. I recited five verses from memory. To hear my amplified voice booming through the speakers was a most unnerving experience, but with Grandpa beside me, I knew I would be fine.

In mosques from Birmingham to Brighton, St Albans to Swansea, I stood up and warmed the hearts of worshippers to the Koran, melodiously reciting with well-tuned *tajwid*. In many ways, I suppose I was a sort of Muslim choirboy.

My parents were extremely proud to see their son doing so well in Muslim circles. For me, there was more to my travels with Grandpa than studying Koran recitation. I mingled with first-generation Muslim elders up and down Britain. I carried Grandpa's books and sometimes his humble, untied turban while he was rushed from house to house, mosque to mosque, teaching, preaching, praying, blessing, and advising. In city after city I witnessed people sit at his feet, men and women, and vow allegiance to God, taking the *bai'ah*. This was a form of repentance, followed by initiation into Grandpa's branch of mysticism, and through Grandpa to the Prophet Mohammed, and ultimately to God. Day after day I watched Grandpa gently close his eyes and remove his turban, and with his head humbly covered with a Muslim skullcap, hold out his loose turban to those before him, and, in a mixture of Arabic and Urdu, help them repent and swear faithfully to uphold God's commands.

He would then, almost always, shed tears with his hands raised to heaven.

I still remember the words of advice he always gave to his new initiates, or *murids*. He would teach them daily Koranic litanies and then advise them to do two things. First, to pray as though they saw God. They were to prostrate themselves and bow during prayer to show peace and humility. This, he explained, brought inner tranquillity to the life of a believer. Second, and key, was to avoid envy and jealousy of others who were doing better in life. 'Be happy for people when you see them advance,' he would say. 'Pray that God gives them more. Do not harbour jealousies for it will cloud your life with darkness.'

Observing Grandpa and his spiritual constancy gave me a better understanding of who God, Allah, was. If Mr Coppin had cornered me now and shouted, 'Where is Allah now then, eh?' I would have said, 'In my heart, accompanying me, strengthening me against the tyranny that is you.' Based on the teachings of the Prophet Mohammed, Grandpa taught me that 'God is as His servant perceives him to be. If a servant perceives God to be close, then God is so. If God is seen as remote, then God is so.' Grandpa's mission in life was to take God's creation closer to God.

I thoroughly enjoyed these trips, visiting hundreds of Muslim homes, seeing different mosques in different cities, as well as making detours to English heritage sites. I loved the food that people offered Grandpa and those who accompanied him. I savoured the long journeys, usually in luxurious cars. Most of all, I enjoyed the private lessons.

All of this was teaching me about a mainstream, moderate Muslim ethos rooted not in Britain but in the eastern Muslim tradition of seeking guidance and religious advice from an elderly sage. I was learning to be an erudite Muslim; Grandpa and his disciples instilled in me a certain way of being gentle and

God-revering. We prayed five times a day, kept the company of a holy man who healed people's hearts, and moved among the Muslim masses teaching spirituality and devotional growth. I had not only learnt my religion from books, but seen it in action in a man who took his faith from nineteenth-century Indian sages, who had taken it from those who preceded them, and so on back to the Prophet Mohammed.

In the summer of 1990 my father invited Grandpa to stay with us while he was in London. My parents were overjoyed when he accepted. I was now fifteen and in my final year at school, so could not travel as much as I had done previously. I was to sit my GCSEs, for which I had not prepared in the least. For me there were other, more important developments.

Saddam Hussein, the former Iraqi president, had invaded his small neighbour, Kuwait. Grandpa would return home every night and ask me for the latest news. The first time he asked, I had no idea where Iraq was located on the map, let alone what its leader had done.

Very quickly I sharpened up my geography of the Middle East. But that was not enough. The following day he asked me how the international community had responded. What was going on at the UN? What were other Arab governments saying? Astounded, I wondered how I was supposed to know. But I knew I *had* to know. Pleading ignorance was not an option.

I grabbed pen and paper and started watching news bulletins in the mornings and afternoons. I took copious notes. I did this for about five months while Grandpa stayed with us, providing him with the details of Saddam's rhetoric, Tareq Aziz's interviews and John Simpson's bomb-ducking analyses. I told him about George Bush's remarks, Norman Schwarzkopf's peace deals, and Colin Powell's press briefings. Before my sixteenth birthday my father's interest in current affairs and Grandpa's delegation of news monitoring to me meant that I had become politicized. Grandpa always listened to everything I said very carefully. His concern had always been for the innocent people caught up in the war, and for the tombs of revered saints in Baghdad, many from his own spiritual order.

That year I grew extremely close to Grandpa and his family. His two sons had joined him on that trip, and they stayed with us too. Grandpa often returned home late from his duties, but was awake long before sunrise, locked away in his room, only silence and the occasionally creaking floorboard indicating that he was awake: bowing, prostrating, reciting. We all knew he was not to be disturbed – he was with his Lord.

When Grandpa left later that year after a long tour of Britain my family went to see him off at the airport. As a parting gift he gave me a small bottle of perfume that he periodically applied in remembrance of the Prophet.

As he approached the departure gates at Heathrow a crowd of his devotees surrounded him for a last blessing, a touch, a farewell. I kept at a distance, not comfortable with the pushing and shoving. He raised his head and saw me standing in a corner. He beckoned me towards him. I rushed over, as the elders made way, and embraced him. I felt a tremor in his body and knew he was crying. An overpowering wave of emotion overcame me; perhaps I would never see him again. He was now nearly eighty years old, increasingly frail, and unlikely to visit Britain again. Amid a crowd of grown men sobbing, women weeping, children crying, he wiped his tears and headed back to his village.

Two weeks later Grandpa's youngest son, a Dhaka-based journalist we called Uncle Husam, called my parents from Mecca. En route to Fultholy, Grandpa had stopped over at Mecca, Islam's holiest city. Uncle Husam was in total panic. He was desperate to speak to me and establish if I was well. I had no idea why. Baffled, I spoke on the phone, though the echo on the line between Mecca to London made communication almost impossible. My parents gazed at me after the call. *What had I done?*

That night my mother told me that in Mecca Uncle Husam had dreamt that I was sitting on the branch of a large tree. Suddenly, without cause, I fell down and died.

2. Teenage Rebellion

A young boy's company determines his destiny.
  Eastern proverb

At school, I was now even more of a misfit. My classmates had learnt that my father was a close disciple of the sage from Fultholy. I was now perceived as a boffin with connections to an elderly *pir* who went travelling around Britain with unfashionable, religious people. Somehow their approval no longer mattered to me. I knew Grandpa to be a generous, benevolent, worshipful man of God. If the Bollywood-hooked brigade of Bangladeshi boys did not appreciate him, it was their problem, not mine. I became resolute. Besides, I knew my Koranic Arabic better than they did, I was familiar with early Muslim history and had gained a good basic knowledge of Islam. Nevertheless I knew that there remained much more for me to learn.

Keen to know more about my faith, I approached my school's religious education department and asked if I could study Islam and Christianity out of school hours. In those days very few pupils expressed serious interest in study of any sort; the RE teachers were nonplussed. Mrs Rainey, head of the department, kindly volunteered to give twice-weekly extra-curricular tuition to me and another student at her home in Wapping.

I enjoyed studying with Mrs Rainey more than anything else at school. She made it clear to us that she was of the Church of England, but that did not stop us from trying to convert her.

The other student who joined me was Abdullah Falik, whom I slowly got to know well. In line with religious notions of respect I used to call him Brother Falik, while he called me Brother Mohamed.

Brother Falik was a rather serious, observant young Muslim. Every lunchtime he helped rearrange the furniture in a classroom to ensure that other Muslim students could perform their midday prayers. After a while I started to help him in what seemed like a noble task.

I now wanted everything to do with Islam. There was one problem: Grandpa and my parents had taught me by setting an example, by *living* faith. Mrs Rainey taught us with books.

The first book I read about Islam in English was *Islam: Beliefs and Teachings* by Gulam Sarwar. My parents and Grandpa had taught me Islam without books, but via an oral tradition, partly because of a lack of books in English on Islam for children, but also because they believed Islam was an internal condition, to be instilled in human hearts by teachers, not lifted from dry pages. But I had always been an avid reader; and now warmed to the idea of reading about Islam in English. Sarwar's book filled a gap.

At school, Sarwar's was the main textbook for those studying R.E. I set out not only to read it but to ensure that I understood it thoroughly. Whether I succeeded or not, one part of the book has stayed with me.

I had been taught that Islam was a path that would draw me closer to God. During my reports of the political situation in the Middle East, Grandpa had never spoken about an 'Islamic state'. In all his discussions about his most beloved Prophet, Grandpa had never portrayed him merely as a founder of an Islamic state, a political leader. In all the books Grandpa read, the chapters he discussed with his students, he never raised a subject known as 'Islamic politics'. Yet, in Sarwar's book, there was a chapter on the 'Political System of Islam'. From a young age I had been exposed to politics: my father's addiction to the news, Attlee's statue outside my local library, family visits to

Gandhi's Kingsley Hall, discussions about Churchill, and my father's acquaintance with our local MP, Peter Shore, all meant that I had strong political roots. At no time, however, did I hear complaints from the thousands of Muslims I met while travelling with Grandpa about the need for (or the absence of) an 'Islamic state' or a 'political system of Islam'.

The first lines of Sarwar's chapter read:

Religion and politics are one and the same in Islam. They are inter-twined. We already know that Islam is a complete system of life ... Just as Islam teaches us how to pray, fast, pay charity and perform the Haj, it also teaches us how to run a state, form a government, elect councillors and members of parliament, make treaties and conduct business and commerce.

In concluding his introductory chapter Sarwar wrote that there was no Islamic state in the world today in which Islam was a system of government. He commended the efforts of several organizations that were dedicated to the creation of 'truly Islamic states' and mentioned several groups by name, including the Muslim Brotherhood in the Middle East and Jamat-e-Islami in the Indian subcontinent, which were working for the 'establishment of Allah's law in Allah's land'.

Today, in British schools, Sarwar's book continues to be used in RE classrooms. In mosques and Muslim homes across Britain it is promoted as an introductory text for young Muslims. What I did not know at school was that Sarwar was a business manage-ment lecturer, not a scholar of religion. And he was an activist in the organizations that he mentioned. Sarwar's book was not the dispassionate educational treatise it purported to be.

He was also the brains behind the separation of Muslim children from school assemblies into what we called 'Muslim assembly', managed by the Muslim Educational Trust (MET). What seemed like an innocuous body was, in fact, an organization with an agenda. In my school, a Jamat-e-Islami activist named Abdul Rabb represented the MET and awarded us trophies and medals for our performance in MET exams. Ostensibly it all seemed harmless, but the personnel all belonged to Jamat-e-Islami front organizations in Britain. Their key message was that Islam was not merely a religion but also an ideology that sought political power and was beginning to make headway. The spiritual Islam of my parents' generation was slowly giving way to something new.

I, at sixteen, was already wondering why my parents had never spoken about this most important aspect of our religion, the Islamic state. In all my discussion with traditional Muslims during the recent Gulf war, why had no one made it clear that religion and politics are 'one and the same in Islam'? And why had none of us sought to 'establish Allah's law in Allah's land'? And if this was what movements such as the Jamat-e-Islami and the Muslim Brotherhood were aiming to do, well, what was wrong with that?

Sarwar wrote about 'Islamic movements' in the Muslim world as perfectly normal developments. But I recalled Grandpa and his students, many of them clerics trained in madrassas in India and Bangladesh, talking about the Jamat-e-Islami in disparaging terms. I had heard many of these conversations taking place between imams in various towns, and they complained about the increasing influence of Jamat-e-Islami activists in their mosques. They had sought clarity from Grandpa about the nature of the Jamat-e-Islami, and Grandpa had spoken repeatedly about a man named Abul Ala Mawdudi.

Born in 1903, Mawdudi was a Pakistani journalist who translated the Koran according to his own whims, without reference to or within the paradigm of classical Muslim scholarship. He developed and promoted a new brand of Islam, highly politicized and deeply anti-Western. Mawdudi, who died in 1979 during a speaking tour of America, was the first Muslim to reject Islam as a religion and rebrand it as an 'ideology'. This 'ideology', political Islam, was actively propagated by the organization he had started in 1941 in British India: the Jamat-e-Islami. Seeing the name on the pages of my school textbook began to make the Jamat-e-Islami seem respectable. *Perhaps Grandpa was wrong*, I thought.

Brother Falik and I continued to attend classes in the evenings at Mrs Rainey's home. He was always punctual, hard working, and just as committed to being a good Muslim as I was. In fact I thought him a better Muslim, because he was also involved with the Young Muslim Organisation UK (YMO) and spent much of his spare time helping to run events at the East London mosque. While I was busy trying to be a 'good son' to my parents by studying the Koran, helping them with the shopping, and staying away from the gangs, Falik was actively contributing to the Muslim community by organizing football matches, youth camps, and study circles.

At school we became closer. I learnt that Falik had recently completed the Haj and that his father had passed away, leaving him to care for his mother. Like me, he prayed regularly. Like me, he was a misfit at school. Together, we started to assert a new identity: we were young, Muslim, studious, and London born. We were not immigrants and neither understood the mentality of our peers who reminisced about their villages in Bangladesh, nor shared their passion for Bollywood actresses. At lunch Falik and I would take turns to lead the other boys in prayer. After a while I mentioned my new friend to my parents.

Falik used to wear a black and white chequered scarf. While preparing my reports for Grandpa during the 1990–91 Gulf war I remembered seeing Yasser Arafat wearing a similar scarf: Bedouin headgear conveniently appropriated as a symbol of Palestinian resistance against Israeli occupation. When I bought my own scarf, my father was puzzled.

'What is that?' he asked.

'Brother Falik wears one,' I answered. 'It's to support the Palestinians.'

'How does wearing a scarf support the Palestinians?' he asked, bewildered. 'And who is Brother Falik?'

'He is my friend from school, Dad. He prays regularly, recently did the Haj, and he also attends classes with Mrs Rainey.' I withheld any information about YMO and the East London mosque, knowing instinctively that those names would infuriate my father. The YMO and the East London mosque both venerated Mawdudi and, as a result of Grandpa's teachings, my father loathed anything to do with him. Had my father caught me snorting cocaine he would have found it in him to forgive me, counsel me. But I knew he would not be able to tolerate any association with those he considered enemies of God: Mawdudi's followers, the activists at the East London mosque. Since childhood my father had always taken us to pray at Brick Lane. In many ways, Brick Lane mosque was the rival to the more glamorous, publicity-craving East London, which had received donations from Saudi Arabia, was custom built with minarets and a dome, and employed Saudi-trained imams. Most of its committee members were affiliated to the Jamat-e-Islami.

Throughout the late 1980s, the East London mosque had been the site of conflict between rival factions of the Jamat-e-Islami in Britain (calling themselves Dawatul Islam and Islamic Forum Europe to conceal their extremist connections). Both organizations knew that whoever controlled this strategically placed institution, at the heart of the densest population of Muslims in Britain, would command significant power among Britain's Muslim community. For years the rival factions had been engaged in a bitter and sometimes violent power struggle.

Much of the conflict was to do with provincialism, personality clashes, and financial disputes. Money from Saudi Arabia helped build the East London mosque and its leaders were channelling funds into their organizations and earning salaries as 'ministers of religion' by associating themselves with Saudi Arabia's missionary arm, the Muslim World League. Some of these Saudi stooges came from Sylhet in the east of Bangladesh, others from Noakhali in the south, and the difference in culture often led to personality clashes between key individuals. There were accusations of embezzlement which in 1990 resulted in High Court injunctions against the then imam of the mosque, Abu Syed, and other key Jamat-e-Islami figures. Several organizers at the mosque were imprisoned following violent clashes. The humiliating spectacle of the Metropolitan Police breaking up fights between activists led Jamat-e-Islami from Pakistan and Bangladesh to send leading members from their central executive committee in an attempt to end this shameful exhibition of Islamist infighting. But to no avail. The expelled imam Abu Syed held Friday prayer congregations under police guard outside the mosque for several weeks while his opposition, led by the newly formed Islamic Forum Europe, prayed inside the mosque. (In later years Abu Hamza would follow this precedent, praying outside rather than inside after clashing with the authorities at Finsbury Park mosque.)

All the while, over at Brick Lane, worshippers shook their heads in disgust at Jamat-e-Islami politics being fought out on the streets of Britain. Grandpa's warnings, it seemed, were all too necessary.

'This Falik sounds like a really good young boy,' my father said. 'Perhaps you should invite him round for dinner one night. What do you think?' My father's words surprised me. Since I had left Sir William Burrough I had brought none of my friends home, mainly because they included no one of whom my father would have approved. But Brother Falik was different – as long as I could hide the East London mosque connection.

One evening Falik and I arrived at Mrs Rainey's to find a note on her door saying that she had had to take her cat to the vet.

'Why don't we go to the mosque and study together instead?' asked Falik.

'The mosque' was, of course, the ill-reputed East London. *What would my father say?* Even to set foot inside East London mosque, which was regarded by my family as a centre of political activity for Jamat-e-Islami rather than a place of worship for ordinary Muslims, seemed practically sacrilegious. Then again, I did not want to alienate the first genuine friend I had had in many years.

'All right, then,' I said. 'Let's go.'

As we headed towards Whitechapel Road I confessed to Falik that I had never visited the mosque before. 'We always pray at Brick Lane,' I told him.

'Yes,' he said, in a sympathetic tone. 'The recent violence at the mosque and the High Court case has scared many people away. It's perfectly safe now, you know. I know people in the community speak about the sniffer dogs the police used when they entered the mosque, searching for weapons, but the carpets have been washed since then.'

My friend had just told me more than I knew. I had no idea that police had raided the mosque with sniffer dogs. (I was later told that weapons had been kept there as a precaution against attacks from the rival faction but that, after a tip-off, they were moved to the homes of unsuspecting families in nearby Old Montague Street.)

'But my father's been praying at Brick Lane since well before the violence. He says the mosque is a centre for Jamat-e-Islami, a political organization, not for worship.'

Falik looked at me, bemused.

'You know the Jamat-e-Islami?' he asked, as we walked along.

'Yes. According to my father they're a sinister political organization, use Islam as a political tool and demean the Prophet's original teachings.'

Falik was rather shocked by such blunt accusations. His older brother was a member of Jamat-e-Islami and, as far as he could make out, they were upright Muslims trying to 'bring Islam' to Pakistan, Bangladesh, India, and Sri Lanka. Perhaps I should meet some people from the organization and decide for myself, he suggested.

For me, that was an acceptable answer. Now I could discover at first hand whether Jamat-e-Islami did indeed loathe Muslim saints, denigrate the Prophet, and want to politicize Islam.

That evening, inside enemy territory, I was given VIP treatment. My schoolmate, it transpired, was extremely well connected. He knew all the movers and shakers behind the office walls of the East London mosque. Most worshippers removed their shoes and put them on rails adjacent to the main prayer hall; I was privileged, along with Brother Falik, to put my shoes behind closed doors in an area reserved for activists of the YMO and the Islamic Forum Europe.

Falik rang the mosque's security buzzer and we were admitted without interrogation. Inside the mosque the atmosphere was incomparably different from Brick Lane. There I was a young boy, in my father's shadow; here the place was buzzing with young, trim-bearded, English-speaking activists. There were no sombre and elderly worshipful Muslims in these offices – pious Muslims belonged only in the prayer hall – rather a sense of organization and discipline; everybody seemed to know their place.

Falik introduced me to no fewer than fifteen people that night, some set to emerge as national 'moderate' Muslim leaders in the years that followed. Almost without exception they took an interest in me, my studies, my family, and my future plans. I could relate to them. I respected them for their seniority, dynamism and commitment to Islam. They seemed like worthy role models: English-speaking, educated, and rooted in faith.

I felt that I could easily become part of this highly organized robust network of brothers who led a mosque-centred life. At Brick Lane mosque the elders only stroked my head to acknowledge me. It was my father they engaged with; I was merely his little boy. The people here were interested in *me*. To an isolated schoolboy, that mattered.

Brother Falik showed me round the mosque. I was most impressed with the prayer area for women, neatly tucked away behind curtains on the top floor. Over at Brick Lane women were forbidden to enter the mosque; that this was not the case at East London seemed like feminist progress.

Then Falik showed me the mosque bookshop. He warned me that the small shop was controlled by the rival Dawatul Islam, and that I should refuse to buy anything from it. A boycott would soon put them out of business, he explained, although their lease was due to expire soon anyway and Islamic Forum Europe, who now controlled the mosque, would refuse to renew it.

I was startled by this unexpected display of rancour and animosity from my trusted friend. We ended the evening with the last congregational prayer of the day, the *Esha*. While most of the worshippers performed their ablution in a large washing area in the basement of the mosque, I, with Brother Falik, again had the privilege of using a different area reserved for mosque activists. I felt very special.

In the prayer hall there were more differences from my father's mosque. At Brick Lane we all wore skullcaps, similar to the Jewish *keppeh* but white rather than black. Muslims wear skull-caps in remembrance of the Prophet Mohammed, and other prophets who went before him, as a sign of humility. But I had left my cap at home, thinking I was attending an RE lesson. How could I pray without one?

Then, as the young activists I had met earlier stood to pray, I saw that their heads were bare. This came as a shock to me, but I reasoned that if they, in their twenties, surely knowing more than I did, and well versed in their religion, could pray without covering their heads, then so could I. What did it matter?

That was my first act of rebellion. I prayed that evening with confidence, with a feeling of difference, of greater ease. And free from the need to ruin my carefully arranged hairstyle.

The East London mosque was more than a place of worship. It housed the infrastructures of activist organizations, hosted meetings and weddings, and offered other facilities for the local community. The prayer hall was for worshippers, the offices were for the many voluntary managers of the mosque who were from Jamat-e-Islami. They referred to themselves as the 'mosque committee', elected not by the worshippers but by a group of selected individuals known as 'members'. I later learnt that leading managers of the mosque such as Dr Abdul Bari and Chowdhury Mueen Uddin★ did not live in Tower Hamlets but in Haringey. Their control of the mosque came from their allegiance to Jamat-e-Islami, not as local Muslims.

Back at school Brother Falik and I continued to hold and lead midday prayers, with help from other students. And at home my father occasionally asked how my friend was doing. He continued to ask me to invite him and I kept delaying. 'I'll do it in the summer holidays,' I said.

Meanwhile, Mrs Rainey's husband, who was in the army, had returned from a posting abroad and she could no longer teach us after school. Instead I spent time at the East London

---

★Dr Bari later became a leader of the Muslim Council of Britain, while chair of the East London mosque and Islamic Forum Europe. Mueen Uddin chaired Muslim Aid and manages Islamist events and leaders from behind the scenes, occasionally stepping into the limelight.

mosque, hanging out with 'brothers' from the YMO and Islamic Forum Europe.

I left my parents under the impression that I was still studying with Mrs Rainey every Wednesday evening while I went with Falik to the Fieldgate Street offices of the YMO, manned voluntarily by its members. We would phone individuals on our contacts list and invite them to YMO events, ensure the office was tidy, and help with the accounts – all members of YMO paid a monthly subscription to illustrate their commitment.

In the room next door there were meetings of the Central Executive Committee of the YMO, an all-male gathering of long-time activists. The Central Executive Committee organized youth camps, national football tournaments, and fundraising events for the mosque, thereby maintaining a tight grip on the lives of its members. My Wednesday evenings taught me much about the organization and the tight-knit community surrounding East London mosque. I looked forward to my visits and quickly became familiar with leaders of the YMO such as Siraj Salekin, Mosaddeq Ahmed, and Habibur Rahman.

The person I warmed to most was Siraj Salekin, whom I had seen at school careers advisory sessions and at other community events in Toynbee Hall in Aldgate. As a youth worker he had a high profile in the locality and the more I saw him, the more he acted as my mentor. He gave me small gifts, memorabilia from his trips to Bangladesh. I was genuinely impressed by his tender and brotherly behaviour. I was the eldest child in my family, with no older sibling to look up to. Brother Siraj quickly filled that void. As the weeks passed by he gave me lifts home and took an interest in those I loved most: my parents. Had Siraj, a seasoned activist of Mawdudi's form of political Islam, realized that the way to a potential recruit's heart was through his family?

Falik never openly tried to recruit me to what was increasingly referred to as the 'Islamic movement', an array of organizations ideologically linked to Mawdudi. However, as I spent more time in the company of activists from the movement, the questions in my mind started to trouble me deeply. Ours was an open family, we ate together, spoke about almost everything without reservation, and yet I was betraying my parents, beginning to lead a double life. I wanted to tell my father about my new companions at the East London mosque, the YMO, but I could not. I had made friends there whom I did not want to lose. I knew my father would challenge my new beliefs, so I wrote the leaders of the YMO a letter. I sought clarity on what they thought about the arch enemy of traditional Muslims, their founder, Abul Ala Mawdudi. I asked what they thought about famed saints across the Muslim world, including Grandpa. I asked why traditional Muslims accused Jamat-e-Islami and its offshoots, such as the YMO, of denigrating the Prophet Mohammed.

I sealed my four-page letter in an envelope and gave it to Falik to pass to the Central Executive Committee, hopeful of receiving a written response which I could show to my father, even Grandpa if need be, proving that there clearly had been some misunderstanding.

A few days later Falik informed me that Siraj Salekin would like to see me. The following Wednesday, with Falik in tow, I met Siraj at Fieldgate Street in a small, threadbare-carpeted room in which stood a desk and telephone, several chairs, and a corner bookshelf stacked with English books. He went through my letter, thanking me for asking such detailed questions and wondering how I knew about Mawdudi, Jamat-e-Islami, and, most of all, who had taught me. I answered honestly, telling him about my time with Grandpa and the spiritual Islam practised by my parents.

He told me how he had family members who admired Grandpa, and how he had no problems with the spiritual form of Islam taught at Brick Lane, but he preferred an 'Islam that was a complete code of life'. To his credit, Siraj admitted that he did not know much about mystical orders of the Muslim world.

He also said he knew Jamat-e-Islami leaders at first hand and they were not the corrupt, politicized deviants most Muslims labelled them but were decent, morally upright workers of the Islamist movement. On the subject of denigrating the Prophet, he seemed genuinely shocked that the YMO could be accused of such a thing. I said that Mawdudi had compiled unauthorized, amateur exegetical works; that he had made serious mistakes. Siraj pointed to four volumes of Mawdudi's exegesis and said, 'Please show us where the mistakes are and we will change them. Also, we don't think Mawdudi was perfect, he made mistakes. You can disagree with Mawdudi, and yet join the Islamic movement. Our aim is to change the Muslims, to make them live Islam as a complete code of life, not as a mere religion. Islam is more than a religion. We want to see Islamic government, Islam taken out of mosques and homes, and into all areas of life.'

I liked Brother Siraj's open-door policy, his willingness to be critical of Mawdudi. He invited me to attend their weekly meetings on Saturday evenings, known as *taleemi jalsa*, and ask any questions I wanted. The YMO had given me friends, a place in the world. Now, as they had answered my questions, their place in my heart was confirmed. At the time, as a result of the months-long violence in one of Britain's largest mosques, the YMO had gained a reputation in Tower Hamlets and beyond as being tougher than the toughest gangsters. The Brick Lane Mafia, Cannon Street Posse, and Bethnal Green Massive shrank to the stature of playground bullies when compared with the rising star of the YMO. YMO had several members in prison. They won fights, deployed kung-fu experts in the mosque hall, defied the police, and were 'bad boys', too. They just liked to call themselves 'practising Muslims'. YMO football tournaments were renowned for mid-game interruptions to perform prayers. In their ranks they had martial-arts experts such as the locally well-known Abjol (now a Respect Party councillor in Tower Hamlets). They were as bad and cool as the other street gangs, just without the drugs, drinking, and womanizing.

At school Falik and I were now openly known as brothers from the YMO. After five years, I had found both a friend and a cause to which I belonged.

My GCSE exams faded further into insignificance as I became involved in organizing a national youth camp at Gilwell Park in Essex. We produced T-shirts, put up posters in Muslim areas of London, persuaded parents to encourage their children to attend our events. I took particular pride in ensuring that there were several posters on the doors of Brick Lane mosque. Where others respected the rivalry between East London and Brick Lane, I was now keen to bring my father's mosque, or at least its younger worshippers, over to the Islamist movement. And I began to lie to my parents a little more.

I told my father that I wanted to revise for my GCSEs with Falik and that there was a good revision programme at East London mosque on Saturday nights. My parents were hesitant about the benefits of revising for school exams at a political centre, but somehow, reluctantly, my father agreed that I could go.

I still remember my very first *taleemi jalsa*. It was not in the main hall of the mosque but in a large rectangular room with green carpet. About fifty young men sat on the floor in a rough circle, with two men sitting at the head. The main speaker was a young undergraduate, a rarity in Tower Hamlets at a time when few young people of Bangladeshi origin went to university.

'Islam is the source of all knowledge,' he told us. 'Before Islam the world was in darkness. Today the West is proud of democracy, but where did it come from? The first democracy in the world was in Medina, when the Muslims elected caliphs in free elections. So much of what the West has today comes from Islam, especially democracy . . .'

That insight into history stayed with me. The unquestioning assertion of Islam's, or more precisely Islamism's, political superiority over the West was a constant theme in YMO events. In other *taleemi jalsa* gatherings similar themes of Islam's ascendancy over communism and capitalism were also a subject of study. Often speakers would quote extensively from Mawdudi's *The Islamic Movement*, stressing the importance for Muslims of striving together to create a true Islamic society in the world. In explaining the 'main objective of Islam', quoting Mawdudi, one speaker read, in English:

These aims cannot be realized so long as power and leadership in society are in the hands of disbelieving rulers and so long as the followers of Islam confine themselves to worship rites, which all too often depend on the arbitrary patronage and support of those very rulers. Only when power in society is in the hands of the Believers and the righteous, can the objectives of Islam be realized. It is therefore the primary duty of all those who aspire to please God to launch an organized struggle, sparing neither life nor property for this purpose. The importance of securing power for the righteous is so fundamental that, neglecting this struggle, one has no means left to please God.

His scathing attack on 'disbelieving rulers' and promoting his own followers as 'Believers' and criticizing those who 'confined' religion to worship made me think about my own approach to Islam. Most compelling was Mawdudi's conviction that the struggle for removing 'disbelieving rulers' and creating a society ruled by 'the righteous' was the only 'means left to please God'.

As I heard more references to Mawdudi, I started to read his books for myself. The loathing for Mawdudi instilled within me by Grandpa gradually evaporated.

I bought a copy of what was mandatory reading for all Islamist movement activists, *Let Us Be Muslims*, from a Leicester-based Islamist think tank, the Islamic Foundation. The Islamic Foundation was staffed by leading intellectuals of the Islamist movement, men trained personally by Mawdudi, such as the late Khurram Murad, the Pakistani economics professor Khurshid Ahmed, and others such as the director Manzair Ahsan.* The Islamic Foundation was committed to propagating the ideas of the Islamist movement, and translated and published the writings of Mawdudi. *Let Us Be Muslims* was prominent among them. I started to read the book with keen interest. Sarwar's *Islam: Beliefs and Teachings* had already got me thinking about the need for an Islamic state, and a political system of Islam. It was the summer of 1991. My evenings were filled with YMO events and meetings, my time at school in organizing and leading prayer meetings, encouraging others to join the YMO. I was sixteen years old and I had *no* white friends. My world was entirely Asian, fully Muslim. This was my Britain. Against this backdrop, the writings of Sarwar's guru, Mawdudi, took me to a radically new level.

*In recent years the Foundation has employed people at junior levels from non-Islamist backgrounds.

3. The Ultimatum

Islam is a revolutionary doctrine and system that overthrows governments. It seeks to overturn the whole universal social order.

Abul Ala Mawdudi, Islamist ideologue and founder of Jamat-e-Islami

I knew my father would not tolerate Mawdudi's books under his roof, so I put paper covers on them, blacked out the author's name, and secretly read as much as possible. While fellow teenagers were smuggling pornography into their rooms, my contraband consisted of books written by Islamist ideologues.

Now I was not a mere *Muslim*, like all the others I knew; I was better, superior.

The Muslims in my life were to be compared with a new category of people my parents never introduced me to: *kafir*. In our home, my parents never distinguished between Muslims and *kafirs* or *kuffar*,★ an Arabic term as derogatory to non-Muslims as 'wogs' is to non-whites.

Mawdudi's works drew comparisons with *kuffar* in order to place Muslims on a religious pedestal. In the East London mosque we used the word regularly in gatherings. We were believers, Muslims; all others were *kuffar*. And we were no ordinary Muslims, but superior to others. As Mawdudi explained:

★ Other plural forms are *kafireen* and *kafiroon*, depending on where in a sentence the word appears.

We have already seen that the only difference between Muslims and Kafirs is in the matter of knowledge and actions. Men who call themselves Muslim but whose knowledge and actions are the same as those of Kafirs are guilty of blatant hypocrisy. Kafirs do not read the Koran and do not know what is written in it. If so-called Muslims are equally ignorant, why should they be called Muslims? . . . If Muslims behave the same as non-Muslims, what difference is there between them and Kafirs?

Mawdudi taught that there were 'partial Muslims' and 'true Muslims'. 'Partial Muslims', Mawdudi explained, confined religion to prayers, rosary beads, remembrance of God's name, piety, and dress. I agreed with Mawdudi's definition, for the majority of the Muslim population I had encountered in Britain was of this variety, the silent majority. However, in Mawdudi's understanding, they had fallen short of the mark. They were not 'true Muslims'.

'True Muslims', Mawdudi wrote, allowed their 'desires, their ideologies, their thoughts and opinions, their likes and dislikes, all [to be] shaped by Islam. Allah's guidance holds complete sway over their hearts and minds, their eyes and ears, their bellies, their sexual desires, their hands and feet, their bodies and soul.'

My frequenting of YMO meetings, helping Brother Falik in the office, and attending *taleemi jalsa*, meant that I was considered part of the Islamic movement. I had taken no vow, nor sworn allegiance to a leader. That happened only after years of activities and proving one's total loyalty. For now, I was a member and was expected to work within YMO, slowly move up the ranks to become a *rukon* (Arabic for pillar), or senior member, and then on to the National Executive Committee.

My readings of Mawdudi were not altogether inspired by genuine intellectual curiosity, although that played a part. As a YMO member, every evening I had to account for my day's activities. Brother Falik had given me an A4 sheet of paper with 'YMO Daily Routine' written across the top. Listed on the sheet were activities I had to report on every day, including how many of the five daily prayers I had read in congregation at a mosque; how much of the Koran I had recited; how many pages of Islamic books I had read; how much time I had spent with family; how many hours I had dedicated to the movement; how many new members I had targeted for recruitment. I kept my routine sheet hidden in my coat pocket, wary lest my parents should ever discover it.

At the end of every week I attended a meeting where we reported our week's achievements. We wanted to outdo one another, and those who underperformed were often subjected to strict questioning. I found this environment of scrutiny, analysis, questioning, and commitment to do better enjoyable. My readings of Mawdudi's books were boosted by the praise I received at these meetings. Week by week, Falik and I crammed more and more on to our sheets while others failed to keep up with us.

My routine sheet had one shortfall: I rarely attended congregational prayers in a mosque. We did not live in the hub of Tower Hamlets and the closest Muslim place of worship, Shah Jalal mosque, was a twenty-minute walk away in Stepney. In those days, YMO was attempting to branch out into other areas of Tower Hamlets, beyond the East London mosque, and targeting areas across the East End. Stepney was one such area.

Towards the end of summer 1991 I started to say my dawn prayers in congregation at the mosque in Stepney. I would wake before sunrise, prepare for prayers and walk over to the mosque. There were about seven of us activists who prayed at the mosque, but there was more to our presence than prayers. We were never content with merely praying – we had to do more.

After most people had left, Sami, the university student who had taught us that democracy started with the Muslim caliphs, would deliver lessons from the Koran. For about thirty minutes after the morning prayer, half asleep, I sat and listened to his impromptu commentary on the Koran. The idea behind such early-morning study sessions was to establish a YMO presence in the mosque and, gradually, win acceptance of the elderly congregation. That way, recruiting their sons to YMO through public events at the mosque would be easier.

While I targeted others' children, all was not well at my own home. My parents were becoming seriously concerned about my sudden outburst of religious fervour. Even in a pious family like ours my behaviour was at odds with my parents' faith. My father wondered what drove me to walk so far, so early in the morning. Was it merely to pray? Surely, God was at home too. My God, however, was no longer at home; he had to be sought out in activism, drive, energy, mobilizing and expanding the Islamic movement. I had to be a 'true Muslim', completely enmeshed in Islam, not a 'partial Muslim' like my parents.

While I supported this new endeavour of YMO to expand seriously beyond our East London stronghold, there were others who were watching me. The then imam of the mosque in Stepney was a disciple of Grandpa. I had assumed that he had forgotten me, a face among so many faces who had surrounded an elderly, frail Muslim scholar. I was wrong.

The imam had remembered me. He tried to make eye contact with me several times, while I sat among the YMO members. As with most mosques in Britain, imams, sadly, tend to be meek. They are bullied by the all-powerful mosque committees with their loud-mouthed chairmen, and are dependent on the congregational collections for their meagre incomes. As such, and contrary to popular opinion, with a small number of exceptions imams very rarely rock the boat. The YMO were perceived in Stepney as a well-connected, well-organized, educated group of young men, outside the domain of a mosque imam. He humbly led the prayers, then left us to listen to the lectures of Sami. It never occurred to us that if it was genuine knowledge we sought, it should have been the imam, the person who had *studied* Islam, to whom we should be listening, not an undergraduate.

My parents knew that the time for GCSE revision had long passed, but still I went to the East London mosque with Falik. This was of real concern to my father, but he was waiting for the right moment to ask me what I was actually doing. Sensing his deep unease, I tried to avoid him as much as possible in the evenings; I kept myself away from the dinner table, locked inside my bedroom, citing all sorts of excuses.

In the past I had always enjoyed spending time with my parents. If I went out I always told them where I was going and, when I returned, the first thing I did was to tell them I was home. Now I was desperate to change that. I did not want my mother to know when I left, where I went, or how long I stayed out. That way I could spend more time at East London mosque without having to explain myself. My strange conduct worried my parents.

One Saturday I sneaked out as usual to attend the weekly *taleemi jalsa*. We were spread in circles of five and were learning how to recite the Koran. There were half a dozen teachers from Islamic Forum Europe, children of men from Jamat-e-Islami, who were teaching us *tajwid*. This was an area in which I had no need of instruction – Grandpa had personally ensured that my *tajwid* was well developed. I was sitting in the main hall of the mosque, late in the evening, among a group of sixty or so activists when suddenly the mosque caretaker, Mr Khan, popularly known as Khan *sahib*, walked into the hall, his large bunch of keys jingling on his waist loops. I looked up to see him walking across the hall, more slowly than usual, and looking straight at me. He raised his arm discreetly and pointed to the main doors behind him that led to the prayer hall.

There, in the distance, stood my father with his hands in his pockets, his face long and wary, his eyes fixed on me, the son he had now lost. My heart was pounding. I froze, unable to move or say anything. Before others could notice, my father turned round and disappeared. As I saw him walk away, I knew that was the end: I had abandoned him, destroyed any hope he had had of raising a decent Muslim son. Khan *sahib* came up to me and tried to make conversation but I was elsewhere, in my father's mind. All those moments he had spent, training me at Grandpa's feet, had come to naught. I knew my father's hurt was deep.

That night I lost my sturdy confidence among my fellow activists. I was sad and desolate at knowing, feeling, my father's pain. Several YMO members tried to comfort me.

'This is the way God tests his servants,' said one. 'Your parents will be an obstacle to your commitment to God's work, the Islamist movement. Ours is the work of prophets, and they were opposed by their families. Abraham was rejected by his family. And in turn Abraham rejected his father.'

Another said, 'Partial Muslims like our parents will never understand what we are trying to do. Be patient, brother. You are from among the true Muslims.'

They were wrong, I thought. My parents were different: overly protective, exceptionally caring, and committed to God as much as, if not more than, those who claimed to be doing the work of the prophets. Those arguments did not wash with me. These were difficult moments, yes, but not a test from God. Still, I decided to be patient.

As time passed, my parents and I were hardly on speaking terms. I continued to spend long hours at East London mosque.

I had not done particularly well in my GCSEs. Uneasy about my involvement in Islamism, relatives advised my parents that perhaps I ought to be sent off to work in an Indian restaurant far away from East London mosque.

My parents, though, wanted me to continue studying, and my father wanted me to resit my exams at Tower Hamlets

College. However, he also wanted a promise that I would study and not spend my time with YMO or visit the East London mosque. It was a promise I could not make, for deep down I had committed myself, my life, to the Islamist movement and, like my brothers at the mosque, I would let nothing stand in the way of following Islam as a complete life code. My father and I engaged in long hours of heated debate about the nature of Islam. He told me that the men who spoke at the YMO conference were Jamat-e-Islami activists from the days when Bangladesh was still East Pakistan. These included Delwar Hussein Sayedi, a prominent speaker from Bangladesh who rivalled Grandpa in his ability to draw crowds and spoke as a chief guest at YMO conferences.

'That night I saw you in Whitechapel, you had no need to be there. Did I not teach you *tajwid*? What can YMO teach you about Islam that you do not already know?'

I tried to answer his questions but he was in no mood to be taught lessons on Islam from his son. I tried to explain to him that Islam had been misunderstood by most of the people he knew. I dared not mention Grandpa in this context. Noticing my newly developed confrontational attitude, both my parents looked on, stupefied.

'You've changed,' my mother said, her lips quivering. 'You're no longer the son I raised.' I wanted to hear no more. Abruptly, I got up and walked out of the living room. My parents shouted after me; never in my life had I walked away from my parents while they were speaking to me.

They were both vehemently opposed to my version of Islam and made their dissatisfaction clear in no uncertain terms. My father spent hours trying to explain that Islam was spiritual, internal, and about drawing closer to God and not about radical politics, assassinating politicians and trying to set up an imaginary Islamic state. 'If you want politics,' he would say, 'go and join the Labour Party.' But British politics was man-made and I was aspiring to a politics that was God-made.

And so I continued to attend events at East London mosque while studying to resit my exams. I raised money for the mosque on Fridays, regularly helped the caretaker with small tasks, and, most importantly, started to help Sami set up a library in the mosque. We spent hours sifting through cartons of books we received from an American high school, and others from Muslim publishers. This was our attempt to create a more studious environment for our brothers.

The atmosphere at home was horrid. In January 1992, when I was seventeen, I minimized my involvement with YMO for a two-month period in an attempt at conciliation. I wanted to regain some of that old warmth and love my parents had showered on me, but I did not want to lose my brothers, my friends at East London mosque. Falik was now studying with me at Tower Hamlets College and he kept me up to date with events at the mosque. I still maintained my daily routine sheet, and read bulletins issued by Jamat-e-Islami. These bulletins carried pictures of thousands of people gathering in Dhaka for protest meetings, Islamist brothers fighting against leftists, many of whom were martyred. Every month we received these from Jamat-e-Islami in Bangladesh.

Then, in March 1992, the leader of Jamat-e-Islami, a political science professor named Gulam Azam, was arrested in Bangladesh on trumped-up political charges. For the next six months the atmosphere within YMO and Islamic Forum Europe changed completely. Our sole aim was to secure the release of the elderly professor from prison. We launched a campaign, during which I helped put up posters across Tower Hamlets late into the night, organized protest meetings, and distributed leaflets demanding justice. One of our key arguments was that the British government issued visas for visiting Jamat-e-Islami leaders and MPs. If they were extremists, as my father and others claimed, then why did the government permit them free rein in Britain?

That summer my father saw on my desk at home a pile of the leaflets I had been handing out. As far as my father was concerned, that was the last straw. He had seen me drift further and further away from the family; he had spent hours trying to engage with me, explain to me that Islam was not politics, but about purifying our hearts and drawing closer to God.

He was shaking with anger.

'What is Gulam Azam doing in my house?' he shouted, before launching into a monologue about the Islamists, their shrewd manipulation of religion to suit their political needs, their hatred of traditional Muslims, and their disregard for Muslim saints. He called them 'the enemies of the Prophet, the cursed of God, allies of the devil, and the rejects of the Muslims. From this day onwards, you will have nothing to do with them! Enough! Enough of pretending to study, then lying to us, deceiving us . . .'

He slammed the door and left. My mother stood in the room alone with me and wept profusely, repeatedly asking in a broken, shaking voice, 'Why? Why?'

My disagreements with my parents were now so deep, their revulsion for my Islamism so powerful, and my commitment to ideological Islam so uncompromising, that my father had little choice but to give me an ultimatum: leave Mawdudi's Islamism or leave my house.

'We raised you as a Muslim, you understand Islam. If you want to stay under my roof, then you will be a normal Muslim, none of this politics in the name of religion.'

I turned to my friends in YMO for advice and they told me again that this was a test from God.

'You must choose between family and God's work. The Islamic movement is more important to us than our families,' said a leading member of YMO.

My father continued to apply pressure on me. He was worried that I would be a negative influence on my siblings. All the while my friends in the Islamic movement were critical of my parents, suggesting that they were not true Muslims. Only those who accepted Mawdudi and his Egyptian counterpart, Syed Qutb, understood 'true Islam'.

Unable to accept two authorities, one night, late in the summer, I wrote a farewell note to my parents, left it on my pillow and crept out of our house while they slept. I left home for the Islamic movement without a penny in my pocket and with only the clothes I was wearing.

Outside in the still, dark night I walked along Commercial Road towards East London mosque and the brothers I knew would help me. It was a long, silent journey. Occasionally, cars drove past, but I ignored them. What if my father had driven out after me? Strangely, I did not feel that God was on my side. I felt it was a fight between my father and me: I had to win. By challenging me, my father had challenged the Islamic movement. I reached Whitechapel and made for the mosque's rear entrance in Fieldgate Street. It was locked. There was not a soul in sight. I sat on a bench for a while and then a black hearse pulled up. A small, white-bearded old man got out and slowly opened the mosque gates. He did not say anything to me: he, I knew, like my father, despised Islamism and Islamists.

He was Britain's first Muslim undertaker, Haji Taslim Ali. His offices were attached to the East London mosque and he was one of its earliest associates. However, under Islamist influences, I was too arrogant to respect him. In the eyes of an Islamist, he was not part of the Islamic movement and therefore not worthy of deference.

I followed Haji Taslim Ali into the mosque for dawn prayers. Soon the popular caretaker of the mosque, Khan *sahib*, appeared in the main prayer hall. Khan *sahib* knew that I had problems at home and immediately understood that I had run away. Why else would I be at East London mosque at 4 a.m.? While I prepared for prayers, he made up a bed for me in one of the offices. He even made me a cup of tea, switched on the boiler for hot water, and asked what I would like for breakfast. I suspected that he had done this all before.

Around 7 a.m. my immediate superiors arrived at the mosque. Siraj Salekin was especially considerate; that morning he treated me like a family member and took me along with him everywhere all day. He was a youth worker, so the sight of a confused teenager accompanying him to work was no great surprise to his colleagues.

That morning my mother called the mosque and accused its activists of kidnapping her innocent, naive son. She asked to speak to me. I was sitting in the office but the clerk said I was not there. My mother phoned back several times that day until, reluctantly, I took her call. All I could hear on the other end of the line was incessant sobbing and prolonged gasps for breath. My mother could not utter a single word to me.

Now it dawned on me just how much pain I had caused. In my arrogance I had given no thought to the consequences of running away. And since arriving at the mosque my seniors had shown no disapproval of what I had done. Deep down I wanted to go home, but that would be seen as backing down in the face of parental pressure. I had to win. The Islamic movement must prevail.

Still, my much-coveted freedom to engage in YMO activities unhindered suddenly no longer seemed so glittering a prize. I attended meetings with a heavy heart and began to miss my family. What did my two younger sisters think? What was going on at home? How were my parents coping?

My distraction became apparent to my brothers. I think they were now convinced that I had passed God's test and should return home. In my absence, communication was established with my father and my repatriation was discreetly arranged. Siraj

Salekin deposited me back in Limehouse after three nights away. Contrary to my expectations, my father behaved as though nothing had happened and conversed with Siraj Salekin and me without a hint of confrontation. He had misjudged my fanaticism: his ultimatum to me had backfired. Nevertheless, I was moved by my father's ability to forgive.

My mother, on the other hand, had found her voice. She had never expected that I would leave and was now effectively washing her hands of me. From today, she said, I was free to do as I pleased. She and my father on the Day of Judgement, before God, would no longer be responsible for my involvement with Islamism. From today I was answerable only to God. I had got my way and I was free to do what I wanted without my parents' interference. I was glad.

With my parents defeated, there was no stopping me. At Tower Hamlets College I became active in the college's Islamic Society, managed by members of YMO. By secret ballot I was elected president. I had rather hoped that my friend Falik would be elected, but my commitment and drive to Islamism outdid even his. The college had a majority Muslim population and the Islamic Society had an extremely high profile. The events I organized attracted crowds of over 200 students. In essence, I was running an Islamist front organization operating on campus to recruit for the wider Islamist movement and maintain a strong Islamist presence. With the help of my members I was successful on both counts. With parental obstacles out of the way, my zeal and commitment to Islamism were unconfined.

4. Islam Is the Solution

I have written *Milestones* for this vanguard [Islamists], which
I consider to be a waiting reality about to be materialized.

   Syed Qutb, Islamist ideologue

Karl Marx and Friedrich Engels had declared in the *Communist
Manifesto* that the 'History of all hitherto existing society is the
history of class struggle'; as Islamists we believed that history was
a clash between good and evil. We represented the former, the
West the latter, and we had to prevail. Assassination attempts on
Mawdudi's life and the stories of martyrdom that reached us
from Afghanistan of jihad against the Soviets convinced us that
'true Islam' had to be in perennial conflict with *kufr* – the dis-
belief of the *kuffar*. And so we were critical, derogatory even, of
organizations such as the Tablighis who engaged in missionary
activities in the Soviet Union – true Muslims should be persecuted by the Soviets, not accepted. To us, being a Muslim
meant being in conflict with non-Muslim society. How could
an atheistic society allow the Tablighis to preach Islam? That
very fact allowed us to pour scorn on the Tablighis. Some of
our leaders even claimed that the Tablighi group was sponsored
by Moscow to pacify Islam. The Tablighis retorted by saying
we were sponsored by Saudi Arabia and, thus, America to politicize Islam during the Cold War.

   Our discussions inside the mosque and in various meetings
did not come out of the abstract. Those of us who read material
from Islamist writers knew that the world we espoused was

underpinned by the writings of Mawdudi and another, more crucial, character: Syed Qutb.

Syed Qutb was a name I first heard from YMO. I knew that Mawdudi had laid the intellectual basis for drawing the battle lines between Islamism and all other systems of thought. Just as his ideas were propagated in English-speaking countries by the Islamic Foundation in Leicester, they were disseminated by several Arab organizations in the Middle East in search of an ideological alternative to Arab socialism, nationalism, and Nasserism. Syed Qutb, a middle-aged Egyptian bachelor and literary critic, rose to the challenge.

When Hasan al-Banna, the leader of the Egyptian Muslim Brotherhood, was assassinated in 1949, the Brotherhood became an orphan movement. Qutb became more than its adoptive father – he became its chief ideologue. Hardened by social isolation in the United States, he became an ardent anti-Westerner. His stance was further radicalized by his terrible experiences in Nasser's prisons from the late 1950s onwards. The horrendous, inhumane torture Qutb and other members of the Muslim Brotherhood experienced resulted in Qutb smuggling *Milestones*, the *Communist Manifesto* of Islamism, out to the wider world.

In YMO *Milestones*, along with Qutb's personal commentary on the Koran, was mandatory reading. When I read *Milestones* I felt growing animosity towards the *kuffar*. True Muslims had been defeated by the imperialists and their agents, the rulers of the Muslim world. We had to regain the upper hand in Muslim countries and reject the culture of the West. Qutb spoke about his own experiences in America, and declared that a total jihad was the only way to remove the disbelieving presidents and princes of the Arab world.

From what I understood, Qutb had adopted Mawdudi's paradigm, but developed it much further. Mawdudi was prepared to make concessions to the West, gain power for Islamism via parliamentary democracy while infiltrating the army simultaneously to ensure that, once power had been grasped, the military would be supportive. Qutb, however, declared all-out war. There was no room for gradualism in Qutb's prescription for changing the world.

Egypt's prisons in the 1950s and 1960s served as a networking forum for Islamists of various persuasions. Qutb, heavily influenced by Mawdudi's writing, met a group of Muslims who helped him further crystallize his thinking. Soon I was to learn who this particular group of people were. *Ideas, intellect, thought, challenge, systems, concepts, destruction, construction* were key words discussed by them with Qutb which he then introduced in *Milestones*. For writing this book, Qutb was hanged by the Egyptian government in 1966.

The Koran repeatedly reminds us that the vast majority of the world's population will not become believers, in the Muslim sense. It accepts religious diversity, creedal plurality. Koranic verses include such Prophetic declarations as 'to you your religion, and to me mine'. However, to Qutb, this was unacceptable. 'Islam is not merely "belief",' he wrote. 'Islam is a declaration of the freedom of man from servitude to other men. Thus it strives from the beginning to abolish all these systems and governments which are based on the rule of man over man.'

We sat in the East London mosque and discussed at length how Hasan al-Banna and Qutb had given their lives to the movement; how they had stood steadfastly against the disbelieving governments of the Muslim world; and how we had to gain popular support of the Muslims to remove these regimes, and create God's government on God's earth, or, as Mawdudi put it, 'Allah's law in Allah's land'. However, seizing political power by the ballot box was not our only option. The Islamization of powerful elements of society would ensure that in the end, if need be, our counterparts in the Muslim world would take power by force.

Now I was convinced that Grandpa and the majority of the world's traditional Muslims were on the wrong path. How could they coexist with *jahiliyyah*, the ignorants, as the Koran called the pagan Arabs of pre-Islamic Arabia? Qutb taught us that the Prophet had declared war on the infidels of Mecca because it was in the nature of Islam that it must dominate. In *Milestones* the world was divided into two: Islam and *jahiliyyah*, or *Dar al-Harb* and *Dar al-Islam*. Just as in seventh-century Mecca, today's world was divided into these two camps: the half-believing Muslim world and the rest of the non-believing world, on whom we declared war. Where Mawdudi advocated gradual change by takeover of parliament, the military, and various arms of the modern state, Qutb declared jihad against the *jahiliyyah*. Where Mawdudi questioned the belief of the Muslim rulers, Qutb declared them infidels, on a par with pagans. It was the expression of these sentiments, and the ferocious advocacy of violence against the Egyptian and other Arab governments, that led to his death, and the birth of a fully formed Islamist ideology.

Qutb was a martyr, a hero. His life and death gave us inspiration to continue with the work of changing the world, bringing Islamism to power, as he and Mawdudi had wanted.

In the malaise of the 1960s Middle East, the confusion of conflicting ideologies, the Muslim Brotherhood had coined the popular phrase, '*al-Islam huwa al-hall*', 'Islam is the solution'. To ordinary Muslims this had a certain resonance. The power of Islam over its adherents is absolute and, as people who played politics with Islam, we knew how to deploy religion to manipulate the emotions of its followers.

On my bedroom wall I had a sticker from Jamat-e-Islami which bore the following quote from Hasan al-Banna:

Allah is Our Lord.
Mohammed is Our Leader.
The Koran is Our Constitution.
Jihad is Our Way.
Martyrdom is Our Desire.

One day my father saw that sticker and broke out in tears. He was in no position to threaten me, but neither could he silently watch me manifest my commitment to the Islamic movement. He said to me, 'My son, the Prophet is not our leader, he is our master, the source of our spiritual nourishment. Leaders are for political movements, which Islam is not. The Koran is his articulation, as inspired by God, not a political document. It is not a constitution, but guidance and serenity for the believing heart. How can you believe in these new definitions of everything we hold so dear? Jihad is a just war against tyranny and oppression, fought by the Prophet after persecution, not "a way". Why do these people call for martyrdom when their sons are in the best universities across the West?'

Then, in highly personal terms, my father spoke about the sons of leaders of the Islamist movements, almost all of whom had received a good education in Britain or another Western country. He cited Gulam Azam's son, a graduate from Manchester University and working for Hackney Council, and others who were in business. He argued that ordinary Muslims like me were caught up in jihad and martyrdom. Factually, my father was right. Hasan al-Banna's own offspring lived in the comfort of Switzerland. But I knew that al-Banna and Qutb had dedicated their lives for the movement; they were my examples, not Gulam Azam's sons. That night I heard my father weep profusely and pray in a loud, pained voice to God after dawn prayers.

At Tower Hamlets College a revolution of sorts was underway. During my first year there a group of student Islamists had come up with a novel idea for a high-profile event at the main campus in Poplar. Their advertising technique was adapted from that used by motor manufacturers when launching a new model: initially covered in a white sheet, it is slowly unveiled before a curious public. The president of the college Islamic Society at that time was a mature, sedate student who was also a member of Islamic Forum Europe. Although there were other Islamist groups at the college with whom we were in conflict (such as the despised Dawatul Islam group), we were keen to present a united front, particularly to the detested *kuffar*. To a large extent we achieved that objective; indeed, the presentation of a united Islamist front to the outside world continues today.

Away from the bickering elders of the East London mosque, as time passed the YMO contingent at Tower Hamlets College worked well with our rival Islamists. After all, we shared a common ideology and veneration for Mawdudi and Qutb and we all despised traditional Islam.

Together we worked under the religious banner of the Islamic Society, knowing full well that it was a front organization for political Islamism. We began our campaign with posters on every college notice board, classroom door, and staircase which read:

Prophets of Islam:
Adam
Noah
Abraham
Jacob
Joseph
Moses
Jesus
Mohammed
What is Islam?

Within days, there were complaints from Jewish teachers and students that these were Old Testament prophets. Immediately, the seeds of conflict were sown. In an attempt to promote Islam we had offended Jews, even Christians, by claiming that their religious figures were, in fact, ours. The Islamic Society was the subject of conversation in every class. We drew back the sheet a little further each time with a series of provocative posters, all of which ended with the 'What is Islam?' punchline. The revelation came in our final poster, again plastered all across the college and even on lampposts in the street outside:

Islam: The Final Solution

There was uproar on campus. The entire teaching community was outraged. Time and again the principal's assistant came to see us in the prayer hall (our gathering place) to remind us that the college was a secular institution. For most of us the word secular had no meaning. We were Muslims – full stop. Our Islam we wore proudly on our sleeves.

Islam was *the* solution for all the world's ills. As Islamists, our contention was that the world had been failed by capitalism and communism, as Qutb had so eloquently put it in *Milestones*. Islam's era had now arrived. But we knew that it would not come to pass peacefully.

Our teachers pointed out that Adolf Hitler had made exactly the same claim as a prelude to murdering 6 million people, mostly Jewish, in the Holocaust. In our minds, that was coincidental. We failed to comprehend the totalitarian nature of what we were promoting. Besides, deep down, we never really objected to the Holocaust. Indeed, in the prayer room we were convinced that the college principal, Annette Zera, as well as several other members of the management, were Zionist agents. Without question we despised Jews and perceived a Jewish conspiracy against our nascent Islamic Society.

Our student event, billed as the largest in college history, was a phenomenal success. The main dining hall was filled with students and teachers who sat and listened to Imam Murad Deen, an American whose powerful presentations were a regular feature at Speakers' Corner in Hyde Park on Sunday afternoons. To avoid hecklers, we announced that any questions would have to be written. A mature student, the president of the Student Union, walked to the stage from the back of the hall and handed the imam a piece of paper.

Before the student had returned to his seat the imam had read the questions and shouted, 'I knew you were a faggot by the way you walked up here!'

Laughter broke out among the students, then jeering and hissing, and finally a heated argument between the imam and the gay student, whose question, we discovered, had concerned homosexuality and Islam. The event descended into chaos.

The following week the management committee went to great lengths to drum into the Muslim students at college that homophobia, a new word for us, would not be tolerated. Homophobia and sexism, just like racism, were disciplinary offences. We, however, failed to understand that the secular liberal ideals that allowed Muslims to congregate at college in Britain were the very same ideals that tolerated homosexuality. It was secularism that allowed Muslims to build mosques, worship freely, and live in harmony – not Christianity. But my appreciation of secularism came only later in life; for now, we had Jews and gays to battle.

In the prayer room, we suspected that the college management was dominated not only by Jews, but by homosexuals too. How else could they possibly reprimand us and condemn our imam for standing up to homosexuality? So now we were convinced that there was a gay–Jewish conspiracy to undermine our efforts.

Among the students, however, we were hugely admired.

They thought the speaker, his American accent and direct mannerisms, were *cool*. In accordance with Islamist rigidity, I was convinced that the imam was right to say that faggots would go to hell. After all, what was Sodom and Gomorrah all about?

In classes, our politically correct teachers tried to imbue us with lessons in tolerance and plurality. My response, without hesitation, was 'God created Adam and Eve, not Adam and Steve', which fellow students always applauded.

As Islamic Society president I had a ten-member committee, which met once a week, planned events, and then critically evaluated the successes and failures of every gathering. I chaired the meetings, minutes were taken, and decisions were acted upon. We ran the Islamic Society like a military operation: we had a chain of command and a clear vision of where we were headed. Last year's successful campaign was still in the air and we were determined to build upon it. I was now promoting Islamism every day, at college, in my private life, and in public with the YMO.

However, there was more to it this time round. Before the term started, the then president of the YMO, Habibur Rahman, an IT lecturer at CityPoly, had gone to great lengths to arrange a two-hour meeting with me. I had no idea why. We sat at the large meeting room in East London mosque and he asked, 'How is your daily routine sheet?'

'It could be better,' I replied. 'You know, my parents still aren't altogether happy with me, so I have difficulties helping out in office hours, or praying at mosques, or attending the *taleemi jalsa*.'

'How long do you envisage this situation will continue?' he asked.

'My father has eased up since I went back home, but now I feel as though I should try, at least, to maintain some peace there.'

'OK. I understand your parents have problems with the

Islamist movement, but where do you see yourself in, say, ten years' time? Do you still think you'll have problems at home?'

'Hopefully, by then, my parents will have overcome their fears. You know, my parents are planning to move out of Tower Hamlets very soon, mainly to get me away from this mosque, though I'll continue to travel here anyway. But honestly, in the long run, let us pray that my parents relax more.'

'How are your studies?' he asked. I was both intrigued and flattered by his interest. To get so much attention from the leader of YMO was an honour for me; he was a busy person, with nearly a hundred young, committed men at his command.

'Not bad,' I replied.

'And how is college life?'

'Well, as you know, we held that talk last year. This year we're hoping to hold more such events. Introduce Islam to the students, do more *da'wah* work.'

Da'wah was an Arabic word I had learnt while I was at YMO. The Islamist equivalent of evangelism, it literally means 'invitation', a call to Islam. I remember Grandpa was always against *da'wah* to Muslims, the primary work of the Islamist movement. He always asked how we could call to Islam those who already believed. Yes, Muslims may need reminders of their sense of duty to God, like believers of any religion, but *da'wah* was not a term I heard used among Grandpa's community of moderate Muslims. In YMO, however, *da'wah* was key. We organized everything, from tournaments to camps, for *da'wah*. Our events at college were *da'wah*, calling students to Islam, or rather Islamism.

The Islamic Society at college was an avenue for us to carry out more *da'wah* work. We never stopped to ask how we could possibly be doing *da'wah* in a college that was predominantly Muslim. And if it was our non-Muslim teachers we sought to convert, then presenting Islam as the 'final solution' was hardly the best way to do it. No, in our context *da'wah* really meant getting people to join YMO or Islamic Forum Europe, become part of the Islamist movement or at least support it. I, as Habibur Rahman pointed out, had lost sight of this aim, seeking only to ensure that Islamism was the dominant force at college. The YMO president wanted more.

'And how do you anticipate the *da'wah* will be this year?' he asked.

'We have a strong Islamic Society committee. *Inshallah*, most of the brothers are members of YMO, though we have three who are from other groups. But as president I call the shots, approve the speakers and events.'

'OK. You organize events, create a stir, and then what?'

'What do you mean?' I asked, genuinely confused.

'You are a member of YMO. What is the connection between the work you will do at Tower Hamlets College and YMO?'

Now I got it. Or so I thought.

'To be frank, it is because of the training I got at YMO that I am able to manage the Islamic Society. Organizing events was something I learnt from my involvement with YMO. And most of the Islamic Society's committee members are from YMO. So I suppose that link is there.'

He gave me a wry smile. I still had not understood what he meant.

'I appreciate that,' he said. 'And we from outside the college are happy to support the *da'wah* in whatever capacity. But there needs to be a clearer aim for YMO workers like those of you who are leading the Islamic Society at college. All those young people who attend your events, what happens to them afterwards? Yes, you create an interest in Islam, hopefully in the Islamist movement, and then where do they go? Do you see what I mean . . . ?'

Habibur Rahman's purpose had now become clear: I was to use the Islamic Society as a recruiting agency for the YMO.

We discussed how this could happen. How it would aid

YMO's desire to expand into the wider Muslim community outside the East London mosque. I was sitting with the head of YMO, planning a recruitment campaign for the Islamist movement. My aims were now clear. I had my orders. Habibur Rahman ended the meeting with a smile, his initial anxiety laid to rest. I had reason to be happy too: my main arena for *da'wah* work was no longer East London mosque but Tower Hamlets College. My parents would be relieved when I told them that, henceforth, all my attention would be focused on my college work.

During enrolment week in 1992 Falik and I plastered the college with posters making it clear to new students where the prayer room was. We also published a magazine: *The Reality*. Every new entrant was welcomed by Brother Falik, me, or another member of YMO, under the guise of the Islamic Society. Right from their very first contact with the college they went away with our literature, knowing who we were.

Most students travelled to and from the Poplar campus by bus, walking from the bus stop on the East India Dock Road via Poplar Park. There, they walked past gold-painted graffiti proclaiming 'Islam is the Solution' and, beneath that, 'YMO'. There was no mistaking who was the dominant force in Tower Hamlets College. It amused me to see the faces of some of my old classmates from Stepney Green as they wondered at my transformation from school misfit to powerful student leader with hordes of adoring followers.

At college, as at Stepney Green, *all* of my friends were Asian, Muslim, and male, but now it no longer seemed odd that I, born in Britain, did not have a single white friend. The happy melting pot that Ms Powlesland had stirred at Sir William Burrough was no more than a distant childhood memory.

*

That year changed the lives of many, not only inside Tower Hamlets College, but within the wider community too. Large numbers of Muslim students were now attending vocational and academic courses at college for the first time. The children of Asian immigrants to Britain had come of age. Initially, I expected to create an awareness of the Islamist movement at college and, I hoped, introduce YMO and gain support for our work, guiding young people to participate in our activities at East London mosque. In fact, the immediate success of our hard work surprised many of us.

Falik and I worked tirelessly, often going without lunch, attending meetings, planning events, visiting printers for flyers, spending hours designing the most attractive posters, organizing daily distribution of leaflets to students, liaising with college management, and meeting tens of students on a daily basis. Often we missed our classes. We became popular at college as the activists who knew what we were doing in life. We were young, seemingly well rooted, and understood the problems faced by the mostly young Bangladeshi student community in Tower Hamlets.

Many came from patriarchal families, others had problems of a financial nature; some wanted to share their problems with us, others wanted guidance in how they could persuade their parents to accept their girlfriends or boyfriends. Underlining all of our social work was the banner of the Islamic Society. Soon it became common knowledge among students that we were from the East London mosque. Many started to express an interest about what went on there.

We organized fortnightly talks on Wednesday afternoons, video presentations, and hard-hitting seminars: 'Hijab: Put up or Shut up' was one controversially titled discussion on wearing the veil.

Again our teachers were outraged, but our work was yielding results. To packed halls we brought speakers from different

Islamist groups who explained why women must cover their hair, be different from non-Muslim women, and earn God's approval.

At the time there were a handful of young Muslim women at college who wore the hijab. This commanded my full support, but questions from teachers, and sometimes students, made the practice increasingly confrontational. We put pressure on un-veiled Muslim women to join the 'sisters' who wore the hijab or risk being seen as un-Islamic rather than practising, proud Muslims. The resultant upsurge of hijab wearing took even us by surprise as scores of fashionable free-flowing hairstyles disappeared from view. (If the hijab was supposed to make a woman less attractive, then it clearly had not worked. Several society members commented to me that the women looked extraordinarily feminine and more desirable in the scarf than without. I shared that sentiment, but dared not express it.)

In every classroom, common room, and public area in college there were clusters of Muslim women in hijab, confident in their mannerisms and superior in their bearing. They were our sisters, linked to the most powerful and dynamic student club: the Islamic Society. We, in turn, were attached to the YMO, and so to Jamat-e-Islami, part of the world-wide Islamist move-ment whose aim was to make our ideology supreme. We acted locally, but were connected globally.

At prayer times, the small prayer room provided by the college management so generously the previous year no longer sufficed. We needed a larger hall, and demanded it from the college authorities. At first, in meetings with the management, I was told repeatedly that Tower Hamlets College was a secular insti-tution and would not provide religious facilities. But that was a difficult argument to sustain. Moreover, by providing us with a small prayer room in the newly refurbished building, despite there being a community mosque a minute's walk from college, the management had set a precedent. We did not want to pray at the mosque because there we were powerless; at college, we could organize our own speakers and rally the Muslims around us.

Several meetings with the vice-principal came to nothing. His refusal to provide us with larger prayer facilities emboldened our sense of purpose. The Islamic Society committee had lengthy meetings about what to do next. For us to back down would be a defeat for the Islamist movement, not something I was prepared to consider. Our response to management inflexibility broke new ground.

One lunchtime we gathered about seventy students outside the prayer room, gave the loud call to prayer, the *adhan*, and prayed in the open space in the centre of the campus. Most of the students were ordinary Muslims, not Islamists, but we provided direction and leadership. As president of the Islamic Society I led the prayers. As we prayed I sensed our numbers growing as others started to join us. I ended the prayer and caught a glimpse of the horrified members of the management team looking on, unable to believe what they had witnessed. It was like a scene from Tehran on the grounds of a 'secular' college in London. How were they to put the genie of Islamism back in the bottle?

Management demanded to see the committee immediately. Again, we missed our classes and held protracted negotiations. I was told not to make threats, but I knew I held the whip hand: with prayers under attack at Tower Hamlets College we could mobilize the wider Muslim community, rally East London mosque and YMO behind us, and cause major embarrassment for the college. In the event, management backed down, provided us with a larger room, and even agreed to clear the furniture for us before Friday prayers. We had won.

Exultant at how easily we had cowed the sensitive, liberal establishment of the college, we grew from strength to strength. To be a member of the Islamic Society was now a mark of pride, an association with the college's most successful fraternity. We became the largest student body on campus with over two hundred members.

To counter our total Islamization of the public space at college (open prayers, Islamist posters, women in hijab), the management increased the number of youth workers, counsellors, and social workers. From our perspective they were pouring in money to divert the students away from our *da'wah* and towards Western hedonism.

A core group of students allied with the youth workers organized raves and discos and played loud music in the student common rooms. These were *haram*, forbidden in Islam. As long as I was president of the college Islamic Society, such behaviour would not be tolerated.

We devised defensive strategies. Brother Falik and I knew that all the students at the college respected us, venerated us even, because we were associated with something they held high in their hearts: religion, particularly Islam. Although we believed Islam was more than just a religion, and that they were partial Muslims, we never hesitated in mobilizing their support when we needed it. Most of the students attended our events, read our magazines, supported our work, and would oblige us if we asked them to do something. However, being lesser Muslims, they also attended the disco.

On the day of the disco, leading members of the Islamic Society took it in turns to maintain a presence near the entrance. We didn't prevent anyone from entering – we didn't have to. Muslim students arriving at the disco saw us there and, out of respect rather than fear, simply walked away. To offend us was to offend God. We had played on their sensitivities of guilt, shame, and humiliation.

The organizers were aghast. They called on the college management to remove us. How was that possible? On what grounds? We stayed put. The disco was a failure. The following day, there were stickers all across the basement common room that read: 'Islam is the *only* way – YMO.' Nobody was left in any doubt as to who had orchestrated the previous day's events.

One youth worker at the time was an active member of the radical Socialist Workers' Party (SWP). In spring 1992 he organized a meeting on 'Islam and Socialism'. He had seen our rise and, like most staff at the college, was deeply anguished to see Islamist domination of its social and public life. He wanted, I think, to respond to our claims that Islam was the '*only* way' or the 'Final Solution'. If Islam claimed to be a solution, well, so was socialism.

Most meeting rooms on Wednesday afternoons, the traditional free period, were booked by the Islamic Society. Occasionally the sisters booked rooms for their own activities too. The SWP made a mistake and organized the meeting at 12.30 on a Friday. We were determined to make a point: at Tower Hamlets College, nothing should clash with our Friday prayers. We held our own private meetings to respond to this new threat from socialism and decided to teach the SWP a lesson.

The speaker from the SWP arrived on time and found a packed lecture theatre. The main organizer was delighted that there were so many of us. Perhaps the SWP would now also make serious headway into the student community at Tower Hamlets. What he didn't know was that his audience consisted almost entirely of members of the Islamic Society. Just as the speaker was beginning to warm up, to deliver his challenges to Islam, our plan of action came into play. I had placed one of our key members, Abdul Jalil, also a member of YMO, at the point furthest from the podium. As the speaker began he got up, walked across the front of the theatre, and headed for the door. One by one, the rest of us got up too. The speaker reddened in embarrassment. The organizer was livid.

'Where are you going?' he asked, looking at me.

My members were all disciplined. No chaos broke out;

nobody exulted at sabotaging a socialist meeting; all waited silently for me to respond.

'It is Friday prayer time. In future please don't organize meetings. If you do, make sure you don't clash with our prayers.'

Over fifty of us walked out of the room, leaving just a handful of people in the audience. The event collapsed and, with it, socialism at Tower Hamlets College. Soon the SWP even stopped selling their newspaper outside.

In six months we had changed the entire atmosphere at college. The dynamism we had created at Tower Hamlets was now spilling out into the community. The sisters who wore the hijab put their mothers and older siblings to shame. The wearing of the headscarf by my mother's generation was not usually practised until later in life, much like women in some Orthodox Christian countries, but the fact that young, educated, confident women at Tower Hamlets College wore the hijab in droves sent a message to the wider community. They saw our sisters on buses, on the roads, and at weddings, and slowly the hijab became a symbol of defiance of Western values and of a return to Islam.

It was, again, much later in life that I learned where the hijab really came from. The headscarf was worn by Christian and Jewish women in the Levant. The Prophet Mohammed had not invented hijab, merely adhered to the dominant dress code of his time. To this day, observant Amish, eastern Orthodox and married Jewish women wear hijab, too. We were ignorant of these facts: to us, it was Islam at its best, something the Prophet had invented.

Our dynamism had reverberations in sections of the student population that we had not known. Our magnetism and vitality drew people to us. A college security guard, after detailed discussion with our members, converted to Islam. Soon his wife converted too. A female student who had attended some of our events, and spoken to me at length about Islam, also converted.

There were plenty of others who looked on dismayed at what we had done to the college: a visible Muslim presence everywhere, women veiled, ubiquitous posters of Islam, and the student population, almost without exception, under our control.

5. We Will Rule the World

We need weapons, not food and aid. In war, we can eat our
enemies.

  Omar Bakri, leader of Hizb ut-Tahrir in Britain

The social ethos among Britain's young Muslims was such that
the more extrovert we became in our perceived expression of
Islam, the more highly valued we were among our peers. Young
girls whom I had seen arrive at college in trousers and blouses,
moderate enough, now thought they had been immodest sin-
ners. Now many wore headscarves and long dresses we called
jilbabs. Some started to cover their faces with the *niqab*. However,
the traditional dress worn by our sisters was modelled not on
elderly piety but on a style of hijab wearing which reflected
trends in Egypt. There was no room for the odd, careless
moment when a light covering fell off one's head, as in the case
of the Pakistani prime minister at the time, Benazir Bhutto, who
donned her headscarf so graciously. Instead a pinned-down-
tight, face-grabbing style quickly gained acceptance as a perceived symbol of godliness and rejection of the West. Indeed,
the main argument of our 'Hijab: Put up or Shut up' seminar
was illustrated by posters of a woman in a miniskirt and another
completely covered in hijab, *jilbab*, and *niqab*. We asked which
woman was a man most likely to look at and desire? The implied
answer was that the woman in a miniskirt would, undoubtedly,
provoke *fitna*, or moral dissension in society.

  It was not, however, all plain sailing. Falik and I learnt the
very hard way about Muslim women in pious dress. The initial

group of six or so who wore the hijab immediately formed a group among themselves. (We used to refer to them as the hijabis.) Soon, these same sisters started to wear *jilbabs*, and within weeks their faces disappeared behind *niqabs*. When we spoke to them, they looked away from us. Some even started to wear gloves to cover their hands from us. Even as Muslim men, we felt they were radically different from us, somehow too superior for us to address them as fellow believers. Their conduct became increasingly intimidating.

I found it hypocritical that the same 'sisters' readily spoke to the few non-Muslim men on campus; with unbelievers they were at ease! However, they assumed that we Muslim men would somehow treat them differently and thus avoided eye contact and would not respond even to our most basic greeting of peace, *Salam aleikum*. For me, this was going too far. Unable to restrain myself any longer, during one meeting with a fully veiled woman who insisted that she speak to me from behind a screen, I asked her, 'Do I have a contagious disease of some sort? Or do you think I am going to rape you?'

I had spoken my mind but, to her, I was blasphemous. How dare I question her perceived piety? Those were the words of an unbridled teenage Islamist, unable to accept female rejection, perhaps.

Though we had worked among the brothers to recruit people to YMO, we had neglected our sisters since YMO was not a particularly welcoming place for women in those days. The segregation at East London mosque cut into YMO events and then into the Islamic Society at college. Our sisters, we discovered, had been under the influence of Muslim female teachers, trained in the Saudi Arabian Wahhabi school of thinking, which taught that women had a responsibility to protect men from themselves. It was in order that we should not fall prey to lust that they had resorted to such extremes.

The brothers started to call them 'ninjas'. While we had been busy trying to Islamize the social scene at college, the ninja sisters had been in close contact with a group of Muslim male scholars who, we were told, strove to live like the early Muslims, the *salaf*. They claimed that they were now 'free' from men, and were no longer viewed as sexual objects. How were we to explain to them that their perceptions of men were wrong? Among the brothers, many wanted to marry those very sisters who had covered *everything*. They were considered to be the 'truest Muslims' and evoked the desires of many a brother. Rather than ask for a date, as was the practice of the *kafir*, we made marriage proposals. Several of my members who had previously had little interest in women now fell head over heels in love with one of them simply because she had covered all. The craving to unclothe the excessively clothed was cruel. But it was not a one-way street.

Oddly, the ninja sisters openly proposed to several of the brothers too. As courting and dating were considered morally degenerate, my members found partners of the opposite gender under the pretext of marriage. Many were still teenagers. They cited scripture from early Islam to prove that a suitor could approach a potential partner directly, agree the terms, and then ask a woman's parents for her hand in marriage. In theory, and in the medieval social structures of the Arab world, there were such instances. In the modern West, however, I saw my members, male and female, struggle with their new form of 'Islamic love'.

My generation of young British Muslims was torn between two cultures. The mainstream British lifestyle of dating, pre-marital sex, living together, and dissolution of partnerships with comparatively little fuss was not something that appealed to us. Simultaneously, the customs of our parents' generation – arranged marriages with cousins – were equally abhorred. So we paved our own alternative way: approaching sisters directly, without parental interference, judging the merits of a possible marriage on the ground of perceived piety, and then, in many cases, eloping to get married.

Our parents failed to understand where this 'Islamic marriage' had come from. It was neither Western nor Eastern but, like relationships the world over, still often ended in tears when couples realized that simply having a religion in common did not necessarily make for compatibility. Some did end up marrying, often after the sister had run away from home. Often she would discover that he was not the pious Islamist she thought he was. And vice versa: brothers would complain that the sisters had been 'influenced too much by feminism'. It is a sad truth that the rate of divorce among Islamists is far higher than among ordinary Muslims. To my mind, this is due in no small part to the extremist, literalist blinkers worn by many Islamists in an attempt to idealize their lives.

Away from the politics of East London mosque, a younger generation led by Brother Falik and me had our sights set on doing *da'wah* among Britain's Muslims. We were now in serious need of public speakers. YMO and Islamic Forum Europe's failure to provide them opened up avenues for many who were more than willing to lend a helping hand to Britain's most vibrant Muslim community.

Speakers came to Tower Hamlets College representing a host of Muslim groups active in Britain, including JIMAS★ and Hizb ut-Tahrir. In the absence of strong intellectual leadership skills from YMO, these two groups started to gain a following at college and, consequently, in the wider community of Tower Hamlets and east London. JIMAS already had a following among the ninja sisters: they sent black, white, and Asian converts who had studied Islam in Saudi Arabia to live and preach

★ Jamiat Ihyaa Minhaaj al-Sunnah (Movement for the Revival of the Prophet's Way).

in the UK. They spoke passionately about the idea of one God, *tawheed* in Arabic, and ceaselessly warned against *shirk*, or polytheism. We invited them often because they were mostly dynamic speakers, able to stir a crowd and plant genuine interest in Islam. Most impressively, they always referred directly to the Koran or the Prophet Mohammed's wisdom, bypassing fourteen centuries of commentary and scholarship on Islam's primary sources. They covered their heads with the red and white chequered Saudi scarf, often wearing it almost like women. They had huge, bushy beards and their trousers were very short, just below their knees. They looked like people from another era, austere in their ways, harsh in their conduct, and constantly reprimanding us for our own. Where were our beards? Why were our trousers worn long? Why did we listen to music? Why did we not condemn *shirk*, or idolatry?

I had never seen such people, but they were popular among our ninja sisters so I continued to invite them to speak. That was my first major mistake, for they planted ideas among the Islamized students that led those students to reject us. By late 1992 the same students that we had rescued from a life of crime were asking us why we were clean shaven. Why didn't we grow beards in emulation of the prophets? To the followers of JIMAS, literal adherence to scripture, with no thought for context, was of primary importance. Not that we understood context, far from it, but their bluntness, ragged appearance, constant quoting of scripture, and browbeating did not endear them to us. Their womenfolk wore gloves, covered their faces, and displayed a holier-than-thou attitude towards other women. Literalism had gained a foot in Tower Hamlets under my watch.

In addition to these outward differences, they prayed in a way I had not seen in any of Britain's mosques, standing in perfectly straight rows, touching ankles, constantly checking to see that their feet were touching one another, and holding their arms in a martial position on their chests, as 'prescribed' in Muslim scripture. This did not seem like prayer, but a cultish act. What was wrong with the way our parents prayed? Grandpa taught his disciples to pray as if they were in God's presence, and to be mindful of this. How did this square with constantly looking to see if one's feet were in place? They flooded the college with books explaining how they prayed and giving 'evidence' and 'references' in support. Literalism may begin with prayer and veiling women's faces, but it leads to terrain that is far more dangerous.

My inability to locate these people on my mental map of Islam led me to turn to that fount of knowledge who disapproved of me: my father.

'They're Wahhabis,' he said, after hearing my description. 'Your Jamat-e-Islami are also Wahhabis, but they don't have the audacity to suggest these ideas of a so-called "return to early Islam" to Muslims in the Indian subcontinent because there the masses still follow spiritual Islam in a framework of centuries-long Muslim scholarship.'

Who were the Wahhabis? I wondered. If I asked my father for more detail he would only attack those I loved: my brothers at the Islamist movement. I recalled vague memories of Grandpa recounting his negative experiences with Wahhabis while he was a student in Mecca. Grandpa, whose health had improved, had recently visited Britain and followed his usual itinerary of *dhikr* sessions, *mawlid* gatherings, and giving service to the followers of the Prophet Mohammed. I deliberately avoided meeting him. How could I see him? How would I explain myself to him? Besides, his activities seemed trivial to me: I was working for true Islam. Grandpa had somehow misunderstood Islam. Only Mawdudi could right the wrongs of Grandpa's understanding.

At college, I asked the speaker at Friday prayers, Abu Aliya, to tell me about the Wahhabis. Abu Aliya had an unkempt beard, flawless English, and a red scarf tied like a turban; he always carried a heavy bag full of Arabic books. Smiling wryly, he pushed up his thick glasses and said, 'They are people who follow the ways of the *sunnah*, or the way of the Prophet.' Deep down, I knew that was not the whole truth. He was hiding something from me. All Muslims claimed to follow the Prophet Mohammed; that answer was deceptive. It was rather like asking, 'Who are the Mormons?' and getting the response, 'Followers of Jesus'.

Whoever its proponents were, many students at college found the literalist approach of Wahhabism attractive, and I soon saw several of my fellow students heading to jihad training in Afghanistan in response to Koranic verses urging Muslims to rise up against violence. That the violence in question was of pagans in Mecca in the seventh century might not be obvious justification of a so-called jihad in the modern world, but who was I to argue with my literalist members? From YMO, we had introduced many of them to *Milestones* – had Qutb not called for a jihad against Muslim rulers on the grounds that they were non-believers? What, then, of the Israelis, or the Serbs, or Indians? Qutb's *Milestones* combined with Wahhabi literalism made a potent and dangerous cocktail.

In the multicultural Britain of the 1980s and 1990s we were free to practise our religion and develop our culture as we wanted. Our teachers left us alone, so long as we didn't engage in public expressions of homophobia or intimidation of non-Muslims. But Britishness and the British values of democracy, tolerance, respect, compromise, and pluralism had no meaning for us. Like me, most of the students at college had no real bond with mainstream Britain. Yes, we attended a British educational institution in London, but there was nothing particularly British about it. It might as well have been in Cairo or Karachi. Cut off from Britain, isolated from the Eastern culture of our parents, Islamism provided us with a purpose and a place in life. More importantly, we felt as though we were the pioneers, at the cutting edge of this new global development of confronting the West in its own backyard.

In early 1993, a thirty-minute video was handed to me about the war in Bosnia, the ethnic cleansing of Muslims in the Balkans. I watched it in horror and then decided that it must be shown to our students to raise money for Bosnian Muslims.

On Wednesday afternoon we booked a lecture theatre under the title 'The Killing Fields of Bosnia'. We warned the students that this was a video unlike any other they had ever seen. That same Wednesday afternoon the youth workers at college organized their second disco, safe in the knowledge that we Islamists would be busy with our own event and unable to keep people from attending. The Islamic Society offered a video on the killing of Muslims by Christians. The youth workers offered dance, drugs, and delight.

To our astonishment, the lecture theatre was packed. The students had voted with their feet. Delighted by the turnout, I delivered a welcoming speech and a stinging attack on the 'enemies of Islam' who had tried to compete with us. Having incited the audience with my confrontational attitude, I then played the video. In the dark lecture theatre there were sobs at what people were seeing; gasps of shock at what was going on two hours away from Heathrow airport: the serving of Muslim men's testicles on trays, Serbs slaughtering pregnant Muslim women, reports of group rape within the borders of Europe. After the video I stood up and, in sombre tone, related this to our situation in college.

'While our sisters are raped in Bosnia, our brothers slaughtered, the enemies of Islam organize disco parties for us here at college. I congratulate all of you for making the right decision and coming here. We must help our Muslim brothers and sisters. Next week there will be a talk on how we can try to stop the horrors of Bosnia. Please pass the word round.'

All that week students were asking us ask what could be done about the situation in Bosnia. How could they help? From campuses across the country we were receiving news of other Islamic societies holding discussions on Bosnia, condemning the United Nations' failure to stop the slaughter of thousands of Muslims, Croats, Serbs. The Balkan crisis truly radicalized many Muslims in Britain. I desperately wanted to help, to *do* something to stop the killing. And we were young; we believed we could change the world.

I began to attend meetings at Queen Mary and Westfield College, where I met young Muslims who collected money and sent individuals to deliver the cash to the *mujahideen*. One student who left for what was increasingly being called a jihad never returned to Britain. He was a martyr. Increasingly there were reports of individual Muslims from different cities going to join the jihad.

At college, doing something for Bosnia beyond collecting for charity became the discussion of the day. YMO offered little guidance but the ninja sisters and the Wahhabis had a clear answer to the slaughter of Muslims in Bosnia: jihad. They cited verses of the Koran that ordered Muslims to fight to defend the weak. Military style boots, Denison smock military jackets, and physical training in anticipation of participation in jihad all gained in popularity.

Word came back from Bosnia that volunteers from Britain were a burden on the *mujahideen* owing to their lack of preparation. The military types among us now started to whisper that Afghanistan, where there were proper training facilities, should be the first stopping point. We believed, we *knew*, Bosnia would not be the last jihad. In Algeria, for example, our Islamist brothers had won elections but had been ousted by the military. We knew that at some time, somewhere, this training would prove invaluable.

Although going off to fight never appealed to me – Abjol, a

YMO martial-arts expert, used to say that I should 'sit in the control tower and guide the troops' – I saw nothing wrong with Muslims preparing for a jihad. Nobody questioned its legitimacy – was this not what Qutb had called upon us to do?

It was in this heightened state that I met members of an international organization dedicated to the overthrow of Muslim regimes and the re-establishment of the Islamic state – the *khilafah* or caliphate: Hizb ut-Tahrir. Mawdudi's literature had trained us to want to create an Islamic state, not a *khilafah*. To Hizb ut-Tahrir, the *khilafah* and the Islamic state were one and the same. One of their members, Abdul Malik, had been invited to the college by a Muslim lecturer to lead congregational prayers on Fridays. The Hizb entered our college not through other students, but by recommendation of a teacher.

Abdul Malik was the son of the leader of our sworn enemies at Dawatul Islam, so we did not take too well to him. Besides, he constantly spoke about the need for a *khilafah*. In our minds the *khilafah* had ended soon after the Prophet passed away. It was a period that belonged to history and at Tower Hamlets College we saw no relevance in its resurrection. Soon we stopped inviting him. However, the three sermons he delivered for us helped us counter-attack the Wahhabis' rejection of scholarly interpretation of the Koran and schools of law in Muslim jurisprudence. Abdul Malik provided us with ample scriptural evidence to oppose the Wahhabi position. Again, where YMO had failed, others were succeeding.

Although we had not warmed to Abdul Malik, members of Hizb ut-Tahrir noticed my restlessness and asked me questions about my commitment to YMO, particularly about our 'methodology for changing the world'. It was difficult for me to defend YMO in the face of Hizb ut-Tahrir. I was disgruntled with YMO's obsession with the Bangladeshi community, lack of intellectual vigour, and complete failure to provide an answer to the Bosnia issue.

The YMO appeared more and more parochial. They concentrated only on maintaining complete control over East London mosque as an organizational base, and engaging in social work, educational events, youth activities, and fundraising with a view to recruitment. True, some senior members maintained close ties with political activism in the subcontinent and provided funds for Islamist politics in the larger cities of India, Pakistan, and Bangladesh, but that was all. Slowly, new rules were brought in. We had to seek permission from YMO leaders if we wanted to attend meetings of other organizations. I found such control-freakery increasingly difficult to stomach.

During this time, at the wedding of a relative, I met an Englishman who challenged my readings of Mawdudi. David, a research student, was a convert to Islam and was stern in his beliefs. A tall, thin man with glasses, he cared little for social graces.

'Why the hell are you in YMO?' he asked without preamble.

'What do you mean?' I asked, taken aback by this display of rudeness.

'YMO are a bunch of losers. They're a branch of the Jamat-e-Islami in the Indian subcontinent, followers of a shallow man, Mawdudi. Jamat-e-Islami have no concerns beyond their individual countries. As Muslims, we must think globally. YMO is a national organization, limited in its scope . . .'

I could not disagree with that. But why was Mawdudi shallow?

'Mawdudi was right to identify the need for an Islamic state as *the* solution for the problems of the world's Muslims,' said David, 'but he provides no answers. How will we bring the state into being? What is going to be its foreign policy? Its education policy? How will it deal with Israel? How will it address unemployment? Do you know?'

I tried to explain to him that Mawdudi believed that we should take power gradually, by infiltration of parliament, the army, and so on. But I had no inkling of how to respond to the questions pertaining to education, foreign policy, and unemployment. Most of us working inside Jamat-e-Islami affiliated organizations had as our goal the seizure of political power, and had given little thought to the minutiae of policy-related matters. If that meant adapting a democratic parliamentary system to our own ends, then why not?

'We can't do that, man!' David said, very excited. 'Democracy is *haram*! Forbidden in Islam. Don't you know that? Democracy is a Greek concept, rooted in *demos* and *kratos* – people's rule. In Islam, we don't rule; Allah rules. Human beings do not have legislative power. The world today suffers from the malignant cancers of freedom and democracy . . .'

As an eighteen-year-old, who was I to argue with a scientist? David continued to rip apart Mawdudi's arguments as I listened, defenceless. Eventually, I asked him, 'So what do you think Muslims should do? If Mawdudi and the Jamat-e-Islami were wrong, and we needed the Islamic state, whom should we work with?'

David was delighted with my question. As we ate tandoori chicken pieces he laid out his alternative of working with a radical political organization: the Hizb ut-Tahrir.

'The Hizb has a clear methodology for dealing with all of the problems of the world. From Bosnia to the Gulf War, from poverty in Africa to high crime rates in the West, we have solutions. Islam is God's system of government. Jamat-e-Islami and other groups may say the same, but we are the only group in the world who really will implement it. Our members in different Muslim countries have penetrated Muslim armies and soon we will establish our own government. Not through democracy or parliament – all that belongs to the *kafir* system. We will deliver the Islamic state through a military coup. Very soon, God willing. Our members orchestrated coups in the 1960s and 1970s in several Arab countries, but the time was not right. Now, the time is ripe. The West will shake and crumble. The flag of Islam will rise above Downing Street . . .'

David's sense of conviction was overpowering, his oratory unmatched by anything I had heard in Muslim circles before. Still, I interrupted and asked how he would relieve poverty in Muslim Africa, for example. The rest of Africa did not interest me: it was only Muslims that mattered.

'Huh! Easy,' he said. 'The Hizb will redistribute the wealth of the future Islamic state. Remember, the Muslim nation is one nation, one *ummah*. We were divided by Britain and France but under the caliph, the leader of the coming Islamic state, we will be united again. So we don't believe that the wealth of Saudi Arabia or Kuwait should be limited to those artificial constructs. The riches of Saudi Arabia belong to the whole Muslim nation, the *ummah*, controlled by the Islamic state. We will first distribute this wealth to poorer Muslims in Africa and then invite other non-Muslim nations to Islam. If they accept, we will alleviate their poverty too.'

I continued to question David, and he fired off responses. His ability to answer any question that I put to him, his brimming confidence, and radical vision for a future world order were attractive to me, a disillusioned teenage Islamist. We discussed the conflict in Bosnia, and the silence of Western and Muslim governments in the face of Serb atrocities. 'Put it this way,' said David. 'If there was an Islamic state, a caliphate, then Bosnia would not have happened.' David took down my contact details and invited me to attend a conference at the London School of Economics (LSE), where the leader of Hizb ut-Tahrir in Britain, a Syrian-born Muslim cleric named Omar Bakri, would be speaking about Bosnia.

My nascent conviction and increasing commitment to Hizb ut-Tahrir was not based on mere teenage naivety, although that played a role. There were other, more important factors at play. At Hizb events they argued that Bosnian Muslims were white, blonde, and blue-eyed and had coexisted with Serbs for centuries, yet Serbs massacred Muslims in their thousands. What chance of survival did we have in Britain? The British government had played a key role in colonizing Muslims in India, Egypt, and other countries: it was a sworn enemy of Islam. It would not tolerate a strong Muslim community in Britain. Among second-generation immigrant Muslims, that was a powerful argument.

Hizb ut-Tahrir activists narrated grisly tales of Muslim men having their scrotums roped to motorbikes by Serbs who then sped off, leaving the castrated men to bleed to death. We were told of pregnant Muslim women being raped by Serbs, who then cut their unborn babies from their wombs. Television news bulletins reinforced the message of Hizb ut-Tahrir: 200,000 people lost their lives in the conflict, millions more were made homeless. The Hizb organized meetings and demonstrations right across the UK on the theme of Muslim slaughter in Bosnia. I admired their passion about the killing fields of the Balkans and their desire to halt the massacre of Muslims in Bosnia. Hizb ut-Tahrir, unlike Islamic Forum Europe, had a clear idea of where it was headed.

Without seeking permission from YMO leaders I attended the conference at the LSE, where a procession of speakers variously proposed that we should lobby parliament, write to MPs, and put pressure on Muslim governments to force the UN Security Council to take some sort of action. Omar Bakri – the charismatic, pugnacious leader of Hizb ut-Tahrir, not yet demonized by the *Sun* – wasted no time in condemning the proposals of those who had spoken before him. His solution was at once radical, historical, and practical: an Islamic state with a powerful army. He took the main lecture theatre at the LSE by storm. No Muslim country, not even Saudi Arabia or Iran, was a true Islamic state. None implemented Shariah law in its entirety, so did not qualify as 'Islamic'. They did not fight Serbs and Jews, sworn enemies of Muslims. A tired crowd, bored after listening to mundane political speeches, suddenly jumped to its feet, shouting 'Jihad for Bosnia!' Omar Bakri knew how to rouse people.

Where others cited UN resolutions, Omar Bakri cited history. He spoke about the power of the Abbasid and Ottoman caliphs to protect Muslims against non-Muslim aggression, and poked fun at the regimes of King Fahd, Hosni Mubarak, Colonel Qaddafi, King Hussein of Jordan, and Saddam Hussein. The then Secretary General of the UN, Boutros Boutros-Ghali, was a Coptic Christian, a lifelong adversary of Muslims. How could we expect help from our enemies?

In the eyes of the Hizb, there was no point in fundraising for charities operating in Bosnia – the Bosnians needed military support, not money. Omar Bakri famously declared that it was *halal*, or permissible, for Bosnian Muslims to eat Serbs, because they were at war, so there was no question of sending money for food. What Bosnia's Muslims needed was the assistance of the army of the Islamic state.

At college we had not looked beyond sending individual and usually poorly trained fighters to join the jihad. David and others from the Hizb now explained to me that Muslim armies around the world were sitting in their barracks, polishing their guns, while fellow Muslims were being slaughtered. It was not the responsibility of individuals to go and fight, but the duty of the Muslim armies to unite under a single state, the caliphate, and *then* declare a jihad on the Serbs. We had the guns, we had the military capacity, and we had the wealth of the Gulf States. What we didn't have was a centralized political leadership. This was more like it, I thought.

Omar Bakri and many of his contemporaries in Hizb ut-Tahrir had entered Britain as Arab political asylum seekers. There was not a non-Arab Muslim in the land who could argue with the

wit and articulacy of Omar Bakri. I witnessed how easily he
overran the arguments of his opponents. As for the other Arab
asylum seekers, limited in numbers and grateful to Britain for
shelter from their oppressive regimes, they had heard Islamist
rhetoric in their home countries and did not have much time
for Hizb ut-Tahrir. It was mostly second-generation British
Muslims and converts who were seduced by the 'Tottenham
Ayatollah'. His mastery of the Arabic language, his ready and
seemingly relevant quotes from the Koran and other sources,
silenced us impressionable Muslims of Britain. Moreover, a particularly effective stratagem of Hizb ut-Tahrir was to convince
its members that 'working towards establishing an Islamic state
is an Islamic obligation', on a par with five daily prayers and the
Haj. Not only were we trying to help the Muslims of Bosnia
and establish an Islamic state, we were also fulfilling our religious
duty, a *wajib*. Arab Islamists, products of the repressive political
cultures of Syria, Jordan, and Saudi Arabia, succeeded in Britain.
Who dared question the mighty Omar Bakri and suggest he had
misunderstood the Koran? After all, Bakri and the Hizb were
true Muslims. The few who disagreed were swiftly branded as
lackeys, lap dogs, or puppets of the British government.

6. Inside Hizb ut-Tahrir

The Islamist does not flatter the people, is not courteous to the authorities or care for the people's customs and traditions, and does not give any attention to whether people will accept him or not. Rather, he must adhere to the ideology alone.

Taqiuddin al-Nabhani, founder of Hizb ut-Tahrir

My interest in Hizb ut-Tahrir came at a critical time. At college there were others who were also coming under its influence. From outside, Hizb members ensured that our interest was not a passing phenomenon. There were seven of us, all members of YMO or sympathizers, who wanted to know what the Hizb was really about. Wahhabis had put out information that the group was 'deviant' in creedal matters. Many in the East London mosque believed that they were Shiite, and Sunni Islamists believed them to be infidels. Arab Islamists familiar with the Hizb from the Middle East suggested the Hizb were American agents. Who were they really? I had liked what I heard from David about Bosnia. His refutation of Mawdudi's Islamism had been pungent. Omar Bakri at the London School of Economics was the only speaker who offered what seemed like a practical solution to the conflict in Bosnia. Now, I wanted to make up my own mind.

From its literature and by asking members of the Hizb I learnt that in 1952 Taqi Nabhani, founder of the Hizb, had applied to the Jordanian Interior Ministry to establish 'a political party with Islam as its ideology'. The Hizb was, from its inception, committed to establishing an Islamic state dedicated to propagating its ideology. The Jordanian monarchy rejected the application on the grounds that the Hizb was committed to overthrowing the king. Right from the outset, the Hizb was banned. Uncowed, it gained momentum in neighbouring Arab countries and was eventually outlawed in every country in which it operated. Its aims were considered seditious, its plans destructive, and its politics iconoclastic. And yet the Hizb survived and thrived in the prisons of the Arab world, filled with political detainees of various Islamist groups.

Nabhani, born in 1909 in Ijzim in Ottoman Syria, now known as Palestine, came from a noble family of Arabs who were close to the imperial hierarchy. Unlike Mawdudi and Qutb, Nabhani was a trained Muslim scholar from al-Azhar, though he later broke ranks with traditional scholarship. He read widely and his writings were of a deeper nature than Mawdudi's. He adopted Mawdudi's idiom of ideological Islam, but developed it to suit the milieu of 1950s Middle East in which Israel seemed like a temporary reality, new kings and presidents appeared transient, and the birth of political movements ranging from Bathism to Nasserism was the norm. Amid this kerfuffle, Nabhani researched and preached the need for a political party with Islamism as its core.

Nabhani and other founders of the Hizb were convinced that the organization would secure political power within their lifetime. They were making history. That mindset of immediacy, urgency, political desperation was visible in the conduct of the Hizb members I associated with in London.

Nabhani in his wildest dreams had not envisaged that the Hizb would one day function in London, capital of the reviled British Empire that had handed over Arab territory to the Israelis in 1948. Hizb members had requested political asylum in London during the 1980s. A member had been shot dead by the Libyan secret service outside Regent's Park mosque late in the decade.

Their primary zone of activity had always been the Middle East – until the early 1990s.

Falik noticed my fascination with Hizb ut-Tahrir's ideas and literature. 'You have important duties in the Islamic Society and YMO and you should continue with those,' he admonished. 'You shouldn't waste your time with these people.'

Falik was a YMO stalwart. Under no circumstances did he wither. When successive Muslim groups came on campus, and many of us took an interest in what they had to say, Brother Falik stood firm, always believing that the way of Jamat-e-Islami was the only path to his personal salvation and that of the Muslim world too. I found that sort of certainty mind-numbing.

Two men, Farid Kasim and Jamal Harwood, were now central figures inside the Hizb. Farid was a Sheffield University-trained town planner and worked for Islington Borough Council. Jamal was a Canadian who had converted to Islam and worked as an accountant with J. P. Morgan in the City. Along with Salim Fredericks, another longtime member, these were the men who introduced the Hizb to British Muslims. Under their leadership, and Omar Bakri's guidance, the Hizb targeted Tower Hamlets with steely determination. For the Hizb, Tower Hamlets was no ordinary borough: it was Britain's most densely populated 'Muslim area'.

The Hizb had three members studying at the Whitechapel-based London Hospital Medical College (LHMC). One of them, Patrick Ghani from Southend-on-Sea, was particularly active. Every week he organized talks with titles such as 'The Hidden Pillars of Islam', 'The Economic System of Islam', or 'Solution for Bosnia' at the Royal London Hospital in Whitechapel. Students from Tower Hamlets College attended in large numbers and some of us started to realize that the Hizb was of a much higher intellectual calibre than affiliates of the Jamat-e-Islami in Britain, YMO and Islamic Forum Europe in particular.

At one meeting Jamal Harwood, the Hizb's in-house

economist, offered solutions to government debt in the Muslim world, suggesting that Muslim countries should withdraw from the World Bank and arguing for nationalization of Saudi, Kuwaiti, Iraqi, and Qatari oil wealth. The 'Muslim oil argument', in which oil is used not as an economic lever by OPEC but to increase the wealth of the *ummah*, was developed by Hizb ut-Tahrir.

Seven years later Osama bin Laden and his assistant, the Egyptian Ayman al-Zawahiri, were to make the very same arguments (failing, incidentally, to attribute their ideas to their ideological teachers at Hizb ut-Tahrir).

I found the talks Patrick organized at LHMC enthralling. I could see that at college we had created a certain emotional hype about Islam, but here was a strategic vision, an alternative to the Jamat-e-Islami's nebulous Islamism. After the talks I would spend hours in discussion with members of the Hizb, questioning them on matters ranging from the dialectical materialism of Marxists to abstruse points in Muslim jurisprudence. Whatever questions I asked, Hizb members *always* had answers. Nothing was unknown to them.

I was responsible for the Hizb ut-Tahrir entering Tower Hamlets College. Although its members had addressed the students before, their reception had been lukewarm until I, as Islamic Society president, offered them direct access to the Islamized youth on campus – a fact that escaped me at the time.

Sensing a fertile recruiting ground, the Hizb moved key members into a flat in Chicksand House, a two-minute walk from Brick Lane.

Within weeks the flat became the Hizb's headquarters in Tower Hamlets, housing members of the Hizb such as the Kenyan radical Abdullah Hameed, who studied at Brunel University, and the SOAS undergraduate Burhan Haneef as well as others from Greenwich University.

Burhan, whom we called Bernie, was studying politics at the University of London's School of Oriental and African Studies (SOAS). Originally from Slough, he was an exceptionally warm, witty, and wayward member of the Hizb. His door was always open to us. At college I was emerging as an ardent supporter of Hizb ut-Tahrir, increasingly dissenting from the YMO disciplinarians, not advertising YMO events and displaying little reverence for YMO leaders.

At East London mosque, they were aghast. Who were these people? How had they so successfully undermined YMO's recruitment drive at Tower Hamlets College? How could they be stopped? Unable to counter the Hizb with ideas, Siraj Salekin even told Patrick 'to go and fish in other waters'. I learnt later that such protectionism stemmed from a spate of defections. Several leading lights in YMO had departed for various other organizations, unable to accept YMO's intellectual simplicity and obsession with Mawdudi.

Soon YMO members were holding briefings about the 'deviation of Hizb ut-Tahrir'. Warnings were thrown at me from all sides about why I should avoid them.

Azzam Tamimi and others from the Muslim Brotherhood advised YMO to leave Hizb ut-Tahrir alone and it would disappear of its own accord, as it had done in the Arab world. But Azzam Tamimi and his Muslim Brotherhood comrades had missed one key point: Britain offered the Hizb the freedom to express its ideas freely and recruit uninhibitedly. The Hizb was legal in Britain, but illegal in the Arab world. It would not disappear unless the British state wanted it to disappear. In the absence of governmental disapproval, the Hizb would continue to recruit and campaign unmolested for another decade.

I had many, many questions about Hizb ut-Tahrir to ask Bernie. Allegations that were made against the group by others, I clarified with him during late-night meetings at Chicksand House.

At the same time Patrick visited me regularly at college. Occasionally Bernie would speak at our events too. Now I began to ride roughshod over the structure imposed on me by YMO: the committee, the minutes, the organizational framework. All this I saw as a way of trying to control my behaviour.

To me, it became crucial that we explain to Muslims at college that they had an important role to play in the world. We were not little Tower Hamletters, as YMO had made us, with links only to the Indian subcontinent. The Muslim nation was a global nation, and we all had a religious obligation to establish a global state that would rival the United States and Europe. This was not fantasy. Not all that long ago the Ottoman Empire had roared at the gates of Europe; we would not only repeat history, we would make it.

Following long sessions with Bernie and Patrick, I and seven members of the Islamic Society had created a separate Hizb faction at college. No longer was I just the president of the Islamic Society, I was also the local leader of Hizb ut-Tahrir.

Patrick had given me some literature to read, including *The Way to Revival* written by the founder of the party, Taqi Nabhani. Like me, Nabhani had once been a member of a less radical Islamist organization. I was with YMO; he had been with our Arab counterpart, the Muslim Brotherhood. However, he left the Brotherhood disillusioned and soon started Hizb ut-Tahrir as a result of his own independent analysis of the Muslim condition in the 1940s. I related to Nabhani. Like him, I was a member of another Islamist organization and felt disillusioned by their ossified thought.

My *taleemi jalsa* sessions and other training programmes at East London mosque had always been lacking in evidence or substance, and too centred on Bangladesh. After all, I had never even visited Bangladesh; why should I concentrate simply on supporting Jamat-e-Islami in Bangladesh, Pakistan, and India and the Muslim Brotherhood in Egypt? Mawdudi's writing had instilled in me a deep commitment to 'Islam as a way of life', but what did that mean in reality? We believed that if only Jamat-e-Islami could win elections in either Pakistan or Bangladesh, then the whole country would become an Islamic country and gradually we would solve its people's problems. We were committed to gradual Islamization, and being pragmatic and gradual was crucial to us. This, on the whole, was based on *realpolitik*, and had no scriptural support.

In my discussions with David, Patrick, and Bernie, ideas I had accepted at *taleemi jalsa* were ripped to shreds. Sami had taught me, before my sixteenth birthday, that democracy was first developed by Muslims in seventh-century Arabia. Now, under Hizb tutelage, I firmly located democracy in the Greek city-state of Athens. And not only was it Greek, at the Hizb we considered democracy as idolatrous, since it did not allow for the One God to control mankind, but allowed human beings to choose their own destiny. How was it possible for Jamat-e-Islami educators to make such terrible mistakes?

Patrick pointed out to me that Jamat-e-Islami and its Arab counterpart, the Muslim Brotherhood, had strayed from the ideas set out in *Milestones*. Qutb, Patrick explained, had written his book under the influence of Hizb members he had met during his imprisonment in Egypt. Indeed, Qutb referred to being in discussions with a certain group of Muslims in prison in the first letters he wrote to his family. Those letters, later published as *Milestones*, were the ideas of Hizb ut-Tahrir: that Arab governments should be forcibly removed, that Muslims had no nationality, and that no other civilization had anything to teach us. Qutb adopted the same repertoire of expressions as Nabhani: *ideas, intellect, thought, challenge, systems, concepts, destruction, construction.*

I had graduated from studying the works of Mawdudi and Qutb and was now ready to receive the wisdom of the last ideologue of modern Islamism: Nabhani. In *The Way for Revival* Nabhani outlined three key stages through which Hizb ut–Tahrir wanted to lead the Muslim nation.

The concept of the 'Muslim nation', as opposed to a number of disparate ethnic communities, was key. To the Hizb, Indians, Malaysians, Turks, Indonesians, Arabs, Africans were all part of a single, global Muslim nation, an *ummah*. We were weak because we were divided. Muslim lands (not countries) were poor because the Muslims of Sudan, Somalia, Bangladesh, Kashmir did not share in the oil wealth of the Gulf countries. Oil, we argued, was a gift from God to the Muslims, all Muslims, and not just the Gulf Arabs. Muslims were 'One Nation, under One God'.

Where Mawdudi had been vague, almost dismissive, about the means by which an Islamic society might come about in Pakistan, Nabhani was exact in his three-part methodology. Moreover, all this was linked, it seemed, to the life of the Prophet Mohammed.

At college, the Wahhabis had been bashing us in the YMO for our lack of scriptural evidence for our Mawdudian *da'wah*. Hizb ut–Tahrir, through Nabhani's literature, provided me with ample evidence to counter such arguments. In fact, I was able to go on the offensive against the Wahhabis, arguing that they were British agents who plotted against the last caliphate, the Ottomans. Wahhabis had declared most Muslims to be 'infidels' and gladly accepted British support in rising against the Turkish sultan. From 1932 onwards, the British government maintained Ibn Saud as king of 'Saudi' Arabia until oil was discovered in the 1950s.

Worse, Wahhabis supported Saudi Arabia, a satellite state of the US, and most Wahhabi clerics were Saudi trained. Of their crimes, the Saudi clerics, under American pressure, had declared that making peace with and recognizing Israel was acceptable. I blasted the Wahhabis and, increasingly, Jamat-e-Islami for the lack of precision in their plans to establish the Islamic state. They agreed with me that it was *wajib*, a religious obligation, but had no 'methodology' to implement this 'duty'. The Hizb, in stark contrast, even had a draft constitution ready for adoption.

I quickly learnt that as long as Muslims accepted the Hizb's premise that the Islamic state was a *wajib*, just like praying, fasting, almsgiving, we were in the ascendant. The acceptance of that principle, that radical politics was the same as prayer, meant that whereas traditional scholars provided guidance in prayer, we provided leadership in political matters. And we knew it.

Moreover, we unashamedly aspired to be the 'intellectual leaders' of the Muslim nation. Mentally, I had already signed up to the idea, the religious duty, of establishing an Islamic state, a caliphate. My readings of Mawdudi and Qutb had already established that, but Nabhani's writings provided the details of how to achieve it.

Nabhani argued for a complete destruction of the existing political order, particularly in Muslim countries, for it to be replaced by the *khilafah* system. We were single-minded in our pursuit of establishing a distinct Islamic state, for in the obtaining of political power lay all the answers to the problems of the Muslim nation. Our arguments were powerful and, at first, undefeatable. 'If we had the Islamic state, then the caliph would send the Islamic army to slaughter the Serbs,' was our answer to the Balkan conflict. The international community said they refused to arm Bosnian Muslims to prevent the escalation of the conflict. But we knew that there was a conspiracy to reduce the numbers of Muslims in Europe.

Bosnia acted as a catalyst for extremism among large numbers of young Muslims in Britain. It was a serious political wake-up call for hundreds of us, semi-radicalized by the emotional Islamism of Jamat-e-Islami but given a clear, radical outlook on life by Hizb ut-Tahrir.

Looking back, I am still astonished by how I became so confident so quickly following my affiliation with the Hizb. Almost everybody I met there was young, articulate, self-assured, and an intellectual of sorts. YMO, once so attractive, now seemed little more than an insignificant local group of unsophisticated young Bangladeshi men trying to assert power by retaining control of East London mosque and funding their would-be martyrs and brothers in Jamat-e-Islami.

Hizb ut-Tahrir helped me to escape this narrow, imprisoned mindset of being in Britain yet associating with Bangladesh simply because I happened to live in Tower Hamlets. Hizb ut-Tahrir was an international political party; my new priorities were global. I was now part of an *ummah* transcending colour, nationality, and language.

I needed to know more about the economic, political, and social system of what we called the 'Islamic state'. Yes, to establish the state was *wajib*, but there was more. The Prophet's mission was wholly committed to establishing political superiority for Islam and Muslims. Right from the outset, the Prophet was a master politician and devised a strategy to ensure political dominance, first of Arabian tribes and then the entire region. This, Nabhani argued, was the purpose of each and every Muslim: to regain political ascendancy by establishing a powerful Islamic state. The Prophet had established a political party to realize his aim: his own companions. The Hizb was following in his footsteps.

It was explained to me that once I had reached this 'deep level of thought', realizing the need for political Islam in the modern world, then it was also *wajib* for me to join the Hizb, to study further its ideas and concepts and to swear allegiance to it. We bent the principles of Muslim law to our own ends. For example, *wajib*, or religious duty, was traditionally applied to individual acts of worship such as prayer and fasting, not politics, yet inside the Hizb we believed that the pursuit of political power was also *wajib*. Before formally joining the Hizb I underwent a lengthy interview with Bernie from SOAS. He made sure that I understood clearly the three-part strategy of the Hizb aimed at taking political power.

First was the 'secret stage' of building a political party with a core group of activists, then the 'open stage' in which the dominant paradigm of political and social constructs would be attacked in an attempt to substitute an alternative worldview. Once this was in place, the Hizb would seek what we called the *nusrah*, or assistance from powerful sources, to take political power. This would, in all likelihood, be a military coup, the third stage.

All this, we were convinced, was based on the *sira*, or the life of the Prophet Mohammed. He had bequeathed a political system for us to implement, a total ideology for global domination: Islam. This ideology would be carried to other parts of the world by means of a jihad, which was the *raison d'être* of the army of the future Islamic state. More precisely, our foreign policy was to conquer and convert. If countries refused to convert, then they would pay the Islamic state a tax, known as *jizyah*, to ensure their safety and protection by the Islamic army.

After confirming that I was intellectually convinced, Bernie introduced me to the cell structure of the Hizb. Every member, from novices still studying the literature of Nabhani to sworn members, attended a weekly gathering of around five people. The Hizb's secretive structure meant that I would be phoned by a mysterious 'Shabbir from Walthamstow', who would direct me to my particular cell, or *halaqah*, of the party.

That weekend, Shabbir phoned me and we met at a house in Shaftesbury Road, off Green Street in east London. Shabbir was a fast-speaking, slim IT consultant. He made me swear that I would never disclose the name of my instructor, or *mushrif*, or the location of my *halaqah*.

Our *halaqah* was to take place every Thursday evening, for a minimum of two hours, at the Chicksand House flat. At first I thought perhaps Bernie would be my *mushrif*, but no. Again, I was underestimating my importance, or the significance of the East End to Hizb ut-Tahrir. The party sent its most intellectual, high-profile, charismatic, controversial, media-savvy personality, to Tower Hamlets to train a new generation of Hizb apparatchiks: it was Farid Kasim himself. With Farid as my *mushrif* I knew I was going to be a big favourite in the Hizb.

Farid had been frequently interviewed by Channel 4 News and the BBC, cited regularly in British newspapers, and was the Hizb's official spokesman. At my first *halaqah* he took great pride in saying that he was banned from Saudi Arabia, Egypt, Libya, Iraq, and a host of other countries. It was almost as though he was suggesting that this was what we should aspire to. Then he said that he was like a father to all of us, and we should refer any problems in life to him. That instruction made me cringe. My own father, though I disagreed with him, was enough for me.

Farid spoke with a slight lisp, wore thick glasses, and had curly brown hair and, in his own words, 'beady eyes'. He was staunch in his Islamism, uncompromising in his attitude, and openly confrontational whenever the opportunity presented itself. He read the newspapers avidly, carrying the dailies around with him in his leather briefcase. The town planner with Islington Council always spoke about his latest projects when we met.

At the same time there was something particularly unappreciative in his attitude to life. Farid had multiple sclerosis and occasionally suffered from stiffness and spasms. He was regularly given time off work to rest and recover, but there was no interruption to his political activities. As a student at Sheffield he had been a member of the Socialist Workers' Party and he brought that radical zeal with him to the Hizb. Even during periods of convalescence he would attend our *halaqah* in a wheelchair.

Farid's unstinting dedication to the work of the Hizb was an inspiration to us all. Despite his illness and many other commitments, he was always on time for the *halaqah*. Some days he was extremely jubilant, on others very serious. Farid was convinced that he was participating in the making of a new world order.

Gathered at Chicksand House with our copies of Nabhani's *System of Islam*, we would never discuss anything trivial. We had to be serious — we were the leaders of the Muslim *ummah*. Like student accommodation everywhere, the flat was sparsely furnished. We sat on the floor in Bernie's untidy bedroom, under the black and white flag of the Hizb, with Farid as our focal point. One of us would read aloud from the pamphlet and Farid would explain its deeper meanings.

He often spoke in cryptic terms, giving us the impression that there was something in the offing, somewhere in the world. To us, the emergence of the Islamic state was simply a matter of time. The caliphate by next Ramadan was not a slogan: it was a statement of intent.

'The Hizb is organic,' Farid would tell us. 'Our ideas do not require offices, mosques, schools, charities, institutions for dissemination. They spread like wildfire. It is our duty to carry these concepts and use them to strengthen the Muslims, and destroy the West and its puppets in the Muslim lands.'

My involvement with the East London mosque became minimal. I occasionally went to pray, but targeting the Muslim masses was more important than helping manage a mosque.

As Hizb activists, we had to make 'hundreds of contacts' from among the Muslims, fill the *ummah* with our ideas. Every member of the Hizb, Nabhani stated, was equivalent to ten thousand Muslims. Without doubt we considered ourselves several cuts above the masses.

Farid abhorred with a passion the Muslim Brotherhood and all its offshoots. Islamic Forum Europe, the UK Islamic Mission, the Islamic Foundation were all different teeth of the same beast. He used to compare them to an octopus which always survived the amputation of a limb. 'The so-called Jamat-e-Islami and Muslim Brotherhood', Farid used to say, 'have many arms and many names in many places, but in the end, it is all shallow. They do not have thoughts and ideas with which to challenge the West, capitalism, and Arab socialism. It is only the Hizb that can overthrow these bastard regimes and install the caliphate. Our duty is to get this message to the *ummah*, to move them to support us.'

Encouraged by the examples set by Farid Kasim and Omar Bakri, we openly attacked the leaders of the Arab world: Saddam Hussein, Muammar Qaddafi, Hosni Mubarak, King Hussein of Jordan, President Asad of Syria, Yasser Arafat, King Fahd of Saudi Arabia, all came under our verbal fire regularly. With large numbers of Hizb campaigners now appearing on the radar in Britain, we took aim at others.

Omar Bakri, during the first Gulf war, called for the assassination of the British prime minister John Major. According to the *Mail on Sunday*, Bakri declared: 'Major is a legitimate target. If anyone gets the opportunity to assassinate him, I don't think they should [waste] it. It is our Islamic duty and we will celebrate his death.'

In Hizb circles we took pride in that command. After all, the CIA was involved in assassinating heads of state across the world, not least its botched attempts on Fidel Castro. So why not encourage Muslims to take out political leaders?

Farid's *halaqah* sessions were extremely potent. He injected us with ideas, brought to life by his years of experience and underpinned by the books we studied.

A second cell met in the bedroom next door, though we never saw them nor they us. Such strict secrecy and discipline, cemented by the ideas of the Hizb, made it an exceptionally powerful network.

Our seriousness and commitment were judged by the level and content of our questions. Farid would often test us. Once he mentioned that he would be attending a wedding at the weekend. A member asked, 'Who's getting married?' To which Farid replied, 'Why does that concern you?' He had mentioned the wedding only to indicate that he would be busy; it was not for us to enquire about the details.

There was a group culture inside the Hizb that no question should be asked unless it was relevant to our global aims. Our focus had to be total, unwavering, and zealous. Irrelevant enquiries resulted in accusations of 'shallowness' and the repetition of the same material in the *halaqah* rather than moving on to study new ideas. When Farid reprimanded me for asking too many questions about the life and death of Nabhani, I realized that I had strayed. We should not be interested in Nabhani the man, but Nabhani the ideologue and his vision for a future world.

The *System* was a core text, as were some of Nabhani's other books, including *Mafaheem*. The *Mafaheem*, or *Concepts*, was in many ways a more important text than the *System*. In part it was a refutation of the dominant Arab political ideologies of Nabhani's time, but more importantly it cast in stone the vision of the future state the Hizb wanted to create for the Muslim masses. Our constituency was the *ummah*, the global Muslim nation, and the *Mafaheem* taught us that in the pursuit of this constituency we should disregard both the views of other Muslim groups and the consequences of our actions. What mattered was our ideological supremacy, the strength of our strategy; in Nabhani's words we were the 'flaming heat under the kettle'. 'The water would warm and then boil, becoming a stirring driving vapour.' We were to be 'a flame whose heat would transform the society to boiling point, and then to a dynamic force'. The Hizb was 'fire and light, which will burn and enlighten, and definitely reach boiling point'.*

---

*Quotes from the English translation of *Mafaheem* (undated).

Nabhani's words certainly lit a fire under us. Our passion was underpinned by other ideas spelt out in the *Mafaheem*. Nabhani informed us that traditional Muslim scholars, the *ulama*, were 'confined to shallow sermons' on Fridays; we, as activists of the Hizb, were an altogether superior sort of Muslim. It was we who called for the resumption of Islamism as a way of life rather than a mere religion, and for that way of life to be enshrined in the power of a state.

The Islamic state, Nabhani taught, was a 'launching point' for a jihad. The *ulama* had failed to understand jihad over the centuries and reduced it to a means of fighting tyranny alone. Nabhani, like Qutb, argued that jihad should be a tool used by the state to advance the propagation of Islamist ideology. He cited the historical conversion of countries such as Egypt and Persia as a model for the advancing army of the future Islamic state. This state was to be set up first in Arab countries, from where it would spread to other nations. 'Jihad', Nabhani declared, was 'a war against anybody who opposes the Islamist call'.

We understood fully why almost every Arab government had banned us from our inception, why Nabhani had led a life on the run, and why Farid could disclose little about him other than that he was a chain smoker who could think deeply only when he had a cigarette to hand.

Immediately after the *halaqah* members would light cigarettes and walk together, discussing what we had just studied. I have never smoked, but in the Hizb I came very close to taking up the habit, which most observant Muslims avoid but most in the Hizb embrace with enthusiasm.

Pious Muslims generally avoid profanity, but in the Hizb it was the norm while arguing with Islamists, condemning the *kuffar* (often referred to in the Hizb as *koofs*) or even disagreeing with fellow members. How did this square with our aim to lead Muslims to an Islamic state by adopting a *shakhsiyyah*, or Islamic personality? There was nothing particularly Islamic about our personalities.

Upon nearing completion of the study of the *System*, lifetime membership of the party was offered. Delayed membership of the Hizb served two purposes: one was to test our level of commitment to the party, how we responded to the new ideas that we were being exposed to. Secondly, while we studied in the *halaqah*, we could legitimately deny membership. In the Hizb's idiosyncratic terminology, becoming part of the secret cell structure did not constitute 'membership'.

Omar Bakri often taught that if the Hizb was hated, loathed as an organization by other Muslims, it did not matter. What was important was to 'carry the concepts' of the Hizb, support the future caliphate, and work towards establishing the Islamic state. At YMO we had been driven by the organization, the name, the affiliation. Here, it was all conceptual, with a clear vision of where we were headed. Soon organizations as diverse as al-Qaeda and the Taliban would be advocating what was music to the ears of Hizb ut-Tahrir: removal of Arab leaders and creation of a caliphate.

When we were accused at public meetings held by other organizations of being Hizb members, our emphatic denials easily convinced our inquisitors. Such training to deny the truth in public was a key component of Hizb *halaqahs* everywhere.

On various eschatological matters, for example, Hizb ut-Tahrir differed fundamentally from mainstream Muslim thinking. The Hizb, based on Nabhani's excessive rationalism, rejected the role of the Prophet in the afterlife and the time spent before the Day of Judgement in one's grave. Other areas of disagreement, as we shall see, included pornography, insurance and almsgiving, along with other subjects. Other Islamists and Wahhabis attacked us based on what they had heard from their Arab sources. Wahhabi organizations were holding conferences on Hizb ut-Tahrir, and our ideas were being discussed behind closed doors by every single Muslim group in Britain. This was the mid-90s, and Islamism was in the ascendancy among Britain's Muslims.

However, we had anticipated those stinging attacks and were well prepared to defend ourselves or, better still, go on the offensive. There was an inbuilt culture of aggressive argumentation, dogged debate, and an inherent ability to cause offence that helped us thrive. We were taught 'Never defend, always offend'. With our radical ideas of world domination we set ourselves apart from the other Islamist groups in Britain. We caused a storm wherever we went. We challenged the ideas of every British Muslim grouping, even bullied speakers to adopt our arguments or face confrontation with Hizb activists. We provided them with what we perceived to be scriptural evidence for the necessity of the Islamic state. In those early days there were very few Muslims who could stand up to the might of the Hizb, pioneered by its young, articulate, British-educated followers. Moderate Muslims such as Yusuf Islam (the former Cat Stevens) even started to talk about the importance of the Islamic state. And so previously moderate Islamist organizations began to adopt our radical stance of confrontation with the West, establishment of an Islamic state, and commitment to ideological warfare. Long before the War on Terror the Hizb openly declared ideological war.

Once other Islamists began discussing the viability of the Islamist state, they had adopted our agenda. Now all discussions on campuses, in mosques, and at Muslim gatherings revolved around rejecting democracy, removing the rulers of the Muslim world, and the duty of Muslims in the West to help advance the cause of our brothers in Muslim countries (though not by making charitable donations, which we discouraged individuals from doing since this was, in our view, the responsibility of the Islamic state).

In political discussions our Muslim opponents were never able to defeat us. We knew how to deny, lie, and deflect. We discussed much of what Farid taught us with other members in Hizb ut-Tahrir and it was abundantly clear that we were receiving a uniform training. We believed that the Muslim *ummah* was in a state of war with the West, particularly Britain, France, Russia, and the United States, so lying and deception were simply strategies of war. Besides, our enemies were *kafir*, not deserving of our honesty or integrity. We employed the scriptural justification for deceiving the enemy that was used in the seventh century. We failed, however, to understand the context.

Hizb ut-Tahrir believed that all natural events were acts of God (though in some actions man could exercise free will), hence insurance policies were *haram*. Furthermore, the *kuffar* economic system should on no account be supported. Consequently, Hizb members could not insure their cars or mortgage their homes.

However, many members of the Hizb had a penchant for fast cars and now, without having to insure the turbo-powered engines, these cars became increasingly affordable. Hizb members were frequently stopped by police for speeding and many were banned for driving uninsured. The brothers from west London began to provide Hizb leaders with false certificates of insurance to produce at police stations. To this day I do not know how we managed to get away with it so often, but we did. (More pragmatic members circumvented the Hizb stipulation by insuring their cars in the name of a non-Hizb family member, which even at the time felt hypocritical.)

Such deception was not limited to the *kuffar* authorities in Britain. Even among Muslims we were disingenuous professionals. For example, other Islamists accused Hizb ut-Tahrir of sanctioning pornography. Hizb leaders initially advised us simply to ignore such claims, but the accusations persisted until Farid was forced to provide us with a defence.

'The Hizb tests public opinion,' he said. 'Occasionally, in the early years, the Hizb issued leaflets with religious edicts to test if the *ummah* was ready for *khilafah*. For example, when the *ummah*, mostly under Arabist influences, proved emotional we knew it was not the right time. Pornography was one such issue. Shaikh Nabhani always taught that there was no such thing as morality in Islam: it was simply what God taught. If Allah allowed it, it was moral. If He forbade it, it was immoral. There was no such category as "feeling immoral". There is a source where early Muslims looked into the reflection of a woman who was preparing to bathe. In another source, it was permissible to look at a woman before a man married her.' Here Farid stopped and asked if we knew what he meant by 'look'?

'Well,' one of us replied, 'it's obvious, isn't it?'

'Aha!' gasped Farid, as he prepared to enlighten us. 'The verb "look" in Arabic means more than just "look". Nabhani argued it meant a man could demand that he see a potential wife nude and then decide whether he marries her or not. Here, the duty was to prevent divorce later on grounds of bodily blemish. In order to prevent the sinful act of divorce, better to completely view her form before. There are sources to indicate that this was an early practice.'

We all gulped at this. How were we to respond? We were not the *ummah*, we were the elite. We had to remember that there was nothing particularly moral or immoral in life, only God's commands. Our own feelings had nothing to do with it. Based on that premise, our responses would deem us either intellectual (good) or emotional (bad). As leaders of the *ummah*, we were inclined to be intellectual and only express amusement at our new knowledge.

It never occurred to me then to ask Farid what sort of view of women this promoted. Were they mere cattle? Products to be examined, bought? And what if the women disliked what *they* saw when their partner undressed? Those were questions that came to me later. For now we had just been given proof that pornography could be acceptable, and we had an argument to combat accusations on the streets of east London.

But Farid was far keener on the wider issues, advising us instead to 'Be sharp! Change the subject! Our *shabab* [literally 'youth' but in this context 'party activists'] must be sharp. You should easily defeat the arguments of these Wahhabis, and the Jamat-e-Islami people. What do they have to say about economics? Foreign policy? Where is their constitution for the Islamic state? Those are the real issues, not pornography. We'll take our concubines later. I prefer blondes from the Balkans personally, but that is for later. For now, work towards the state. Go out and destroy the thoughts of the West. Expose democracy for the failure that it is . . .'

For Farid, and soon for us, the Islamic state was not an illusion. It was not an abstract idea. It was real, on the horizon, soon to be declared. It was merely a question of time. Farid's remark about Balkan blondes was not fantasy – it was the future he foresaw.

On university campuses across the country our *shabab* were creating a storm. Between 1992 and 1993 *Newsnight* covered our rise. Local newspapers in Britain, including the *Evening Standard*, wrote about the Hizb's activities. The *Jewish Chronicle* campaigned against the Hizb. We circulated newspaper cuttings among the *shabab* and celebrated our prominence. All other Islamist groups looked on bemused. How had the Hizb raised its profile so quickly and so successfully?

Boosted by the intense media interest, we went from strength to strength. Nothing gave us greater motivation than to hear our ideas being amplified in the national media, reaching new audiences of millions. To us it did not matter whether the coverage was favourable or otherwise. We were resigned to biased reporting, but we knew that there was a crucial constituency of Muslims who would look upon us as their leaders, their spokesmen against the attacks of the infidels. It was this recognition we needed more than anything else. The British media provided us with it and more: Arab dictators were now increasingly worried about the rising profile of a group they had banned four decades previously. Britain breathed new life into the Hizb.

When Yasser Arafat and King Hussein of Jordan visited London, our *shabab* were there in large numbers calling for the removal from office of these and other Arab leaders.

Buoyed by media interest, we now had a powerful presence at several British universities up and down the country. I had progressed from being an isolated president of a college Islamic Society to become part of a network of high-flying undergraduates at some of Britain's finest educational establishments.

On campuses we used the platform of the Islamic Society to call for the destruction of Israel and the rejection of the West, and to promote an Islamist alternative. At Queen Mary and Westfield College, for example, we held debates with the Jewish Society during which Farid and others often referred to the 'bastard state of Israel'. Our numbers were steadily increasing as we attacked the West, questioned any possible future for Muslims in Europe in view of what was happening in Bosnia, and denounced the incompetence of Muslim rulers.

We scoured newspapers and magazines for useful data to deploy against our major enemy the USA, underwriter of the state of Israel and prop of several despotic Arab regimes. The Hizb produced tens of thousands of leaflets envisaging the imminent collapse of the USA and the West, and of allied Arab governments. The leaflets cited the worst aspects of Western social freedoms, its financial system, and political immorality as evidence of the coming decline.

At the same time we met stiff opposition from other Islamist organizations, not only for theological reasons, but because we attacked Saudi Arabia and Saudi scholars with unreserved zeal.

It was the Saudi government that had invited the *kafir* US soldiers to the Holy Land. Their clerics had justified making peace with Israel, sworn enemies of Hizb ut-Tahrir. Our politics often isolated mainstream Muslims on campuses, but without doubt we had the loudest voices and the clearest ideas to convey.

We held debates with our teachers, journalists, and other intellectuals. Farid, for example, debated publicly with the likes of Paul Foot at London Guildhall University (precursor to the London Metropolitan University) and also with Fred Halliday of the London School of Economics. He also debated, among large crowds, with the president of the National Secular Society, Barbara Smoker.

She was constantly jeered, mocked, and patronized by a travelling crowd of Hizb apparatchiks who found it rather amusing that the best opposition Britain could offer to the Hizb was a middle-aged woman who was not well versed on Islamism. Nevertheless, she tried to enlighten her fanatical crowd with the virtues of secularism, though without much success. Farid's lack of grace in those debates was notorious. And we loved it.

Our style of debate and discussion was confrontational, designed to provoke outrage, to 'destroy concepts', as we called it. Our strategy was to obliterate those ideas that controlled people's behaviour or influenced their psyche and then supplant them with new ideas: our ideas.

The very first line of the *System of Islam* is 'Man progresses as a result of his thoughts'. Much time had been spent in our *halaqah*, as well as during my long discussions with David, Bernie, and Patrick, grasping the importance of bringing about an 'intellectual change' prior to any other shift in society. Implanting our thoughts into the Muslim masses was our most important aim. Long before Tony Blair spoke about a 'battle of ideas' we were seeding the very ideas that would shake the world.

★

One of our most popular speakers, a medical student at St Bartholomew's, was Abdul Wajid, or Waj as we called him. I still remember Waj's boasts: 'Jordan is ours,' he used to declare. 'King Hussein knows this. Our *shabab* control the army and we can walk into the palace at any time. But Jordan on its own cannot survive as the Islamic state, so we're working in other countries to join Jordan.' Similarly, Omar Bakri used to tell us that every house in Beirut had a Hizb activist. Such statements as these gave me great confidence.

Waj understood the minds of young Asian Muslim students in Britain, their difficulties and concerns. He littered his talks with anecdotes of curry, masala, and Urdu words, and used these to devastating effect to recruit many to the Hizb. Waj was later instrumental in setting up Hizb ut-Tahrir in Pakistan.

Conventionally, the Hizb responded speedily to international affairs by issuing leaflets, circulating press releases, and condemning global powers. Waj changed all of that. He, with help from other British-Asian Muslims such as Farhan at the University of Westminster, decided on a series of leaflets and talks that proved to be a phenomenal success across university campuses in the 1990s.

Waj travelled Britain delivering these talks, drawing huge crowds, bringing into the open subjects that mosque authorities considered taboo and families usually swept under the carpet. The first generation of British-born Muslims were now at universities in large numbers, and suffered from common problems that the Hizb tapped into.

'Sex, Drugs & Rock 'n' Roll' was one popular topic. 'Asian: Born to be Brown' was another. Most successful, however, was, 'Marriage: Love or Arranged?' Hizb ut-Tahrir produced leaflets on these subjects, though unattributed to avoid any accusation of dumbing down and losing its image of radical seriousness. We produced recordings of the talks and sold the tapes for a pound.

At first, college authorities paid little attention to the speakers who spoke at Islamic Society events or the content of their speeches. On the way to one such talk at Tower Hamlets I had asked Waj not to refer too often to the Islamic state since there was a large number of YMO students who believed in the Jamat-e-Islami and Mawdudi method of achieving social change.

'Sorry,' said Waj. 'You know we must pass on the concepts. I'll debate them if they want, though we'll rip them to shreds, but we have to pass on the concepts.'

It was that sort of steely determination to 'pass on the concepts' that led to the development of Hizb ut-Tahrir's distinct identity. Omar Bakri frequently reminded us that even if we were discussing the life of a chicken in a country farm, we were to link the discussion at hand to the caliphate, the Islamic state. 'Impregnate the *ummah* with the Islamic state,' Omar would say. 'And she will deliver the baby.'

The talks went like this: for example, in 'Asian: Born to be Brown' we would begin by cracking a few good jokes, utilizing examples of Indian food, auntie's chapattis, and so on. Such examples were well received by young people who were away from home for the first time in their lives. Then we would speak about racism in British life, that we will always be brown and never accepted. Then we linked this to Bosnia and promoted the Islamist state in which there would be no racism.

Similarly, in 'Sex, Drugs & Rock 'n' Roll' we spoke about clubbing in Leicester Square, getting high and one-night stands, and then realizing that there is more to life than pleasure. How could it be that we lived for pleasure while Bosnia burned? Those were sensible questions that resonated not only with Muslim students but with students of all backgrounds. However, it was our all-purpose solution, the Islamic state, that proved controversial.

Many Muslims students disagreed with our politicization of every subject. Even Ramadan, a month of spirituality, was full

of political meaning to us. Increasingly, Islamic societies dominated by Wahhabis and other Islamists expelled our members.
'Fear Allah, brother,' our members cried as we appealed to their
sense of awe for God and, when that failed, we appealed for
Muslim unity, suggesting that we should allow Hizb ut-Tahrir
speakers to address events and deliver sermons on Friday. Invariably, that appeal failed, too. Interestingly, all Muslim groupings
on campus at that time used self-taught, unqualified individuals
to address gatherings. Wahhabis, less extreme Islamists, most
certainly Hizb ut-Tahrir, all abhorred traditional or moderate
Muslim scholars. In fact, 'tradition' and 'moderate' were dirty
words in all our circles; in that, at least, we were united.

When our tactical appeals to fear God and embrace Muslim
unity had, predictably, failed, we pioneered other *da'wah* activities that stopped our rivals in their tracks. We made full use of
British pluralism and the encouragement to dissent by setting up
alternatives to an Islamic Society. When we failed to win control
of an Islamic Society we simply ignored it and started a host of
other student societies instead, with names such as Thought
Society, Debating Society, 1924 Society, One Nation Society,
Pakistan Society, and so on.

We used these bodies to secure generous funding from the
student union and then held events to promote our ideas and
win converts from rival Islamic societies.

At my own college there was a civil war raging in the Islamic
Society. I had been elected president because I was a YMO
stalwart, and now that I had defected to Hizb ut-Tahrir knives
were being sharpened. Forever naive, I believed that the young
people whom I had helped 'bring back to Islam', as it were,
would at least support me. I understood why they would oppose
my concepts, but not me. But to them, not only was I no longer
a member of YMO, I had joined Hizb ut-Tahrir, and so
I should be ousted.

All the same I worked on expanding the Islamic Society

beyond the Poplar campus to the college's Arbour Square site. After an event at Arbour Square several members of the Islamic Society surrounded me and asked for an impromptu meeting. In typical YMO style there was a chair and a minute-taker, and I was put in the dock. It was an attempt to express dissatisfaction and initiate a chain of events to remove me from office. Looking back, I can't believe that as eighteen-year-olds we were such organized, committed individuals.

I sat and listened to a room full of people accusing me of having introduced dissension to the campus; that as president I should be neutral and not supportive of the Hizb. I countered that being neutral meant being with Jamat-e-Islami. I seized the opportunity to be 'sharp', and pass on the concepts as Farid had taught us to do. I challenged them to produce a methodology for their work, to abandon emotional activism, and to develop a vision for the future Islamic state, the need for which we were all agreed upon. As taught in the *halaqah*, I went on the offensive. But the crowd was not in receptive mood. They had clearly planned this and a protagonist was emerging.

Abjol, the man later to become a councillor for the Respect Party, raised his voice and in rude and personal terms attacked my presidency, completely lacking the respect I expected of him and others. As I listened I could see how those very individuals I considered to be brothers could turn nasty, violent even. There were just a few Hizb sympathizers in the crowd who rallied to my defence.

While the argument raged, I began to feel dizzy. I had committed myself to Islamism because I wanted to be a better Muslim, a complete Muslim, not in order to divide Muslims. I had served the Islamic Society, raised its profile beyond that of any other college in Britain, in order to make Islam superior, not to instigate infighting. At that moment, for the first time in months, if not years, I remembered Grandpa. Abjol stood up and continued to shout, yell, and hurl abuse. Brother Falik sat beside me in stunned silence, not knowing what had happened to his old friend. I wondered the same.

I remembered Grandpa had once warned an imam that if the congregation was unhappy, then it was always better to resign rather than taint the congregation's religious experience with bitterness. I, to all intents and purposes, was the imam of the young Muslims at Tower Hamlets College. I announced my immediate resignation and walked out of the meeting. As I left, I felt pain in my heart, for only a year ago I had recruited many of those who were now unthinking sheep for YMO, *da'wah* fodder for Jamat-e-Islami, and bodyguards for visiting Islamist politicians from Bangladesh. My purpose, I thought, was greater than that.

On the bus home that day, for the first time in years, I cried. We were a few weeks away from the end of my second year at Tower Hamlets, and they could have waited to see me out. But they chose instead this form of brutal confrontation. Where was all the brotherhood we spoke about? Perhaps it had been instigated from outside, by those who had asked me to use the Islamic Society as a recruiting agency for YMO? I would never know. Oddly, the Islamic Society's ten-member committee which I had founded called me to a meeting and told me they had passed a motion of no confidence in me. Rather than simply accept my resignation, YMO had to have the last word by kicking me out.

Soon Hizb ut-Tahrir activists at Tower Hamlets College out-raged the established, prestigious, all-dominating Islamic Society by launching a rival One Nation Society. I still recall the joy with which the college management welcomed this split. Instinctively I avoided the limelight and put forward others to lead One Nation while I operated from behind the scenes. Farid called me a 'real politician'. In Hizb circles, that was the highest accolade one could wish for. Being 'sharp' was laudable, but being a 'politician', as defined by the Hizb, was better by far.

7. Targeting Communities

The art of propaganda lies in understanding the emotional ideas of the great masses and finding, through a psychologically correct form, the way to the attention and thence to the heart of the broad masses.
  Adolf Hitler

As the summer of 1993 approached, the Hizb was determined to ensure that Hizb activities did not cease when the students returned to their homes but that the concepts would be taken into the Muslim communities. A busy, event-packed summer was to follow.

Almost all the *shabab* who were recruited in Britain were rooted in Muslim communities in various parts of the country. Some were foreign, Arabs who were sent back to their home countries to put out feelers to determine whether the Hizb would be tolerated there. British university campuses had been fertile ground, not only to fire British Muslims with our concepts, but to send fresh blood into several Arab dictatorial regimes. Slowly, through contacts made in the UK, Pakistan, Bangladesh, Indonesia, and Malaysia were now on the Hizb radar. While Farid taught us, Omar Bakri was busy teaching Arab students and other 'secret' *shabab*. Many were said to be members of Arab ruling families, military personnel, or civil servants. At one stage Omar Bakri was delivering as many as twenty-nine lectures a week, both in private and in public.

While the British state fed Omar, he sowed the seeds of terror in British Muslim minds. Farid was delivering at least fifteen lectures a week. Similarly, Waj, Bernie, Jamal, and others all had their own bookings on the Hizb's lecture circuit. Our level of activity was considerably higher than all the Islamist groups combined. And where their events were often celebratory, ours had a distinct purpose: to inject the *ummah* with radical ideas.

From 1992, in mosques and community centres across the UK, Hizb ut-Tahrir appeared as a force to be reckoned with: young, articulate British Muslims whose parents had sent them to university for an education returned as dogmatic zealots linked to a network of speakers and brothers across Britain. Most of the *shabab* were given areas to canvass, in which we worked tirelessly to convey our ideas, attract new contacts, and initiate new events. I was placed in Tower Hamlets, which we always called Whitechapel, probably because our activities were focused around Brick Lane and East London mosques.

Whitechapel was vital to the Hizb, and our *masul*, or area leader, there was Farid himself. Gone were the days when he and Jamal Harwood distributed a few leaflets outside East London mosque. Now the Hizb had a core group of about twenty *shabab* who knew the area and the people well. Our duty was to move the masses, challenge Western values, support our brothers in Arab countries, demand *khilafah* in Muslim countries, set up contacts in the military. However, before any of this happened, we had to change public opinion. On campus it had been easy to stage debates, and we had had a ready-made audience of curious individuals. Mobilizing whole communities proved a more difficult task.

Unlike other groups, we deliberately avoided taking over mosques and setting up institutions. Nabhani had warned even against holding frequent conferences because this would create a false sense that something had been achieved. The only achievement we wanted was a radical shift in perception, to politicize Muslim public opinion, to connect it as an *ummah*, as One Nation. Then we could destroy the existing political order in Muslim countries and engage in the conversion or coercion of the rest. The unfinished business of Vienna in 1683, when the Ottomans tried and failed to conquer Europe, had to be completed.

And we were buoyed by media interest, with homophobic and anti-Jewish statements in our party literature. We took our ideas to the wider Muslim community for the first time. Just as we had done on campus, we avoided the name Hizb ut-Tahrir, instead calling ourselves the Muslim Unity Organization as we launched a series of local demonstrations across Britain.

We whipped up Muslim fear: 'Bosnia today, Britain tomorrow', we declared. Our leaflets, however, were always more than just flyers. We used them to 'pass the concepts', always including several lines about the dire need for the Islamic state and how it would solve the problems of the Muslim world alongside the place, date, and time of the meetings they were advertising. The leadership of the Hizb ensured that there was consistency in all our leaflets across the country – either Farid Kasim or Jamal Harwood vetted every one of them. In many ways, what we were trying to do was inculcate a feeling of *ummah* among Britain's relatively well-off Muslims, who saw themselves as remote from the problems of the Arab and Muslim world.

Moreover, as Patrick repeatedly told us, we were preparing an army of support for the future Islamic state. When the caliph emerged, we believed that the Islamic state would come under immediate attack from *kafir* countries, particularly Britain, France, Russia, and America. For these countries we had particular loathing.

In anticipation of this global conflict we were, in all earnest, trying to ensure that the caliph had plenty of support among Britain's Muslims, who would swear *bai'a*, or allegiance, to him and accept his orders. A home front would open up in the coming jihad.

Jihad, we believed, could be of two types: defensive and

offensive. When Muslims came under attack they were permitted to conduct a jihad on defensive grounds. But to declare war on states, and fight national armies, was the responsibility of the Islamic state. As such, a real offensive jihad would emerge when the caliphate was established. Naturally, allegiance to the caliph was *wajib* for all Muslims. Moreover, the caliph's orders were God's orders. The man-made law of the land had no meaning for us.

For the jihad to succeed against the crusader countries (we were talking of crusades long before George W. Bush), Muslims in those countries had an ideological duty to unite behind the Islamic state and be prepared to launch attacks on Britain from within.

During the first Gulf war, there were rumours that Hizb members were planning to attack British army barracks outside London.

In the meantime Bernie, Abdullah, and other visiting members of the Hizb who lived in Chicksand House struck up friendships with the gangs of Muslim youths who hung out on street corners in the evenings. These contacts, along with the many we had built up at Tower Hamlets College, had now to be channelled. Many were attending circles at Chicksand House, but Patrick wanted a public gathering place to which we could invite as many people as possible. His own venue, London Hospital Medical College, was now coming under increasing scrutiny; we suspected that the YMO and East London mosque had lodged a complaint in an attempt to shut us down.

So we moved to the public hall of the Davenant Centre on Whitechapel High Road for several weeks, directly opposite the East London mosque. After our events, we went there en masse to 'drop our prayers'. (The Hizb bred a culture that prayers were a burden, to be 'dropped'.)

The first time I entered the East London mosque with Omar Bakri, YMO members gathered quickly to see what we would do. I had planned simply to enter, pray, and leave; Omar, however, was uncontrollable. When he started to address the congregation the mosque caretaker ordered him to stop.

'But we are worshipping God! We are speaking about Islam, in a mosque. This is not your personal property. Let the *ummah* discuss these vital issues. Bosnia is being massacred, Palestine is under occupation, and you stop us from discussing those issues. Fear Allah, brother. Fear Allah . . .'

The caretaker was unmoved. Several members of the mosque management committee now came to his aid. He said he would call the police, and I knew this was no idle threat: the people at East London mosque had been my own family, giving me shelter when I ran away from home – I knew how far they were prepared to go to protect their personal fiefdom.

I turned to Bernie. 'We must get out, now!' I said. 'Otherwise we'll have the police in here, arrests, and chaos. These guys will fight to get us out, I tell you. Come on, get Omar.'

Bernie got the message to Omar and, luckily, Omar listened, though he had to have the last word. He got up, but he didn't shut up. 'Shame on you Muslims!' he shouted at the committee members. 'You go to the *kafir* police against your own brothers. Shame on you.'

Omar was the first Muslim cleric in Britain to drive a wedge between Muslims and the law. Within a decade his policy of non-cooperation with *kafir* legislation would set many Islamists against the British police force.

As we left the mosque I saw my old mentor Siraj Salekin. Not surprisingly, the old warmth had gone. Bernie and I headed back to Chicksand Street to discuss what to do next. On the way we discussed how wise it had been for Omar to confront the East London mosque authorities so directly.

'I'm glad he did it,' said Bernie. 'The *ummah* can see how corrupt these people are. They have no right to stop us from speaking in the mosque.'

I agreed. We dominated Muslim groupings on campuses up and down the country; nobody threw us out. We always found an alternative way to enter, to regroup, rename ourselves, and find a different pretext. But we were also concerned about Omar's application for political asylum. I worried that the Hizb's high profile in Britain might jeopardize the chances of him staying in Britain. I raised this with Bernie too.

'Oh no,' he said. 'On the contrary. The British are like snakes; they manoeuvre carefully. They need Omar in Britain. Most likely Omar will be the ambassador for the *khilafah* here or leave to reside in the Islamic state. The *kuffar* know that – allowing Omar to stay in Britain will give them a good start, a diplomatic advantage, when they have to deal with the Islamic state. Having Omar serves them well for the future. MI5 know exactly what we're doing, what we're about, and yet they have, in effect, given us the green light to operate in Britain.'

Bernie's words about the intelligence service proved to be correct. It was not until the events of 7 July 2005 that British intelligence admitted it had been a mistake to allow Islamists of all shades to put down serious ideological roots among Britain's Muslims.

Farid, now acting as area leader in Whitechapel, had instructed us to organize an area-wide demonstration to protest against the massacres in Bosnia. Our rally was headlined 'Bosnia Today – Brick Lane Tomorrow'. I helped distribute over 30,000 leaflets in houses, markets, and mosques publicizing a protest march along Brick Lane, Whitechapel High Road, and Cannon Street Road which would be followed by a meeting in the local park.

Similar events were being organized in Slough, Birmingham, Oldham, Manchester, and several other parts of London, including Newham and Southall. While the mosque authorities sat and looked on in amazement we generated widespread euphoria on the streets of Tower Hamlets.

This was our largest event yet, and we worked day and night

to publicize it. Our target was not to draw a huge crowd – if that happened it would be a bonus. Nor did we seek to raise the profile of Hizb ut-Tahrir. Indeed, we organized the rally under the banner of 'Concerned Muslims Living in Tower Hamlets'. In Newham, where I now lived, *shabab* there did the same: 'Organized by Concerned Muslims Living in Newham'.

Patrick and I met with local police officers in Leman Street to discuss the rally. Initially, the police were reluctant to allow it, for we had arranged everything without informing them. In the end, though, they had little choice and grudgingly agreed to police our rally.

So easily bending the police to our will made us feel immensely strong. Patrick now wanted to organize a demonstration every month. My immediate concern, however, was to ensure that this first one went well. Patrick's enthusiasm was typical of most Hizb activists, nearly all of whom were born-again Muslims. Being surrounded by so many Muslims in Tower Hamlets was, after his upbringing in white, working-class South-end, almost like living in an Islamic state. I was different. My sobriety came from the fact that Tower Hamlets was my area: I knew it well. More importantly, I appreciated the sensitivities of the people in the area, the families, and the successes of other Islamist organizations. I had worked with YMO and knew what it meant to organize a successful event, and how to avoid failure.

We had to be inventive.

Unlike the YMO, we did not have access to a regular Friday crowd at the East London mosque. I considered approaching the mosque at Brick Lane, trying to capitalize on my childhood relations with the imams there, but the son of the mosque president, Zitu Zaman, whom I had recruited from Tower Hamlets College to the Hizb, advised me against it.

'They still haven't forgiven you for joining YMO. Leave them out of our calculations,' he said.

With the two largest local mosques out of our reach, how

could we convey our concepts and invite the Muslims of Tower Hamlets, the largest concentration of Muslims in Britain, to join us in our protest meeting?

I drew on my childhood experiences and remembered that the local MP, Peter Shore, used to canvass us for Labour inside and outside the Brick Lane mosque during and after Friday prayers, using a megaphone. In the Hizb, the idea of non-Muslims entering mosques was anathema to us: how dare they lecture us?

But I did learn some things from Peter Shore. I suggested we fit a car with megaphones to announce our forthcoming demonstration. We started our megaphone canvassing on Friday afternoon, when over 20,000 worshippers would be at one or other of the major mosques in Tower Hamlets. We placed *shabab* outside each one to distribute leaflets and we created an ambience of activity and radicalism by flooding the streets around them with our supporters.

Patrick and I took it in turns to shout into the microphone. Amjad, an easygoing medical student from St Bartholomew's, drove us around in his mother's red Volkswagen Polo. We chose his car because it had two distinct advantages: it ran on diesel and, most importantly, it was insured by his mother. We knew that the police, as representatives of the *kufr* system, would stop us, so we had to take every precaution.

As we had expected, the police pulled us over. The car was briefly searched, but white lab coats and innocent-looking medical students helped allay any fears the police might have had. Besides, we told them, their man at Leman Street knew all about it.

Everywhere we went we drew a crowd, and we publicized the demonstration every evening in the week preceding it.

'O *ummah* of Islam,' I would shout. 'Your sisters and mothers are being raped in Bosnia, and yet you simply pray. You have a duty to protect your brothers in Bosnia. Come! Demonstrate!

The only solution for Bosnia is *khilafah*! Jihad for Bosnia! Jihad for Palestine! This Saturday, one o'clock, at Altab Ali Park. Jihad for Bosnia! Come and join us!'

We didn't pray at that time; the call to jihad was more important.

Today the call to jihad is heard more or less daily by large segments of British Muslim youth, but at the time this was extreme rhetoric. More than any other group, Hizb ut-Tahrir introduced the notion of jihad to the streets of Britain. Our call for one in Bosnia was not limited to east London but heard all across the UK. As we predicted, the *ummah*, once given the idea, delivered. Home-grown British suicide bombers are a direct result of Hizb ut-Tahrir disseminating ideas of jihad, martyrdom, confrontation, and anti-Americanism, and nurturing a sense of separation among Britain's Muslims.

I attended other demonstrations in Slough, central London, and Newham. At each the format was identical: the black flag of the Hizb with a truck to lead the crowd, stirring speeches, and stewards to direct the people and lead the chanting.

Key individuals attended most of the demonstrations and whipped up the crowd with slogans:

'Crusader, Invader! Saladin is coming back!'

'USA! You will Pay!'

'Israel! You will Pay!'

'Jee-had for Bosnia!'

'Jee-had for Palestine!'

We had gathered crowds for Bosnia, but the events were boiling with the rhetoric of jihad, the duty of the Islamist state. We did not believe that individuals should go off to fight. That was too small scale for us. We wanted the Muslim armies to move in the Middle East.

Wahhabi jihadists came to the scene much later. We introduced jihadi rhetoric, but wanted to channel the emotions to establish the *khilafah* that would do the fighting for us. However, the jihadi genie proved to be a difficult one to control. Going off to fight in Bosnia became increasingly acceptable and training in Afghanistan earned street credibility among young Muslims we had radicalized.

At Whitechapel, in numerical terms, we had not been as successful as I would have liked. We drew just under a thousand people. More importantly, the media covered our demonstration as I led it from the park on to Brick Lane, through Hanbury Street, and then on to Whitechapel High Street, past East London mosque and eventually to the third largest mosque in Tower Hamlets, which belonged to the Tablighi Jamat, in Christian Street. Our route had passed the three major mosques in Tower Hamlets in an attempt to move the masses against the mosque authorities and in support of our ideas.

A local protest march organized by Muslims was ground-breaking territory. As we marched past, calling for jihad, the shopkeepers, the council estate tenants, drivers, and Jack the Ripper route-following tourists, watched us. And so did the rest of the country. I still remember an ITN camera focusing on my face as I held a microphone and shouted to the crowd, 'We are entering the streets of the capital of *kufr*, my brothers, let them know "*Allahu Akbar*".'

We had targeted the prayer hall at the Regent's Park mosque some months before, forcefully holding gatherings there on Saturday nights and on an impromptu basis when there was a public event. During most of the 1990s there were always *shabab* at Britain's central mosque. Visiting Arab dignitaries, diplomats – tourists when not resting in the confines of their embassies – prayed at Regent's Park. Every Friday, our *shabab* passed concepts outside the mosque, spoke about the urgency of *khilafah*, and distributed leaflets. The East London management had thrown out Omar Bakri, but at Regent's Park we still had free rein. We were able to speak in the prayer hall at any time of our choosing.

The demonstrations in Slough and central London were addressed by Omar Bakri. I watched him as he walked tirelessly despite his limp, sustained after an injury fighting the Israelis in Beirut in the 1980s. We gained unprecedented exposure in communities across the country with our Bosnia demonstrations. Numbers were smaller than anticipated, but the concepts had been passed. *Khilafah* and jihad were now topics that dominated Muslim discussion.

In central London the *shabab* held regular study meetings at Regent's Park. In north London, we had access to the mosques at Turnpike Lane and Finsbury Park, and once a month we held 'political concepts' meetings for the *shabab* in London there. I went to two Finsbury Park meetings. In Newham we met at Green Street mosque, where Omar Bakri held weekly *tafsir* (Koran study) gatherings. Similarly, in other parts of the country we had entered mosques through two avenues: as young, concerned Muslims returning from universities on a break, wanting to 'talk about Islam', or through personal contacts we had among the large network of Asian uncles, the *Biraderi*.

We were still struggling to produce results from our contacts in Tower Hamlets, but we never stopped trying. Patrick was insistent that we attend Christian Street mosque every Thursday night. The Muslim missionary organization, the Tablighi Jamat, held weekly gatherings there.

'There is a ready-made crowd of three thousand there every week. Guys, we must make contacts. These people come from across Britain; send them back to the cities, not with Tablighis, but buzzing with our ideas.'

It became official policy in Whitechapel. At YMO it was an unwritten rule that we never interfered with the Tablighi Jamat gatherings, and the Tablighis reciprocated by not disturbing YMO events, but Hizb ut-Tahrir broke that mould. We attended and tried to control everybody's events. If we failed, we ensured that there was sufficient heckling to effect maximum disruption. There was nothing Muslim about our conduct.

Christian Street mosque, managed by the missionary but highly literalist Tablighi Jamat, had two floors and vast prayer halls to accommodate the Thursday night crowds. The Tablighis were well-mannered, humble people: we abused those traits ruthlessly. Humble minds, trained in mosques, were no match for our oratorical skills, sharpened at debating fora throughout the British university system in confrontation with atheists, Marxists, and other Islamists.

The first floor was crammed with elders who came to listen to speakers in Urdu. We rarely entered the first-floor prayer hall – that never interested us. We targeted instead the young minds that often sat idle on the second floor, waiting for a translation of the Urdu lecture into English. These speeches often started after evening prayers, but for hours beforehand youth from all over Britain, and sometimes Canada, South Africa, or Australia, would sit patiently and wait. Many of them were sent there by their parents.

The targeting and recruitment of contacts was easy. The Prophet had taught his followers to say *salam aleikum* as a first greeting. That was exploited by us as an ice-breaker. It was effortless to shift from saying the *salam* to asking, 'How are you, brother?' and from that to, 'Which city are you from?' and from that to the message we wanted to give. The maxim 'He who questions, leads' was utilized by us to the full.

We knew the people we had to avoid – those who were hardcore, wearing the subcontinental long shirt, skullcap, and long beard, we avoided. It was their junior followers in jeans and T-shirts, new kids on the block, that we had in mind. On several nights we entered the second floor of the prayer hall and split up into pairs, sitting among the youth and conducting impromptu circles, rather like Speakers' Corner at Hyde Park.

The young men were already in a religious frame of mind,

sitting in a mosque waiting for a lecture to commence. We gladly entertained them with our ideas. Farid encouraged us to speak as often as possible at Christian Street. He had sharpened his own delivery there.

Farid and his sidekick Zulfiqar would jump on a bench outside a mosque, or stand on a car bonnet wherever Muslims gathered. Farid would address the crowd with no preparation whatsoever. This style of spontaneous zealous public performance, taken from fundamentalist Christian preachers and Marxists, was developed among Muslims by Hizb ut-Tahrir: we always had something to say. Other groups leafleted, booked venues, hired speakers, invited people. We went to the crowds: wherever there were people, we spoke. At university refectories we spoke aloud among ourselves, exploiting the British habit of eaves-dropping.

At Christian Street we had free access every Thursday night for at least three months. The elders from the first floor were delighted to see that the young people upstairs were divided in groups and 'speaking about Islam'. However, as expected, we were soon detected. We made the mistake of distributing leaflets and some of the *shabab* even handed out their phone numbers. That immediately alerted the elders.

A 'no discussion' rule was imposed on Thursday nights – from then on, only the main speaker would speak and we were all supposed to listen. But we were not ones to obey man-made rules. A young lanky, long-bearded Tablighi politely asked several of us to leave the mosque one Thursday night.

'Why, brother?' asked Patrick. 'How can you ask a Muslim to leave the House of God?' We knew how to play to Muslim sensitivities. The guilty fellow reconsidered his actions.

'OK. Stay. But please don't speak.'

'Why not?' asked Patrick, realizing that his tactics were paying off. 'We're speaking about Islam. About Muslims in Bosnia. How can you silence us? Fear Allah, brother.'

Before Patrick could end his argument, which was clearly heading towards a successful conclusion, a Tablighi elder came along and patted Patrick on the back, saying, 'Please leave. No discussions.'

The elders were harder for us to engage with. They were not easily persuaded, nor susceptible to our well-tried 'Fear Allah' blackmail.

The following week we returned with our megaphones and the Volkswagen Polo. We circled Christian Street mosque attacking the Tablighi Jamat and their introvert, apolitical form of Islam.

'Praying and fasting is not enough, O Muslims! What use are your prayers when the Jews slaughter your brothers in Palestine? Today it is more important to establish the Islamic state, the *khilafah*, to honour your faith. Wake up from your slumber! Bring back the army of *khilafah* . . .'

Oddly, for the first time, there were police sirens behind us. I was in the back seat, with Patrick at the front. The last thing I wanted was for us to be arrested or questioned in front of the mosque, presenting ourselves as a scene for amusement for Tablighis. I asked Amjad to drive to the end of the road, where, with the police car behind us, we stopped.

'Please step outside, gentlemen,' an officer requested.

The usual recording of names and addresses followed. Upon learning that we were all students, two of us medical students at leading London university hospitals, the police were lenient with us.

'There have been complaints from the mosque,' said the officer. 'I suggest you don't trouble the people inside. If they deem you to be a nuisance, then we will have to take things further.'

'But we're not harming anybody,' protested Amjad. 'We're only megaphoning. What's wrong with that?' Our innate inclination to confront, to argue, could not be dampened even by the courtesy of the British police. We parked the car, put the megaphone in the boot and headed to the mosque. In the meantime, outside the mosque, our *shabab* were causing an uproar.

'How dare you call the *kafir* police,' shouted one. 'Don't you know it's *haram* to get the *kuffar* involved in Muslim affairs? The Saudis invite the US to our countries, just like you. Go running to the *kuffar*.' We had been trained always to link local issues to the global concerns of Muslims. Our *shabab* were doing well, very well. To link our expulsion from a mosque to US troop presence in Saudi Arabia was indeed an intellectual achievement of sorts. In years to come the Hizb would argue that every British Muslim difficulty, from terrorism to poor community relations, was a result of British foreign policy. And to this drumbeat, other Islamists would march.

Among all the shouting and chaos, the call to prayer went off. Most of the Muslims went inside to pray. We were banned from entering, so we wandered off.

Although we were ejected from Christian Street mosque, our presence pervaded Tower Hamlets. We put up posters on the walls, handed out leaflets on the streets, and held regular events at the Davenant Centre. Patrick had made many key contacts in the local media. He selected his 'contacts' carefully, and slowly worked to ensure long-term conviction. Many of those contacts he then handed over to local *shabab* in various parts of the country. In his home-town of Southend-on-Sea, Patrick had recruited over twenty young people to the cause of Hizb ut-Tahrir. Soon Patrick was sent from Tower Hamlets and ended up recruiting in Bangladesh, a result of a contact in Tower Hamlets. He had been in close touch with a university professor in Dhaka, whom he used to set up Hizb ut-Tahrir there. Britain served the Hizb ut-Tahrir as an excellent launch pad for recruitment and the export of Islamist ideology to parts of the Muslim world Nabhani never dreamed would join the Hizb: Indonesia, Uzbekistan, Pakistan, Bangladesh, Turkey.

★

We had fired up Whitechapel to such an extent that summer that our faces were now well known in every mosque and community centre in Tower Hamlets. I began to wonder if I was doing the Hizb a disservice. Should we move to other areas and allow newer *shabab* to take over? Our brothers in the neighbouring borough of Newham were struggling with limited numbers and resources. Perhaps some of us should move there. I wanted to speak to Farid about this when an incident in East London mosque made up my mind for me.

I regularly received reports from several of our activists about their recruitment and development of support for our ideas in East London. However, as a principle, I tried to avoid attending the mosque as often as possible. I had too many memories and knew far too many people there. Besides, I knew Brother Falik had not fully recovered from my defection from the YMO and did not want to rub salt in his wounds. However, after a lecture in the Brady Centre, I was passing by the mosque with a group of our *shabab* when the time for prayer came. It seemed wrong to walk past and not pray.

After prayers I walked downstairs to the large foyer and noticed, as usual, our *shabab* engaged in debate there. The echoes were loud and I was surprised that there were no complaints. Debating with Islamists from YMO was always interesting for us, because we almost always won. A particular weak spot of the YMO and their parent organization, Jamat-e-Islami, was that they, like the Muslim Brotherhood in Egypt, had participated in free elections.

'How could you possibly advocate democracy?' said one activist, interrupting a leader of Islamic Forum Europe. 'Don't you know democracy comes from the Greeks. It is *kufr*. *Demos kratos* is people's rule. In Islam, only Allah rules. Not people. Sovereignty belongs to God, not men. How can you follow man-made law?'

Musleh Faradhi, a leader of Islamic Forum Europe, was surrounded by YMO people unable to believe that their leaders were silent, without argument. Faradhi made an excuse and left. Other smaller discussions were taking place and as I walked over to join one I saw the main doors of the mosque open.

Shoes in hand, in came an old acquaintance of mine. Zachariah had studied at Tower Hamlets College the previous year. He was always stern, but friendly towards his acquaintances. I knew Zachariah fairly well and had heard others speak about his mastery of martial arts. I knew he often trained in the basement of the mosque with other martial arts fans. Khan *sahib* would reserve the rooms for him. 'Zachariah is training' was understood to mean that there were a small group of people in the basement who were not to be disturbed.

I went over to greet him. He was not his usual self, taken aback by what he saw: several activists of the Hizb publicly debating on what he considered to be his own turf. And I, in his eyes a traitor who had left the YMO, was there too.

'What are you doing here?' he asked.

'What do you mean?' I responded, puzzled.

Zachariah walked up to one of the *shabab*, grabbed him by the arm, dragged him down the stairs, swung open the main doors of the mosque, and threw him outside. I could not believe what I was seeing. How dare he?

'Stop it!' I shouted. 'Stop it! How can you attack Muslims? It's *haram*!'

At that moment Zachariah grabbed my shirt collar and violently tugged it, ripping the buttons while bending my neck suddenly. He pushed me down the stairs and out. Within seconds, all the *shabab* were fleeing the building.

I was almost in tears, but I knew this was a moment at which I had to remain strong and provide leadership to those who looked on.

How could Zachariah, a fellow brother in the Islamist movement, commit such a crime? The pain was unbearable, the humiliation unprecedented. Only a year earlier I had run away from home and been given shelter by Islamists at this mosque. In all my life, I had never been treated violently. Even during the racist days of the 1980s, my secondary school years, there had been taunts and the odd tussle, but nothing like this.

We crossed over Whitechapel High Street and I called Farid Kasim. On our very first *halaqah* he had told us that he was like a father to us. Farid's response on hearing what had happened stunned me: 'You must change public opinion in the area. That is the only way to control the mosque.'

There were no words of comfort, no promise to complain officially to the mosque, and we were not allowed to go to the police. It was Muslim business.

Farid's impersonal, indifferent response shook me. How could he? When Farid had been expelled from university campuses, we had stood by him. At SOAS and at Tower Hamlets College we had smuggled him in by changing his name to Abu Yasir, defying the authorities and risking expulsion. And yet, when we were down, he did not care.

What sort of human beings was the Hizb creating? This experience sowed the very first seed of doubt. If Zachariah, a fellow Islamist, was prepared to fight us in a mosque, what were Islamists capable of doing when in power?

8. Inferior Others

The only meeting place between a Muslim and a Jew is the battlefield.

Hizb ut-Tahrir leaflet

My defection from YMO to Hizb ut-Tahrir, involvement in setting up the Hizb in Whitechapel, and managing the college Islamic Society through a turbulent period meant I had little time left for my studies. My mind was on Bosnia and Palestine rather than my studies in Britain. My daily life was dedicated to activism: recruiting new activists, organizing events, distributing leaflets, arguing and debating with those who opposed us.

At home my parents thought that I had left YMO and Islamism and began to express some joy. It was short lived. My disagreements with YMO were not theological, they were political. My father soon pointed that out to me. At the beginning of the previous academic year he had suggested that I study for A-Levels at any one of the three further education colleges in Newham. I refused. I had been elected president of the Islamic Society at Tower Hamlets and had a duty to serve.

Now, exhausted and wary of Islamist factionalism in Tower Hamlets, I decided to study in Newham. The previous year I had flunked my exams and scraped through my resits, using my pass to access the college and attending classes only occasionally. This year, I promised myself, I would study.

I chose history, government and politics, and sociology for my A-Level subjects and applied myself to study. I was fortunate that my request for a transfer from Tower Hamlets to Newham was granted by the leadership. The 'scene', as we called it, in Newham, was totally different from that at Tower Hamlets. There, we fought tooth and nail with rival Islamists from Jamat-e-Islami's offshoots, were in conflict with apolitical Tablighis in Christian Street mosque, and, in my case at least, tried to avoid Brick Lane mosque for fear of clashing with my own father in public. Nevertheless, I left a Hizb that was growing in numbers, confident in its expression and able to maintain a visible public presence with its innovative ideas.

Newham, though a neighbouring borough to Tower Hamlets, was a completely different operation altogether. It had a large Muslim population, but it also had a liberal smattering from other faiths, particularly Sikhs and Hindus. It also had a large African Christian population as well as a significant white working-class Protestant presence. As an Islamist, I saw everyone along religious lines, and all non-Muslims as inferior to us.

During my first year in Newham, 1994, I studied well. I attended classes regularly, took part in seminars and did all of my homework. All the while Hizb ut-Tahrir was creating waves on campuses across the country, coming under fire from Jewish leaders as anti-Semitic, but I kept a low profile. The college's Islamic Society in Newham did trouble me, though, because of the group that dominated it.

The society held weekly lectures. They were not as popular as the ones in Tower Hamlets had been, but a fair number of students attended. The speakers, without exception, were Wahhabis from JIMAS, although these young teenagers with their trademark fluffy beards, short trousers, army boots, and red Saudi scarves preferred to call themselves Salafis, claiming that they followed the Salaf, or early Muslims. In reality, they were far removed from the Salaf. In many ways they were similar to the Amish, but without the key trait of humility. While the Amish are an independent, secluded community, the Salafis are sponsored by Saudi Arabia to propagate Salafism or Wahhabism globally.

I did, however, keep my political activities going in the community. I met potential recruits who were handed over to me by local *shabab*. Every Saturday night I attended a public circle in Shaftesbury Road, in the mornings helped man a *da'wah* stall on Green Street, and attended my weekly *halaqah*. Compared to the manic lifestyle in Whitechapel, this was luxury.

During these activities I met a young Hizb activist, Eisa al-Hindi, a convert from Hindusim. Eisa used to spend nights at Shaftesbury Road and other houses rented by Hizb members. His family wanted him to return to them, if not Hinduism. Eventually they tracked him down and forcibly removed him to India in an attempt to sever his connection with the Hizb. It was too late. The commitment to jihad and destruction had already been implanted in Eisa's young mind. In India he searched for others who held similar convictions. He ended up fighting Indian troops in Kashmir, wrote a book advocating violence which was sold in Britain's Islamist bookshops, and then, after 9/11, his name appeared on the CIA's list of al-Qaeda terrorists who had previously targeted New York.

I remember Eisa in his black bomber jacket and dark denim jeans. He was always keen to socialize, spending long hours talking and attending as many events as possible. We manned stalls together in Asian-dominated Green Street, in Upton Park. He was someone who had entered Islam and started preaching to Muslims about the need for the Islamic state, jihad, and the destruction of the West without having learnt how to pray.

The *da'wah* stall was a creative idea first used by the Hizb. Again, while other Muslim groups were busy organizing along conventional lines, we were pioneering new methods. I think we borrowed that particular idea, as we did much else, from radical socialists. On Saturday mornings, and occasionally at large meetings of other groups, we pitched up with our paste table and some of our most controversial leaflets, tapes, and invitations to our meetings. For about five hours every Saturday morning, five minutes away from West Ham football stadium, we took turns in groups of four to stand by our stall. Similar stalls appeared in many other parts of Britain.

As a result of my relocation from Whitechapel, my *halaqah* changed too. I now had the same *mushrif* as Patrick. Amir Khan was a final-year medical student at King's College London. His younger brother, the whiz-kid behind a coming campaign, was Asif Khan, a scientist at Imperial College London. Both brothers, along with their younger brother, Kashif, were dedicated members of Hizb ut-Tahrir. They lived with their parents in a maisonette off London's Marylebone Road. I attended *halaqah* on Thursday nights, and usually caught a lift with Tahir Malik, a city banker.

This *halaqah* was different. All the students were at top universities in London. There was an American student who was studying at the LSE, and most others were at SOAS, King's, or Imperial. I was the youngest student there and being in such company made me take the Hizb even more seriously.

Amir developed the concepts in the latter part of the *System of Islam* to new heights. He was an enthusiastic intellectual, keen to deliver the ideas to us as succinctly as possible. The details of the Islamic state were contained in the draft constitution composed by Nabhani and offered to several Islamist organizations as a political document. One had been sent to the Iranian revolutionary Ayatollah Khomeini in 1978, though after two meetings with Hizb leaders in Paris he had rejected the constitution. We, however, studied it with more dedication than the Koran, convinced that we would see the 186 articles listed in its fifty pages implemented as state policy very shortly, preferably by 'next Ramadan'.

It was during the study of the constitution that doubts started to creep into my mind as to where we were headed. The draft constitution was not set in stone but a living document – the 'architect's blueprint' Karl Marx wrote about as a prerequisite to political success. In the constitution Nabhani had designed a highly centralized state, controlling almost every aspect of life from the centre. He had detailed the role of the army, the function of the citizen, the purpose of the education system, the running of the economy, and the minutiae relating to the life of a caliph. Much of this was impressive, for we believed this was all Nabhani's own research. Later, at university, I discovered a book by a thirteenth-century Muslim author, al-Mawaridi, who had detailed the structure of the Abbasid Empire; the Abbasids, like their predecessors the Umayyads, had simply adopted the codes of civil government of Byzantium and Persia. The claim to an 'original Islamic political system' was a myth. Nabhani had simply adopted that text without mentioning his source. Nabhani's plagiarism, I was soon to learn, was not limited to his constitution.

Much of the constitution was a futuristic document; although I found several of its articles unpalatable, they were not immediately relevant to my life. However, under a section entitled 'The Social System', Nabhani had several articles I found problematic. Article 114, for example, states: 'Women are forbidden to be in private with any man they can marry, they are also forbidden to display their charms or reveal their body in front of foreign men.'

By 'foreign men' Nabhani meant men from outside the immediate family. And the tone of the article was Koranic. However, in Hizb circles, we mixed with the 'sisters', or female activists of the Hizb, more than any other Islamist group. In YMO, segregation had been rigorously upheld, and one of the Hizb's attractions for me was its comparatively liberal attitude towards women. Many of our *shabab* were in relationships with the 'sisters'. Were we prescribing for other Muslims behaviour that we did not ourselves follow? Nabhani advocated segregation, but our events were far from segregated. Our *shabab* courted many of the sisters. I asked Amir how this could be. His response annoyed me. 'We're talking about the plague, here. Women are like the plague. Avoid them at all costs. I know that many of the *shabab* are in relations with sisters, but we shouldn't be.' Any further questioning would result in me being perceived as shallow and distracted. I had to be careful about the questions I asked, the assumptions I made.

The Hizb had an ingrained culture of smothering thought and questions that it considered might conflict with the grand scheme of overthrowing governments and confronting the West. I had already gone beyond the pale; I had questioned Nabhani.

As one who had two sisters and was close to his mother, I did not take well to this description of women as 'the plague'. And Amir had been far too lenient on the 'relationships' issue. My qualm was about fairness: if we believed in segregation for Muslims and no private meetings between the sexes, then it ought to apply to us too. Meeting in parks, cinemas, cars, and university corridors in the name of 'public space' smacked of hypocrisy to me.

The beginning of 1994 was a quiet period for me. Across the country, however, much was happening. In addition to the hundreds of meetings we held, public and private, not counting the impromptu public addresses by members outside major mosques in Britain, we started the publicity for an unprecedented event.

Our success on university campuses, the previous summer's Bosnia demonstrations, and the headway we had made in local communities gave us great strength. My instructor's younger brother, Asif, began to publicize an international conference to mark the official ending of the Ottoman Empire, the abolition of the sultanate and the introduction of Ataturk's secularism. This we referred to as the 'destruction of the Islamic state'. After the First World War, and Turkey's defeat, the last sultan was removed from office on 3 March 1924. For all Muslims, but for us more than any other group, this date held particular significance.

At several universities, when we were expelled from the Islamic societies, we started a '1924 Society' with the aim of making the events of that year seem recent, relevant, and reprehensible. In Sunni Muslim minds the *khilafah* was associated with the first four caliphs who ruled after the death of the Prophet and, after some turbulence, their successors in the Abbasid Empire, which ended in 1256. However, Hizb ut-Tahrir successfully recast our imaginations, arguing that the rightful caliph of the Muslim world had been the Turkish sultan and that 1994 marked only the seventieth anniversary of the *khilafah's* destruction. Inside the Hizb, there was a feeling that something was about to happen in the Middle East. That we were on the verge of a new world order, that our brothers in the armies of Jordan and Iraq would move to topple the regimes, and empower Islam and Muslims by declaring an Islamic state.

As always, our duty in Britain was to prepare the *ummah* for the caliph, to swear allegiance to the future Islamic state, deeming the Queen and the British government wholly irrelevant to British Muslim life. We planned a major conference, billed as the 'largest outside the Muslim world in history'. We booked Wembley arena.

With the Hizb's network of nearly 300 core activists, and a further web of 'contacts' nearing 4,000, we were confident that we could easily attract a crowd of 12,000. We started the advertising early, seven months beforehand.

As I was attending *halaqah* with Amir, I got regular updates from the motor-mouthed Asif about intense media interest in the event, forthcoming press conferences, and the agonizing of Arab regimes. 'Something massive is about to happen,' he would tell us. 'Take it from me.' There were secret late-night meetings between Omar, Farid, and other tight-lipped leaders of the Hizb.

Asif organized the production of thousands of luminous orange stickers that read *Khilafah – Coming Soon to a Country Near You!* Tahir Malik and I were given a car boot-load of rolls to deliver locally. As we left, Asif was on the phone arranging for others from all over Britain to do the same. 'I want to see these plastered everywhere' he said excitedly. 'Every public lamppost, road sign, notice board . . .' To help us target the right areas, members from every district went to the local library to consult the electoral roll. We were against democracy, and the first Islamist group in Britain to declare voting in general elections *haram*. Yet we had no qualms in using the government's electoral rolls.

Within weeks local newspapers were running articles about our 'vandalism'. The *shabab* had put *khilafah* stickers everywhere. Many sections of the media, like the general public, were bewildered: what was *khilafah*? Who was putting up the stickers?

Those were the very questions we *wanted* people to ask – particularly Muslims – to generate interest in the Wembley conference. With awareness at new heights, we plundered the electoral rolls for Muslim names and went knocking on doors. To our surprise, when those doors opened we were often received with hostility. Many criticized our indiscriminate fly-posting. Others refused to speak to us at all. Some were downright abusive.

We retreated to safer ground, leafleting mosques and selling tickets to our own friends, families, and neighbours.

London was a popular tourist destination for many Gulf Arabs during the summer months, so the Hizb made it their business to maintain a six-hour presence every evening near the hotels they favoured. The intention was to distribute leaflets calling for a replacement of Arab governments and inviting Arab tourists to join the work 'towards establishing an Islamic state', but most of the Gulf Arabs I met on the Edgware Road, many of whom were Saudis, were more interested in calling female escorts from phone booths than listening to a Hizb politico ranting about an Islamic state.

That was more or less my first contact with Arabs outside the Hizb. Their lack of support for what we were trying to do, their indifference to the future Islamic state, and their derisive attitude towards Hizb ut-Tahrir struck me as odd. There we were, trying to liberate them from tyranny, and they could not care less.

One evening, I was called to a press conference in Edmonton, where Omar Bakri had recently started his one-man School of Shariah, teaching rudimentary Arabic and Muslim law. When I arrived I was introduced to a stocky middle-aged Saudi physics professor: Mohamed al-Mas'ari. Farid Kasim presented the professor to a packed room of British journalists as the effective opposition to the corrupt Saudi government. There was great excitement – Hizb ut-Tahrir in Saudi Arabia was active, perhaps on the verge of taking power.

In later years al-Mas'ari became famous as the Saudi dissident whom the British government wanted to deport to the Caribbean island of Dominica. I remember him as jovial, friendly, and considerate. By wheeling him out at a press conference the Hizb hoped to give the impression that 'something big' was about to happen in the Middle East. Mas'ari was scheduled to address the conference in Wembley; we seriously believed it was part of a strategic move to declare the caliphate in one or more Arab countries on the day. Intrigue was further raised on the day of the conference when, for 'security reasons', Mas'ari pulled out.

The *khilafah* conference was a shambolic failure, though at the time very few of us were prepared to admit the fact. Thanks mostly to the *Jewish Chronicle* and London's *Evening Standard*, BBC local news channels, and a host of other media outlets, we gained acres of media coverage. However, attendance was nowhere near the 12,000 that we had expected. In typical Islamist fashion we blamed the Jews for sabotaging the conference by 'buying all the tickets' and thus making them unavailable for Muslims! The possibility that Muslims were simply not interested in our conference did not dawn on us.

Peter Tatchell showed up with a group of people from the gay rights organization Stonewall to protest as 'Queers against Mullahs'. His arrest ensured that the conference at least made the papers the following day.

Representatives of the Hizb from the United States including the Jordanian Abu Talha, addressed the conference, as did Omar Bakri, Farid Kasim, and a crowd-pulling cleric from Pakistan. Large numbers of Islamists from other organizations also attended, primarily to gauge the success of the Hizb. The swathes of glaringly empty seats inside the conference hall sent them away with smiles on their faces. They, like us, had overestimated the organizational ability of the Hizb.

All that day we monitored the news. Between stewarding duties I would watch TV, hoping for breaking news of the Islamic state. We had used the conference to launch English translations of Nabhani's books, particularly his revisionist history book *The Islamic State*. Surely this would be in huge demand now that the state was about to be announced. The *kuffar* would, no doubt, turn to it for information following the months of publicity, a plague of Day-Glo stickers, and a major conference.

But nothing happened. There was no Islamic state, no military coup, and no caliph. There was not even a rush at Waterstone's. Soon, *inshallah*, we consoled ourselves.

Back at college, I now had classmates who were not Muslims. Not since Sir William Burrough had I been acquainted with non-Muslim British students. At Newham I studied alongside Christians, Sikhs, Hindus, and, of course, many ordinary Muslims. They had not noticed anything particularly 'different' about me. Some had seen me on the stall on Green Street and wondered why I sold Islamic tapes at the weekend, but they did not seem to care much.

Patrick had recruited an active core of about twenty young men in Southend-on-Sea and had been holding study circles with them. (They knew him by his Muslim name, Naseem, but his parents called him Patrick.) Most of these young Muslims were in their final year at school and many were children of middle-class Asian businessmen, attracted by Patrick's ideals of an Islamic state in which there would be no racism, Muslims would be first-class citizens, the *kuffar* would be put in their place and an army would declare war.

One acolyte, Majid Nawaz, embraced the Hizb ut-Tahrir's message more tightly than most. After completing his GCSEs he left for London to attend Hizb cell meetings, keen to know more. I had met Majid on a speaking visit to Southend and he had asked me where he should study in London for his A-Levels. I suggested a number of colleges but he opted to join me at Newham, where there was a significant Muslim population and where, to date, I had avoided going public with Hizb ut-Tahrir.

I liked Majid, he was sharp, committed, and open to new ideas. He was also a master barber, and gave me and other Hizb members haircuts to help subsidize his stay in London. Brother Falik, the old friend whom I had lost as a result of leaving YMO, was finally replaced.

In less than a decade Majid would become a national leader of the Hizb in Britain, advocate the Hizb's extremist ideas in Egypt during his Arabic language placement year, and be tortured while serving a four-year prison sentence in the notorious jails of Cairo. But in 1995 we thought only of Newham.

My mother had long promised me a car if I passed my driving test, a promise she kept despite her revulsion at my extremism. In 1995 I became the proud owner of a small but serviceable Austin Metro, in which I was able to take Majid home to Southend at weekends to visit his parents. His was a different home from mine; his parents were not particularly religious. The Hizb was his way of defining himself against his non-practising

Muslim parents. Oddly, the Hizb served the same purpose for me: defining me against my observant parents. We were both rebelling against our parents' beliefs.

Often Majid would eat at my home, where during Ramadan of that year we regularly broke the fast. At the end of the month Majid bought my mother an electric kettle as a token of his appreciation. He was lucky: almost without exception the parents of our members made us feel unwelcome in their homes.

Majid was keen to shake up Newham College, and his enthusiasm combined with my experience at Tower Hamlets would prove to be dynamite. Unlike me, Majid oozed street cred. He wore the latest baggy jeans, expensive trainers, and had good hair. He had once worn an earring and the empty piercing spoke volumes to east London rude boys. Majid was equally at ease among aspiring black rappers and budding Asian bhangra singers. His clothes, attitude, good looks, and street speak made him very popular, very quickly.

Majid and other members of the Hizb often spoke about their *jahiliyyah* days, a reference to the period of time in Arabia before Islam. But how could people born and raised in Muslim homes know *jahiliyyah*? Just as the Hizb had influenced Syed Qutb, Qutb had influenced the Hizb. Qutb had declared modern-day politicians in the Muslim world as non-Muslims, from the time of *jahiliyyah*. For Majid and others, becoming Islamists was rejection of *jahiliyyah*.

We were an odd couple. Majid's clothes all bore designer labels while I wore blazers, shirts, chinos, and thick glasses. What united us were our ideas: a common vision of a new world on the horizon. Having observed their stern Salafi speakers last year, I knew that working with the Islamic Society would prove to be a waste of time, so instead we set up a debating society. While Majid recruited contacts and made large numbers of friends in the college canteen I dealt with the college principal and head of student affairs. I assured them that ours was an intellectual venture, launched to facilitate debate among students and develop their presentation skills. At Hizb ut-Tahrir we knew how to work an audience. While I was soothing any concerns the college management might have had, Majid, with new recruits around him, was whipping up fervour in the common room, canteen, and, increasingly, the classroom.

Newham students, Asian and African, tended to group themselves along ethnic and tribal lines. We aimed to change all that. For us there were only two divisions: Muslims and the rest.

In the library Majid and I would start discussing current affairs stridently so that other students were compelled to listen. When the librarians expelled us, we took a crowd of Muslim students to the canteen or common room and continued speaking. Our primary audience had always been Muslim youth, but confrontation with non-Muslims, particularly Sikhs and Hindus, helped to consolidate Muslim support for us. Since we had provoked the confrontations, and then elicited Muslim support, we always led the masses.

Unlike Tower Hamlets College, Newham had no prayer room. We knew that prayer was something all Muslims held dear and would easily unite behind. Our first confrontation with management, therefore, was to demand a prayer room. Their reluctance to provide one led to accusations that the principal of the college was Jewish and did not want to see Muslims at prayer.

'They slaughter us in Bosnia, expel us from our homes in Palestine, and refuse us the basic right to pray in Britain,' I would say to students in the corridors. Again, just as the Hizb had trained us, we were linking local issues to global politics. We needed to accustom Muslims to talking and thinking about the wider Muslim world, for it was from there that our state would rise. Soon our arguments spread like wildfire among the students. Newham management was increasingly perceived as anti-Muslim and racist. At the same time we opened a second front to our confrontation, this time with Sikhs and Hindus.

Sikhs and Muslims often dated. This mixing of religions troubled me. We were Muslims, superior and different from others. I was determined to get this message out. The caliphate would reinstate our superiority. Muslims who advocated inter-faith dialogue and coexistence we condemned as having a 'defeated mind'. I was convinced that the harmony that existed in Newham was a result of that defeated mind among Muslim youth who saw themselves as Pakistani or Indian rather than Muslim. As far as I was concerned, that had to change. For us, there was no such construct as 'Pakistan', or 'Turkey'. These were imperial creations and deserved no recognition. Muslims were not to associate themselves along national lines – we were Muslims, plain and simple, and not in need of nationality. Our abhorrence of nationalism was something Indian students at Newham College could not understand.

In our debating society Majid and I openly challenged Hindus and Sikhs to put their case. 'No outside speakers,' I used to boast. 'I'll take on any Sikh or Hindu any time. Tell me, what does your religion say about economics? Politics? I'll dismantle your belief system in five minutes.' To compound such arrogances, we declared that India was Muslim land: 'The Moghuls were Muslims and before the British colonized India, Muslims were its rightful owners. The Islamic state will reclaim India, as it will Spain.' Such provocative comments infuriated non-Muslim Asian students, but strengthened the self-belief and confidence of hundreds of my fellow Muslims.

Muslims increasingly defined themselves against Hindus, Sikhs, Jewish management, Christian Africans. We saw ourselves as Muslim more than anything else. Muslim confidence was not only reinstated within months, but a feeling of Muslim superiority was palpable.

The Islamic Society looked on, stunned by our success, as we went from strength to strength. They organized formal weekly talks while we held spontaneous public sessions almost every day in packed canteens, common rooms, and even corridors. Majid or I would start to discuss a topical issue while our sympathizers, spread across the room, directed the others' attention to us.

Soon our success in Newham became known in the local community. We could, at an hour's notice, gather a crowd of nearly a hundred at the main gates of the college. 'There will be a talk at lunchtime today' was sufficient to rally Muslim support. And if the word had not spread, then we began our talks by shoring up Muslim spirit, invoking the mob mentality. Either Majid or I would stand on a bench at the college steps, just as we had learned from Farid Kasim and Waj, and then someone would shout from the back, '*Takbeeeer!*' To which the crowd responded with a resounding '*Allahu Akbar!*' This style came from the Middle East, the shouting of 'God is Greatest!' in martial tone.

In my childhood I heard melodious chants glorifying God and the Prophet, but now we had done away with the Prophet and melody. All that was important to us was God, an angry God. Terrified non-Muslims would pass us, not daring to look. At no point did a single member of staff try to stop us.

Once again I started to miss classes. My sociology teacher, a committed socialist, came to find me. He took me aside and uttered only one sentence, then walked away. To this day, I have not forgotten his words: 'If you want to change the world, then you must get an education first.'

Most of my teachers disagreed with my politics, yet on a personal level we still got on rather well. I owe that teacher a debt of gratitude for those words and his help later, when the defiant ethos we had created came tumbling down.

As had happened at Tower Hamlets, Newham's Muslim women students started to wear the hijab. There was a new level of conviction in their faith, a sense that all others had lost to our arguments. In common rooms Muslims played games of pool in Muslim-only groups. In the canteen Muslims socialized only among themselves. Being a Muslim was a badge of pride.

In addition to the many Muslim students who 'returned to Islam', or became 'born again', several non-Muslims converted to the supreme ideology we had been promoting. A Hindu girl and a Christian boy accepted Islam as a consequence of our Islamization of campus. We drew them to Islam as a force, a power. Today, I doubt very much if they were humble hearts who turned to God.

I was about four months away from my A-Level exams when a Muslim student came to see me accompanied by a lanky black Brit whose face seemed familiar. 'This is brother Saeed. He is looking for Hizb ut-Tahrir.'

'Pleased to meet you, Saeed,' I said. 'I've seen you somewhere before, haven't I?'

As I studied his long face, his deep eyes under his thin black turban, I heard Majid's voice in the background. As Majid and Saeed introduced themselves to one another, I remembered where I had seen him.

'Saeed, we met at Christian Street mosque. Don't you remember? We ate together!'

While I was in Tower Hamlets targeting various mosques, Patrick and I had visited the mosque before our regular Thursday night attendance. Saeed had sat down with us and we had spoken for a long time. I remembered because it was the first time in my life I had eaten from a single plate, sharing with two other people. Patrick, Saeed, and I had had pitta bread with lentil soup, sitting on the floor. I left hungry and uncomfortable. That memory had not left me.

'Yes, of course, brother!' said Saeed. 'I remember!' In my mind, I wondered what a Tablighi Muslim was doing at the college. Did he want to register on a course? And why was he looking for Hizb ut-Tahrir?

Majid and I took Saeed around the college, showing him the classrooms, library, and common rooms. Looking back, it almost was *our* college, our personal property that we were displaying to him.

'I heard Hizb ut-Tahrir run things here,' he said. 'That's good. The *kuffar* need to know that they should not mess with the Muslims.' He dug deep into the outer pocket of his leather jacket and took out a business card bearing his name and phone number. 'If they mess with you, just ring me. I'll sort it out.'

We accepted his card, slightly bemused by his confidence. We 'ran things' at college without help from Tablighi people. The Hizb was enough for us. Besides, we had learnt from Hizb leaders that Nabhani had taught that *all* Muslim groups were 'barking dogs' who should be ignored. We, Hizb ut-Tahrir, were on a fast track to a specific destination. In our speed and single-mindedness, no other Muslim group warranted our attention. Much of our combative attitude towards other groups came from these teachings.

As we walked round the college Saeed handed his card out to every Muslim we introduced him to. He was a visitor with Majid and me, and people noticed him. Many of the younger students took a liking to him, the 'black brother' who was Muslim. Soon I learnt that some of the young Muslims from college had met him once or twice outside college.

The Islamist control of Muslim student populations was not limited to Newham and Tower Hamlets. At Walthamstow and Redbridge colleges similar activities were taking place. At many universities the tactics of confrontation and consolidation of Muslim feeling under the leadership of Hizb activists were being adopted. The Hizb confronted the Jewish, gay, or confidently secular or socialist lecturers. We led Muslim opinion and directed it towards contentious politics, a feeling of global Muslimness, the *ummah*, which needed the leadership of the Islamic state. While we waited for the state to be established in the Middle

East, and the army of the caliph to invite and invade other countries, the Hizb ut-Tahrir would lead Muslims. Of this we made no secret. What dumbfounded us was the fact that the authorities on campuses never stopped us.

On a personal level, my relationship with God had deteriorated. If we were working to establish God's rule on earth, as we claimed, then Hizb ut-Tahrir activists were the most unlikely candidates God could have chosen. My comrades were heady and headstrong young people. We were ecstatic at the thought that soon a 'real Islamic state' would emerge in the Middle East, reverse history, and allow a return to the glory days of Islam.

Yet as I had become more active in the Hizb, my inner consciousness of God had hit an all-time low. The presence of God in my life, a gift from my parents to me, was lost. Externally I portrayed signs of piety to maintain a standing among my target audience, but I was no longer an observant Muslim.

We sermonized about the need for Muslims to return to Islam, but many of the *shabab* did not know how to pray. I witnessed at least four new converts to Islam at different university campuses, convinced of the superiority of the 'Islamic political ideology' as an alternative to capitalism but lacking basic knowledge of worship. Within three weeks of their conversion they were lecturing others about the need for a *khilafah*, the role of the future Muslim army, and the duties of citizens in the future Islamic state. But when it came to reciting the Koran or maintaining basic Muslim etiquette, they were clueless.

When Patrick and Bernie came to ask me about basic verses of the Koran for recital in prayers after they had delivered sermons at prayer rooms in universities, I began to realize how little these people knew about the Koran. I was getting older, and the Hizb seemed suddenly like pretentious, counterfeit intellectualism.

Despite huge political success, I despised myself for appearing pious and upright in Muslim eyes when all the while I knew that there was a vacuum in my soul where God should be. I spoke to several Hizb ut-Tahrir members about this and they were unanimous in saying that this was my personal responsibility and Hizb ut-Tahrir was a political party, not a spiritual order. That response annoyed me. They were shirking responsibility for developing the Islamicness of their Islamic recruits – but content to use these same recruits to promote a seemingly Islamic cause. I was not persuaded.

I went to the top. I found myself alone with Omar Bakri one night in a car on the way to a mosque in Edmonton. I put it to him that we were not sufficiently Muslim in our personal lives, and asked how we could establish the Islamic state if we, as a group, did not master the acts with which we earn God's pleasure. How did we expect Muslims to trust us? Omar was candid: he agreed. He went as far as saying that the founder of Hizb ut-Tahrir believed that members of the group, especially in the 1970s Middle East, were not sufficiently pious. Why else was God withholding the state from Hizb ut-Tahrir? Nabhani had believed that within thirteen years of the Hizb's establishment the Islamic state would be set up. In later life he blamed his members' distance from God for the Hizb's failure to secure the state. But the effort to gain a state never evaporated. If anything, it increased in intensity. Omar said that he had noticed vast gaps in the knowledge of group members in the 1990s. Omar reassured me that something would be done; a training session had to be held. Months passed and nothing happened. I approached Jamal Harwood, a leading Hizb apparatchik and city accountant. He instructed the *shabab* to pray at mosques 'to show Muslims we were serious, to provide leadership'. As usual, prayers were linked to political ambitions, but at least instructions to worship were given. Still nothing changed: members knew that prayers were not the first priority. It was

Islam's first command to Muslims, but not of much interest to Islamism's activists.

We continued to disrupt meetings of other Muslim groups, to plaster the walls of inner-city London with our posters late into the night, come home in the early hours of the morning, and go to bed without saying our prayers. We were too tired to pray; establishing the Islamic state was more important than minor matters such as praying, reciting the Koran, giving to charity, or being kind to our parents and fellow Muslims.

At home, I no longer knew I had a family. By day I was active on campus, and in the evenings I kept myself away from my parents and siblings. I could not bear discussions with my parents any longer. All subjects returned to what my father called my 'going astray to the enemies of Islam'. Those words angered me. My life was consumed by fury, inner confusion, a desire to dominate everything, and my abject failure to be a good Muslim. I had started out on this journey 'wanting more Islam' and ended up losing its essence.

Nevertheless, in public I was still the mighty leader of the Hizb on campus, the challenger of *kuffar* in the name of Islam, the leader of Muslims. I went around college with Majid and many of our new recruits, maintaining our visible presence and making ourselves available to the *ummah*.

Of the many faces I encountered on a daily basis there was one belonging to a girl called Faye that did what mine used to do a lot: smile. As an Islamist I had lost my ability to smile. Every time I approached Faye with an invitation to our meetings, she smiled, accepted, then failed to turn up. Faye confounded me. I wanted to get to know her more. Slowly, we became very good friends.

Faye was no ordinary girl: her genuine and illuminating smile, caring eyes, her endearing face with its olive complexion, her warm ways, drew me to her. I discovered that we had identical ancestral and social backgrounds, a common interest in learning

Arabic, and shared a desire to travel. In time we realized that our friendship was no longer platonic. The new threshold of our relationship was to mark a milestone in many ways.

We would write to each other, and Faye's letters and verses spoke of a God that was close, loving, caring, facilitating, forgiving, and merciful. Faye was close to God: she prayed regularly. I, by contrast, believed in a God who was full of vengeance, a legislator, a controller, a punisher.

I could not envisage a future without Faye. I marshalled sufficient courage to write and ask if she would consider me for her future husband. She paused for thought for a week and eventually said yes, but only on condition that we both complete our studies and pursue careers. Love illuminated beyond all expectations.

For the first time in many years, I was uplifted from within. At *halaqah*, we were told to be serious people – how could we smile? Whenever I saw Faye, how could I not?

I now started to spend more time studying with her in the town hall library, across the road from the college building. One afternoon a new recruit to the Hizb rushed over to ask me to go to the college immediately. Some black Christian boys had been hogging the pool table and were refusing to let a group of Muslims play. Things could get nasty. I rushed over to find a stand-off involving a dozen pool cues and a roomful of injured pride. How dare the inferior Christians refuse Muslims a game? For us, there was no right or wrong here. We were not interested in what had happened; we were there to support our brothers. At that point the fire alarm went off. We all knew what that meant: an invitation to fight outside. College managers restrained the Christian boys, allowing us to exit the building first. Majid and I led the Muslims to the other side of the street, ensuring we had more space if a ruck should break out. We led a crowd over 200 strong, repeatedly shouting '*Allahu Akbar!*' and 'Jee-had!'

Now, as the students poured out into the streets and the fire brigade came rushing in to attend what we all knew was a false alarm, the black non-Muslims looked on, concerned by our numbers and the sheer power of our voices. Amid screams of 'Jee-had' many started to wave their fists too. The college rude boys of the previous year were now completely under our leadership.

Amid the shouting, I felt a tug on my arm. I turned round to find Saeed standing next to me.

'Saeed!' I said, surprised. 'What brings you here?'

'Somebody called me from college. You need my help.'

'Oh, no, no. I think we have things under control. Just a small scuffle over a game of pool.'

'Yes,' reassured Majid. 'Nothing too difficult.'

'They were calling us names, bro',' protested somebody from the crowd. 'The Christian niggers need to be taught a lesson,' continued the speaker without a trace of irony. There was a lot of anger. Saeed did not seem offended in the least: he was no longer black, he was a Muslim.

In the end it all came to nothing. The college managers ushered in the Christian students and we decided not to bother. I asked the students who were involved to walk away and head to the high street. I still did not understand why Saeed was there.

'You brothers are doing a great job,' he said. 'But listen, if anything kicks off, call me. I'll bring Abdul Jabbar with me and we'll settle things down for you.'

'Abdul Jabbar?' I asked, puzzled. 'Who is he?'

Saeed smiled, looked left and right, unzipped the front of his leather jacket, and reached for his inner pocket. He quickly pulled out a dagger, resting inside an ornate scabbard. I caught a glimpse and was immediately speechless.

'Meet Abdul Jabbar,' he said.

★

We spoke about jihad, but we never anticipated real violence. Not yet, anyway. Recently there had been skirmishes between Muslims and Sikhs in Slough and Southall. Hizb activists from Newham and Redbridge had gone there to lend a hand in the fighting, but that was in a personal capacity. It was not 'party policy' to engage in violence before the caliphate came about. We believed that fighting as individuals was futile – our aims were greater. An army would fight entire nations with the military force of the Islamic state, not by vigilante gang warfare.

With A-Levels pending, and under Faye's spell, I spent whole days studying. I was fortunate that my *halaqah* had been cancelled for about two months during that time owing to an organizational restructure between Newham and Ilford. There was also a shortage of *halaqah* instructors as membership swelled. I was allowed a short break before resuming *halaqah* and a new book by Nabhani. It was an unexpected respite. I was no longer distributing leaflets, disturbing meetings of other groups, or shouting down our opponents in gatherings.

One afternoon as I sat in the library, buried in my books, I heard voices outside. On the other side of the street a small crowd had gathered and Dave Gomer, the student affairs manager, was pushing people away. Within minutes an ambulance arrived and from where I stood, I could see a boy lying on the ground next to a pool of blood – one of the Christian boys who had been involved in the row over the pool table.

Something terrible had happened and the library was no place to be. I sent Faye home. Majid arrived and we went outside, where police officers were speaking with Dave Gomer. No doubt our presence was duly noted.

I asked everybody to disperse, to go home and stay in contact by telephone. Majid and I left the scene with heavy hearts. We both knew that whatever had happened at college, as Hizb activists we were responsible. It was we who had encouraged Muslim fervour, a sense of separation from others, a belief that

Muslims were worthier than other humans. And those ideas had been inculcated in us by Hizb ut-Tahrir.

Majid had seen the whole thing. Apparently the boy, a Christian student of Nigerian extraction, had been throwing his weight around and being generally offensive towards Muslims and about their attitudes. Someone had phoned Saeed, who, as he had done previously, turned up within fifteen minutes. The pair confronted each other outside. The black boy drew a knife.

Saeed remained calm, looked the boy in the eye and said, 'Put that knife away or I will have to kill you.'

The boy did not respond. Perhaps he thought Saeed was bluffing. Saeed walked closer and warned him again. Exactly what happened next is unclear, but within seconds Saeed had pulled out Abdul Jabbar and thrust it into the boy's chest. This was murder. And had I not been with Faye in the library, I would probably have been somehow involved. It was a narrow escape.

Early the following morning two police officers came to the door, asking to see me. My mother called me out of bed. I told them I had nothing to say. My father insisted that I co-operate; in all his life, the police had never knocked on his door. 'We need to eliminate you as a potential suspect,' they said.

Although I was no longer attending *halaqah*, I was still intellectually committed to the ideas of Hizb ut-Tahrir. How could I speak to two *kafir* officers and inform on a fellow Muslim? Impossible.

Besides, I was still in pyjamas. They issued threats of arrest, detention, prosecution, but I refused to budge. Reluctantly, they gave me their contact details and left.

The murder was now all over the local press. I felt unremitting guilt at what had happened. As Hizb's representatives, Majid and I had met Saeed when he had come to college that first day and asked for Hizb ut-Tahrir. However, now, under police and

media pressure, the Hizb leadership put out press releases that it
had never operated on the campus.

Dismayed, Majid went to see Omar Bakri, who had visited
Newham days before the murder, and gave him a full explanation of what had happened, explaining that Saeed had acted
in self-defence and asking Omar to stand beside the college's
Muslims. Instead the Hizb leadership issued a condemnation of
what had happened, saying that it was a non-violent party.
This myth was swallowed by investigators who never really
understood the seriousness of the Hizb's form of violence. Even
today, a primary reason for Western failure in the War on Terror
is this same cause: an innate inability to understand the Islamist
psyche.

That murder, the direct result of Hizb ut-Tahrir's ideas, served
as a wake-up call for me. Now, every time I saw a leaflet with
Hizb's flag and masthead posted above photos of the globe I felt
nauseous. It was not mere PR – they wanted to control the
world, to conquer countries.

Soon Saeed was arrested, charged, and convicted of murder.
Since my first meeting with him at Christian Street he had left
the Tablighi Jamat and become what we now mistakenly called
a 'jihadi' or vigilante. Despite their condemnation of vigilantism,
most Islamists are jihadis, particularly members of Hizb ut-Tahrir
and its offshoots. Individual jihadis are driven by ideas that
prompt them to immediate personal action; Hizb ut-Tahrir
encourages individuals to form an army dedicated to a prolonged
military campaign. In essence, the differences from vigilantism
are simply of time and scale.

9. Farewell Fanaticism

The facts of history are nothing; interpretation is everything.
    E. H. Carr, British historian

Just as I had become a member of the Hizb over a period of
time, my departure from the organization did not occur on a
specific date. Attraction and commitment to extremism have
always been part of a gradual process. My first move away was
to dissociate myself from the *halaqah*, a move prompted by the
taking of an innocent life, Omar Bakri's subsequent deceit and
my horror when I realized how poisonous was the atmosphere
I had helped create. Most important of these was the murder –
the Hizb's ideas had led to the belief that the life of a *kafir* was
of little consequence in attaining Muslim dominance. I could
not bear to be associated with such ideas any longer. I was
frightened of where they might lead. Did I really want to follow
a credo that led to violence and murder? I had advocated the
ideas of Muslim domination, confrontation, and jihad, never
for one moment thinking that their catastrophic consequences
would arrive on my own doorstep. It had all seemed abstract
and remote, relevant for Bosnia or the Middle East, not Britain.

Now I began to wonder whether Islam had anything at all to
offer. I had completely confused Islamism with Islam: to me
they were the same. Did God really want government in the
name of religion? I had serious doubts. If God was on the Muslim
side then why had we failed to establish the Islamic state? Why
were the 'enemies of God', as we viewed the West, politically
dominant?

I wanted to find out, and the only way to do so would be to learn Arabic so that I could read the Koran and classical Muslim sources for myself. Had I been duped by both Jamat-e-Islami and Hizb ut-Tahrir in their deployment of Arabic? Like many Muslims, I had learnt from a young age how to read and pronounce Arabic words, but I had no idea what those words meant. What I did not realize was that even in trying to set my mind free, I was taking steps that Islamists take: going direct to divine text without scholarly guidance, believing that I, with the mere understanding of a language, could interpret what Muslim scholars have debated and discussed for centuries.

All the while Faye's companionship and love helped me to maintain my composure. We spoke about the Hizb for hours and there was no doubt that she preferred me out of the Hizb than in. I told her about the arguments I had had with my father and that similar tension existed between nearly all Hizb activists and their parents. Faye reminded me of one of Islam's most basic teachings: be kind to your mother and father. 'How could people in the Hizb reject their parents so easily? Don't they know about the man who wanted to go on a military expedition and the Prophet said that looking after elderly parents was more important that jihad?' In my pursuit of political power I had become remote from such teachings. Had it not been for Faye's guidance and encouragement, I might well have returned to the Hizb.

In an attempt to persuade me that the Hizb was more than Omar Bakri's deceit, that the ideas and concepts were still true, Majid and three other Hizb members visited me. Members of my old *halaqah* came to my home, outraged that I could even contemplate severing my ties with the Hizb. They forcefully explained that as long as I agreed with the 'concepts' of the Hizb, I was part of the Hizb. I was 'carrying their ideas'. 'Carrying' – I felt like a woman pregnant with a violent partner's child.

In my mind, there was turmoil. I was still 'intellectually

convinced' (to use Hizb phraseology) that oppression and subordination of Muslims must be reversed, but I could no longer endorse violence as a means to do so. I knew the Hizb's ideas were designed to confront, subvert, and ultimately annihilate opposition through violence. In my heart, though, I felt that my time inside Islamism had ruined me and my relationship with those around me, particularly my parents. It was time to stand back and think again.

The indoctrination of the Hizb was powerful and it was many years before I was completely free of it. With the help of my teachers I managed to pass my A-Levels, and I chose to read history for my degree. I was offered a place at the School of Oriental and African Studies and Faye was offered a place at Queen Mary and Westfield College, but I knew that the Hizb was active at both institutions. Fortunately we were both also offered places at what was then the University of North London, and decided to accept on the grounds that we would be together. More than ever before, I needed Faye's love and warmth to help me reconcile my mind to the modern world and come to terms with the reality that surrounded me, rather than trying to dominate it in the name of religion. I tried to avoid the Hizb as much as possible. I stopped answering phone calls from former friends, avoided shopping centres in Ilford, Walthamstow, Green Street, or even Whitechapel on Saturday morning because I knew the *da'wah* stalls would be there.

Away from activist Islamism, for the first time in nearly five years I was hopeful of being able to study conscientiously. I had no daily routine to complete, no weekly *halaqah* to attend, no one telling me what to think. I loved my time at university. My understanding of my subject had hitherto been blinkered by the arguments of Mawdudi, Qutb and Nabhani that history was a conflict between Islam and the rest of the world. But I was determined to open up my worldview and slowly, independently, question some of the concepts and tenets I had once held so dear.

It was not easy. At first I still saw non-Muslim academics and their interpretations of history as part of a global conspiracy against Islam and Muslims. Even some Muslim authors I regarded as suspect, remembering how Farid, Jamal, and others had publicly mocked Muslim scholars as government agents, puppets of the West, unworthy of attention. When the Cambridge-based Pakistani scholar Professor Akbar Ahmed produced a BBC documentary series highlighting various manifestations of Islam in different countries, Hizb leaders publicly dismissed it as 'Mumbo-jumbo from bungo-bungo land'. When Muslim scholars from Al-Azhar in Cairo, the oldest surviving university in the world, declared that signing a peace treaty with Israel was in the interest of both Islam and Muslims, the Hizb lampooned them as 'scholars for dollars'. The Hizb's mental barriers were not easily broken down, and only slowly did I become conscious of how deeply the Hizb had penetrated both my life and my teenage mind.

Such a doubtful and rejectionist mindset was hardly helpful to my studies. Hizb activists obtained their degrees by writing what the examiner wanted to see, not what they believed was true. I was determined to avoid this Dr Jekyll and Mr Hyde approach. Nevertheless, of my first essay (on the 1882 British invasion of Egypt) my tutor wrote: 'The author of this paper is culturally and politically committed to Islam'. Mr Hyde was obviously still alive and kicking.

A major influence on me during my time at university was Professor Denis Judd, a British historian who has written several books on empire. More than any other tutor he nurtured my mind with academic rigour, critical thinking, and fresh interpretation. He was a warm, approachable, and respectful teacher who welcomed me to his office whenever I knocked on his door.

After almost a decade I was once again experiencing some of that heartfelt, sincere humanity that I had encountered as a child at Sir William Burrough. Professor Judd taught me much about the British Raj, Victorian and Edwardian Britain, Britain's involvement in the Middle East, and the international fallout that followed the dismantling of the Empire. We discussed British–Muslim relations in India and the Middle East and I learned about the perception of Islam in British minds in Victorian Britain. What struck me most about Professor Judd's subject and his teaching methods was that he, despite being a non-Muslim, did not express enmity or animosity toward Muslims and Islam at any stage. How could that be?

To my Islamist psyche, anyone who did not accept Islam was an opponent of it, a *kafir*. The neutrality towards Islam of Professor Judd and his students left a mark. Where was the 'Islamophobia' or 'orientalism' that Hizb ut-Tahrir had warned me to expect from *kafir* teachers? The exceptionally friendly Professor Judd, openly discussing the merits of Muslim identity in British India and the exploitation of these sentiments by egotistical politicians to later break up India and form a new country, Pakistan, in the name of religion, hardly conformed to that stereotype.

Professor Judd also introduced me to the ideas of Keir Hardie, Harold Laski, and others influential in the Labour movement during the last century. Professor Judd's commitment to centre-left politics reminded me of my father. After Labour's 1997 election victory Professor Judd put a poster on his office door for all to see that read: 'We Won'. I recalled my father's words about joining the Labour Party.

But I was not yet ready to commit to man-made politics or, worse, democracy. In the Hizb we had constantly attacked representative government. We preached 'democracy is hypocrisy' in an attempt to dissuade Muslims from engaging in British politics and so they would not expect the future Islamic state to be a democratic one. To us democracy implied sovereignty for man, whereas Islamism demanded sovereignty for God. I started to read as widely as possible about representative government, freedom, and democracy and realized these were all contested concepts, that the definitions of these ideas were constantly in flux, reflecting different social and political realities in different countries.

Nabhani disliked democracy not because it in any way undermined God but because it was a Western idea. Much like his rejection of *kafir* Western terms such as 'social justice', democracy too was un-Islamic and *haram*. His argument was rooted in separatism and rejection of the West. (For similar reasons, he had declared Islam's greatest philosophers, Averroes and Avicenna, non-Muslims.)

I learnt that rejection of democracy was nothing new: Plato detested it too. But I began to see it as an attempt to govern by consent and to resolve conflicts by peaceful means. Increasingly I developed a nuanced, contextualized understanding of democracy and gradually started to question Nabhani's pedantry and extremism.

All university professors teaching the history of the Middle East were referred to by the Hizb as 'orientalist', professionals who sought to demonize Islam and Muslims and define themselves and their culture and history, i.e. Western civilization, as superior by portraying Islam as inferior. I had thought that history was a collection of facts, a factual narrative of *what happened*. I could not have been more wrong.

Another of my tutors was Professor John Tosh, author of *The Pursuit of History*. His lectures forced me to question my approach to history. One thing history was not was an idle intellectual pastime. Professor Tosh argued that the past created the present, and the past was open to multiple interpretations. What seemed like blasphemy at first slowly began to make sense.

The book that posed the most intriguing challenge to my

conceptions and thinking was E. H. Carr's *What is History?* Carr's pungent lines about the role of a historian made me wonder how his approach to the subject compared with my approach to Muslim history. Carr disputed 'facts', and argued that we knew only what those who went before us wanted us to know. Historical records do not necessarily tell us what happened, but only their authors' perception of what happened, or what they wanted others to believe had happened.

Carr also argued against hero worship, the backbone of Islamism. I believed that men such as Mawdudi, Qutb, Nabhani and others swam against the tide, stood separate from the milieu in which they found themselves, and thus sought to guide us to a better, purer age. Carr hoped to 'discourage the view which places great men outside history and sees them as imposing themselves on history in virtue of their greatness, as jack-in-the-boxes who emerge miraculously from the unknown to interrupt the real continuity of history'.

Were my intellectual heroes cardboard men? My *halaqah* training in the Hizb had always been that Nabhani resisted socialism, capitalism, and other ideas and formulated his own pure Islamic response to the 'onslaught against Islam' at the 'hands of colonizers'. I was to put this idea to the test.

Nabhani had argued that his *ijtihad*, or scholarly reasoning, was based purely on Islam and not influenced by any other source, particularly Western philosophical thought, which he abhorred. This hatred of Western intellectual development was widespread in the Hizb, and we prided ourselves on our 'intellectual purity' as 'carriers of deep enlightened thought' derived from Islam. Away from the *halaqah*, in a free intellectual atmosphere, I now sought to understand Islamism's most intelligent ideologue: Nabhani. Was he really 'pure', as he claimed? Or was Carr right to suggest that we were all products of our time?

Nabhani was most vociferous in arguing that Muslims, under no circumstances, should accept *kufr* influences in their religion, and, by extension, coexistence with the wider world. In his vitriolic rejection of *kufr,* Nabhani was perhaps second only to his fellow Islamist, the Egyptian radical Syed Qutb. While Qutb wrote about the contemporary Muslim world and advocated the violent overthrow of Arab regimes, Nabhani argued for a deeper intellectual reformation of Muslim minds: the overthrow of what he considered 'un-Islamic ideas'. More than any other Islamist ideologue Nabhani concentrated on the mind and intellect. The goal, however, was the same for both men: Islamist domination of the world.

As a Hizb foot soldier I had been most impressed with Nabhani's diagnosis and prognosis. How great, I marvelled, were the 'systems' of Islam. Now I discovered that Nabhani was not as 'pure' as he and his followers claimed. His ideas were derivative, fully formed by Western political discourse but presented in the language of Muslim religious idioms, offering European political ideals wrapped in the language of the Koran in order to gain mass appeal in the Arab world.

My new reading of Nabhani's writings suggested that his conceptual framework of a so-called Islamic state was not the continuation of a political entity set up by the Prophet, maintained by the caliphs down the ages (however debatable), but in fact Nabhani's response to the circumstances he encountered: secular modernity. Of the Western thinkers who influenced Nabhani most, it seemed to me, Hegel was of vital importance.

Hegel was a very systematic thinker; he developed a system of thought based on 'ideas'. In addition to Hegel's emphasis on ideas and thought in human life, he emphasized the role of 'the state' over every other social organization.

Like Hegel, Nabhani did not believe that the state was an end in itself, but rather a means. Hegel's emphasis on the importance of ideas had obviously greatly influenced him. Nabhani, by adopting Hegel's thinking, learnt from the same source as Karl Marx.

Hegel has been criticized for laying the conceptual framework for a totalitarian state, but that was not a cause for rejection in Nabhani's view. Hegel's writings, particularly phrases such as 'The state is the march of God through the world', only emboldened Nabhani.

I also discovered that many of the criticisms of democracy I had heard in the Hizb were not new and original, but based on writings of Rousseau and others. Rousseau called for God to legislate, because man is incapable of legislation. Where Rousseau was unclear in his mind as to how God would legislate, Nabhani, a Muslim cleric, had the answer: the Shariah and Islamic law. Rousseau wrote, 'How can a blind multitude, which often does not know what it wills, because it rarely knows what is good for it, carry out for itself so great and difficult an enterprise as a system of legislation?' Islamists regard (their own) interpretation of the Koran as 'God's law'. Problem solved.

The worst expression of man-made law, according to Hizb ut-Tahrir, was democracy. Yet before the Hizb pilloried freedom and democracy among Muslims in Britain and elsewhere, even Islamists generally accepted that democracy was a positive development in human history. Indeed, at East London mosque I was taught that democracy was a Muslim invention!

Bertrand Russell, writing in the late 1930s, suggested that 'Hitler is an outcome of Rousseau; Roosevelt and Churchill, of Locke.' It seems to me that Nabhani was also a product of Rousseau.

I was not, I had discovered, a believer in any distinct 'Islamic' political system. Nabhani's ideas were not innovatory Muslim thinking but wholly derived from European political thought. In and of itself this was not a negative development. My objection was, and remains, the deception of the Hizb ut-Tahrir in claiming that it was 'pure in thought', not influenced by *kufr*. In their attempt to maintain 'ideological purity' they claimed to have disowned all *kufr* influences. For it was those influences,

Nabhani wrote, that had caused the gradual decline of the cali-
phate. Nabhani had singled out Greek philosophy as a major
perpetrator of corrosive influence on Muslim minds, and went
as far as declaring renowned Muslim philosophers such as al-
Farabi, Ibn Rushd (Averroes), Ibn Sina (Avicenna) to be *kuffar*.
For Nabhani, accepting Greek influences and, more recently,
European impact on Muslim thinking was a 'surrender to the
West' and detrimental to the superiority of Muslims.

Having established the prominence of the state, placed God
at its centre, rejected democracy, and developed a political
system of rule from a misreading of the Shariah law, Nabhani
now needed to develop a strategy to bring it all to pass, the
dream Zion of Islamists.

In an attempt to verify the existence of a single Islamic state
throughout fourteen centuries of Muslim history, Nabhani
argued that all Muslims had sworn allegiance to the Umayyad,
Abbasid, and Ottoman dynasties. However, that simply ignores
the historical fact that millions of Muslims living in Indonesia,
India, China, Spain, Africa, and Iran, had *not* pledged allegiance
to these ruling castes. Indeed, the Persians were at war with the
Ottomans for at least two centuries.

Now, Nabhani wanted to revive this mythological Islamic
state, and he turned, it suddenly seemed to me, not to Islam but
to Gramsci, an Italian Marxist ideologue. The role of the political
party was crucial to Gramsci's understanding of bringing about
political change. In addition to learning about the strategies
of 'destroying and building' new ideas for a political entity,
Nabhani also learnt that the political party was an 'organism, or
complex element of society'. Little wonder, then, that Farid
often spoke about the Hizb being 'organic' and the ideas of the
Hizb as being a precursor to mass political change.

Where Hegel outlined the importance of thought in the
progress of a nation, Gramsci explained how these thoughts
were to be inculcated in the masses, or *ummah* as Nabhani

preferred to call them. It was not sufficient to propagate new ideas, but old ideas had to be 'destroyed' and supplanted by new ones. And that is *exactly* what I was taught in my *halaqah*, and what I tried to execute on the streets of London. Nabhani shrewdly linked Gramsci's concepts to the life of the Prophet Mohammed, and in Muslim ears this found greater acceptance. Just as Jesus had spoken out in harsh tones against the Pharisees, Mohammed had spoken out against the pagans in Mecca. Was this an attempt 'to destroy ideas' and replace them with 'new thoughts'? Did this make Jesus and Mohammed role models for political strategy in the twentieth-century Middle East? In Nabhani's mind, the answer was a resounding yes.

Nabhani's major mistake was to accept an emphasis on the state over other social structures, and then assume that the Prophet Mohammed had struggled to establish a political entity. Rather than approach the life of the Prophet in its proper context of seventh-century pagan tribalism, which the Prophet marvellously reversed to the belief in the one God of Abraham, Nabhani saw only the political office of the Prophet and gave this precedence over all else.

In my mind, Nabhani had fallen from his pedestal. And with him all of Hizb ut-Tahrir's claim to political purity, intellectual superiority, deep thoughts, and the dressing up in religious terms of a political agenda born in the 1950s Middle East. Islamism became an empty, bankrupt ideology. However, its cultural attitudes to the world still resided deep within me. I had shed its intellectual grasp through my studies and my rejection of Hizb *halaqah*, but not its behavioural traits. Thoughts, I learned, were not always linked to action.

10. Entering the World: Which Life?

The life of this world is but play and passion.
  The Koran

The Saudi government funded the Muslim World League, the head office of which is in Mecca. It also occupied a three-storey office building on London's Goodge Street which served as a mosque and funding centre for various Islamist activities in Britain. I had every reason to disagree with the Muslim World League, but heard that they taught Arabic. There, I met a young Tunisian man with a trimmed beard and an artificial smile.

I do not remember exactly what I said to him but he seemed somewhat impressed. He asked me to accompany him to his office on the second floor and quietly closed the door behind him. Within moments he had offered me a full scholarship to study Arabic and full financial assistance in any degree programme of my choice at a university in Saudi Arabia.

'Where does the money come from?' I asked.

'Don't worry about that,' he said. 'Just think about it.'

From being anti-Saudi to being recruited by Saudi agents was not something I had anticipated, even on a visit to the missionary arm of the Saudi government. I excused myself and left. I wonder, though, how many others the Tunisian did recruit. Years later I was to meet British agents of Saudi Islam in Jeddah.

Disgruntled but not demoralized by my encounter at the Muslim World League, I attended evening classes in Arabic at the Muslim Welfare House in north London. In a crammed classroom there were around ten young Muslims studying Arabic with a teacher from the University of Westminster, Dr Shayyal. He was a chubby, warm-hearted, and smiling instructor, but again I knew that my fellow students were no ordinary Muslims taking a language course. One in particular gave the game away.

Zahid Amin was a committed activist of a newly formed group called the Islamic Society of Britain (ISB). Their head-quarters were in Leicester at the Islamic Foundation, Europe's leading Islamist think tank. The ISB was bold in that it broke away from Jamat-e-Islami, particularly its Pakistani arm in Britain: the UK Islamic Mission. Mawdudi himself had attended an Islamic Mission conference in London in 1974. In breaking with its Pakistani Islamist heritage, the ISB was entering new territory. To me at the time, the ISB was a new organization about which I had heard very little.

Islamists in Britain are a diverse and complicated phenom-enon. They are divided by age, ethnicity, class, geography, and their allegiances to Islamists in Southeast Asia or the Arab world. Unravelling the formation of ISB meant going back to 1962, and the creation of the UK Islamic Mission as the British arm of the Pakistani Jamat-e-Islami. In 1971, after Bangladesh divided from Pakistan, the Dawatul Islam was created to cater for Bangla-deshis in Britain, who felt increasingly isolated in a Pakistani-dominated UK Islamic Mission. In 1979 the Dawatul Islam created its own youth wing, the YMO, with strong working-class roots.

In east London, meanwhile, differences based on Bangladeshi regionalism, essentially a form of racism, led to the creation of the Islamic Forum Europe (IFE) in 1990, with YMO siding with IFE in the conflict with Dawatul Islam over East London mosque.

In the 1990s the ISB emerged as a home for predominantly middle-class, professional Muslims who, in the line of fire from the Hizb, closely aligned themselves to the Egyptian Muslim Brotherhood and Palestinian Hamas for educational training and international kudos. If the Hizb was global, well, so was the ISB.

The close association of ISB personnel with Arab Islamists led to the 1997 formation of the Muslim Association of Britain (MAB), a breakaway from the ISB. A bitter relationship has existed between these organizations ever since. MAB maintains close ties to the Arab Muslim Brotherhood.

But though internally divided, they are all in agreement in their veneration of Mawdudi and Qutb. In different but unquestionable ways, they are affiliated to the Jamat-e-Islami of the subcontinent, the Muslim Brotherhood of the Arab world, or Hamas of Palestine. And in recent years they have united as the Muslim Council of Britain (MCB), formed in 1997 at the request of the Tory home secretary Michael Howard. What were isolated, competing, often bitter enemies have come together to present a united front as spokesmen for British Muslims, though the majority of British Muslims are not Islamists.

I remembered Zahid Amin from my days at Newham. When we had demanded a prayer room, and the college principal refused our request, it was Zahid Amin who had advised the principal as a representative of a local mosque. Now that I was no longer an activist of Hizb ut-Tahrir, Zahid was not an enemy. We could and did talk amicably, though I refused to answer any questions about my time with the Hizb, having vowed to avoid the subject. I had no regrets about leaving and pursuing my studies, I never missed any of the activities, except to wonder occasionally if I was neglecting my religious duties. One thing that I certainly didn't miss about the Hizb was its obsession with secrecy. We were always being told that any time now the caliphate would be established, but never when or how.

'In ISB we're totally open,' he said. 'You're welcome to come along any time and see for yourself.'

We exchanged phone numbers and soon Zahid called me.

I had dinner at his place and we spoke about the life of young Muslims in Britain. He knew how active I had been earlier with the Hizb and before that the YMO and said that I was foolish to keep away from all Muslim organizations simply because of my experiences with the Hizb.

'At ISB we are not waiting for a caliph to appear in the Middle East. Some of our members are close to the Muslim Brotherhood, but most are British and want to make Britain more of an Islamic country, to introduce Islam in Britain.' At Hizb ut-Tahrir we believed that the army of the Islamic state would conquer Britain and that 'the flag of Islam will fly over Downing Street'.

Zahid invited me to a three-day camp in Leicester to see what the ISB was all about. At first I refused, simply on the grounds that I wanted nothing to do with any Muslim organization again. Besides, by Zahid's own admission there were people in ISB who were influenced by Islamists, especially by Mawdudi and the Muslim Brotherhood. My Hizb days had given me a particular dislike for all organizational forms of Islam.

But it was difficult to say no to a person like Zahid.

'Just come along and compare us with the Hizb,' he said. 'Give us a chance.' I knew Zahid was keen to recruit me to the ISB, and believed that, broadly speaking, it was part of the same Islamist movement which I had left: activist Islam. But Zahid disagreed. He was genuinely convinced that the ISB were moderate Muslims.

I assessed my choices: I could continue to live in isolation, away from all Muslim organizations with Islam playing a very small role in my life, or I could draw closer to a transparent Muslim organization, and thus try to live as a better Muslim among Muslim friends. At university, all 'practising Muslims' were either part of an organization or associated with a movement. I was the only loose cannon. I dared not admit openly to my Hizb past, and in the absence of clear association I was always suspect. I stood out. For now, I decided to give Zahid and the ISB a try.

The ISB was proudly British. My aversion to nationalism, a result of my Hizb indoctrination, made it difficult for me to accept this at first. I used to believe in One Nation, and Muslims had no nationality except Islam. Seeing these young, educated people increasingly defining themselves as 'British Muslims' rather than Hizb ut-Tahrir's preferred 'Muslims living in Britain', was irksome. I might have left Hizb ut-Tahrir, but had the Hizb left me? As Farid used to say, 'You will carry the concepts for ever.' Well, perhaps not for ever, but they were certainly proving difficult to shed.

One of the major attractions for me of the ISB was their vehement stance against Hizb ut-Tahrir. Among their ranks they had several vociferous critics of the Hizb, not least Sarah Joseph (later editor of *Emel* magazine), the outspoken community leader Ajmal Masroor, and the provocative lawyer Omar Faruk. I had crossed swords with all of them as a Hizb member. Now I felt it was my moral duty to support them. I was twenty years old and needed to flush out the Hizb from within me. Zahid and I had many conversations about the failure of the Hizb, its complete lack of spiritual connection with God. More than any other, Zahid understood me. His own sister and brother were key Hizb people. His sister was later to marry Hizb leader Jalaluddin Patel.

At a three-day conference in Markfield I met several Muslims who would later rise to political prominence. They included Inayat Bunglawala, a democrat, a member of the Conservative Party, and a supporter of Muslim integration in Britain. The Hizb loathed those ideas, and more particularly the confrontational style in which he delivered them. He had been a thorn in the side for the Hizb in east London, myself included. I knew the Hizb activists who had plastered his street with stickers and posters, and vandalized his father's car. Almost as an act of apology, I made it my business not to offend Inayat a second time.

After the Markfield conference, Inayat asked me to attend a weekly *usrah*, something new at ISB. I had attended *taleemi jalsa* with YMO, kept a daily routine, been part of *halaqah* at the Hizb – but what was an *usrah*? 'Come and see,' said Inayat, and offered to pick me up on Wednesday nights. In the meantime the Arabic classes at north London were temporarily suspended and eventually cancelled on the grounds that the tutor was too busy. The ISB suddenly became my sole link to Islam; once again, my focus was becoming more political than spiritual.

The following Wednesday Inayat called for me in his father's green Fort Escort. With him were two others: Sher Khan and Abdul-Rahman Jafar. Khan and Jafar later became involved with the MCB, and Jafar took a leading role in the Respect Party, becoming its mayoral candidate for Newham in 2006. I attended weekly *usrah* meetings of the ISB with them.

Usrah, in Arabic, means family. My *usrah* was in a house in Maryland, east London. The idea behind the ISB gatherings was that they were 'family gatherings' of brothers. It was an idea taken from the Muslim Brotherhood and I felt uncomfortable with it. Inayat introduced me to the *murabbi*, or instructor, a middle-aged, clean-shaven Palestinian called Abu Luqman. We started the *usrah* with recitations from the Koran, followed by his commentary and a discussion on what we had read. Finally, we shared a meal.

The disciplinarian streak of YMO was absent, as were the mind-controlling tactics of Hizb ut-Tahrir. Luqman's family was very hospitable and his wife served a different delicious Levantine dish at every meal. I grew to like *usrah* and I liked Abu Luqman. There was only one problem.

Abu Luqman told us that, during his youth, he had been a student of the firebrand Palestinian cleric Shaikh Ahmed Yasin.

One reason these gatherings were so valued was because we believed Abu Luqman was a true Palestinian, trained by Shaikh Yasin and a member of Hamas. Abu Luqman's deep and powerful hatred of Israelis and Jews was unmistakable. Many times he promised destruction of the state of Israel and the return of Muslim control of the Holy Land. I sat there and accepted this. The Palestinian hatred of the Jews, as occupiers of Palestine, that I had detected in Nabhani was equally strong in Abu Luqman. Neither Inayat nor myself questioned any of this. Jew bashing was an acceptable part of the Islamist curriculum though not necessarily accepted throughout the ISB.

But I should have known better. By then I had studied the history of Jews in Europe, the pogroms, the rejection, the Holocaust. I should have spoken out, but I didn't. Instead, I was now leading a different kind of double life. In private I was a free thinker. Among Islamists I was a 'brother'. I was not to dispute our unquestioned perceptions: hatred of Jews, Hindus, Americans, gays, the subordination of women. I still had two faces, two personalities. Outside the classroom I switched off my critical faculties and accepted the religious and political assumptions that were dominant in the events I attended.

I deliberately avoided any form of serious activism with the ISB, but every Wednesday night Inayat would pick me up and drop me off after a session of Koran recitation, religious discussion, anti-Semitism, and good food.

Members of the ISB went to Palestine and returned with photos of themselves with Ahmed Yasin as a souvenir. Many cherished these links with Hamas members and the Egyptian Muslim Brotherhood. Two leading members of the ISB travelled to Egypt to become official members of the Brotherhood.

At a national conference in Birmingham, ISB leaders proudly told us that a PhD student at Leeds University had concluded that, in the long term, ISB was the 'real threat' to Britain, not Hizb ut-Tahrir. That did not sit well with me. Why the pride in being a 'threat'? The inherent Islamist desire to confront and control was also lurking within ISB.

The short time I spent with the Islamic Society of Britain was confusing; I was caught between British Islamists, Hamas supporters, and Wahhabi sympathizers. The ISB was going through an identity crisis itself: many within wanted to establish links with the Muslim Brotherhood in Egypt while others demanded that we sever ties with Islamic movements. I was among the latter. The society later split: the Muslim Brotherhood brigade broke off and formed the Muslim Association of Britain (MAB) in 1997, which was instrumental in creating George Galloway's Respect Party in 2004.

One day, on the way to the *usrah*, Inayat played a tape of a Muslim speaker, somebody with a soft voice, speaking in an erudite American accent. There was a certain gravity in his words, and attraction in his tone, that kept me engaged for a while.

'Who is he?' I asked.

'An American shaikh. He sounds good; I'm not sure of his name. He's new on the scene. Check the cover in the glove compartment.'

The man was Hamza Yusuf Hanson. *Who was he?* I thought. Inayat kindly lent me the tape and I took it home.

Imam Hanson spoke about things that I had never heard about in my life. He had become a Muslim in 1977 and his grasp of early classical Islam was beyond anything I had heard to date. His words, even on tape, carried a certain weight. He spoke about Islam being a beginner's level, an early stage in one's spiritual growth. Based on questions that the angel Gabriel had asked the Prophet, Imam Hanson explained that the next level was *iman*, and the final level was spiritual perfection, known as *ihsan*.

He spoke about the heart being the receptacle for *iman*, and not the intellect. In the Hizb we were always taught that Islam was an intellectual conviction. In Imam Hanson's estimation,

I was still a beginner! So were most of my Islamist colleagues, for we were still at the Islam level. The deep conviction in his voice indicated that this was a man who spoke from spiritual experience.

I started to ask more questions about Imam Hanson. Very few people knew much about him other than the fact that he had studied classical Islam for more than ten years in various Muslim and Arab countries, had converted at a young age, and was not involved in Islamist movements. The latter was off-putting to us. Although we fought among ourselves between different Islamist factions, and the ISB was a moderate outfit while Hizb ut-Tahrir was more radical, we all understood that we sought political domination in some way. At first, this made me slightly wary of Imam Hanson. But I liked what he had to say and thought it would be interesting to meet him one day. I did not have to wait long.

In the summer of 1996, still at university, I attended a three-day 'Living Islam' family camp in Worcester organized by the ISB. It was a large event, drawing around 3,000 Muslims and their families from across Britain.

That night I had helped with security while the families slept. As I prepared to sleep I wondered if I was getting embroiled in activist Islam afresh. I did not take part in the arguments between ISB and the jihadis led by Babar, but I was troubled by the sight of Islamists arguing among themselves as to whether jihad or political engagement was the way forward in Britain.

After morning prayers I went to sleep in a rabbit shed as most of the tents were taken by families with young children. It was a cold morning: I zipped myself into my sleeping bag and dozed off.

A powerful yet soft voice coming over the loud speakers broke my deep sleep. I listened enthralled to its Californian accent filled with well-pronounced Arabic references to poetry and the Koran. I got out of my hutch, brushed my teeth, and rushed over to the main hall. On stage stood an American

Muslim scholar, speaking passionately about the need to revive the Muslim spiritual condition, escape intellectual slumber, gain knowledge of Islam through classical sources at the feet of traditional Muslim scholars, and renew our personal commitment to God.

I sat in silence and absorbed every word Shaikh Hamza Yusuf Hanson uttered. He spoke about a daily dawn cry from the depths of the earth, *ana khalkun jadeed*, meaning 'I am a new creation'. Our yesterdays, he explained, have gone and we have no power to alter the past. Muslims, he said, should be *abna al-waqt*, children of the moment, trying to maximize the benefits of the present with a view to the future, both earthly and heavenly. I was struck by Hamza Yusuf's eloquence and presence, and his vision of Islam as empowering individuals rather than activist groups.

Free from Hizb ut-Tahrir, I had no rehearsed questions to subvert his message, no leaflets to distribute to his audience, no instructions to sabotage his gathering. There was purity in his speech and a depth to his presence that resonated with me. After having watched Islamists bicker about jihad and Syed Qutb, I wondered how Imam Hanson avoided such politicization of religion.

In response to one questioner Imam Hanson went as far as to declare that there was 'no such thing as the Islamic state'. I liked his courage, his willingness to stand up for traditional Islam when every Muslim organization had become dominated by the need to establish 'a state'. Imam Hanson explained that the Prophet referred to political power in Medina as *hadha al-amr*, 'this affair'. He cited other historical arguments and reprimanded those who adopted modern European political idiom and sought to impose it on a 1,400-year-old tradition. His final argument, that God never bestowed power on those who sought it, meant a lot to me. I had seen enough of the Hizb's remoteness from God to know full well what the Imam meant.

He gave historical examples from the time of the Prophet. To Arabs who wanted to become governors the Prophet gave warning that we do not give 'this affair' to those who covet it. How distant, I thought, the Hizb was from this Prophetic Islam. Imam Hanson's blunt criticism of political Islam only reinforced my doubts about the wisdom of seeking power to 'establish Islam'.

He explained Islam in a way that I could relate to. I bought other tapes by Imam Hanson and these led me to other Western Muslim scholars, including the Cambridge theologian T. J. Winter and the American Sufi Nuh Keller. However, I was not ready to accept them, I was still not sure they were 'right'. I found the subdued, spiritual approach to religion difficult. I could not understand a God-driven Islam. Indeed, Imam Hanson could not be right: he was not from the Islamic movement and therefore suspect. His Islam did not advocate overthrow of governments, indiscriminate jihad, perennial confrontation, but rather knowledge, spiritual growth, and divine love. For me, Islam was still about domination, if not in Nabhani's mode, then in some other vague way. Yet, deep down, I knew these scholars possessed a transcendent form of faith that I wanted to draw closer to.

While I led this double life, between mild Islamism and free thinking, switching off my brain at Islamist gatherings, accepting suicide bombings and supporting Hamas, believing that somehow, someday we would Islamize Britain, I attended a three-day camp at the Islamic Foundation. There I met two key individuals of the Islamic movement in Britain. One was Khurram Murad, deputy leader of the Jamat-e-Islami in Pakistan and translator into English of Mawdudi's writings. He had been ill but still made a point of visiting the ISB gathering and wishing us well. Khurram Murad was one of the first Islamist thinkers to speak of developing an Islamizing presence in Britain, and he saw the work of the Islamic Foundation as key to this objective. He endorsed the ISB as a wholly British-based organization, with few or no links to global Islamism, despite the fact that its *murabbis* (instructors) were drawn from Hamas and the Muslim Brotherhood. As deputy leader of Jamat-e-Islami, Khurram Murad was devising strategies for Islamists in Britain.

The second person I met was Dr Zahid Parvez, a lecturer at the University of Wolverhampton and president of the ISB, who treated us to a two-hour hi-tech presentation on *how* we should Islamize Britain. Responding to the rhetoric of the Hizb, he had drawn up a 'methodology' whereby members of the Islamic movement, or Islamists, would enter key positions in government and the professions, invest in key business structures, and thus slowly exert influence on British public life. Away from Britain, secluded in the quiet, Islamized terrain of the Islamic Foundation, this seemed possible. That night, an extremely cold one, all the men slept together on the floor of the mosque of the Islamic Foundation. The sisters had the good fortune of sleeping in the bedrooms upstairs.

The ISB was different from the Hizb. There was more of a feeling of Muslim fraternity among their members; they were very close as individuals, wrestled with one another, cracked jokes, and seriously debated whether they should cut their ties with the world Islamic movement and go native in Britain.

But despite this closeness, I was never able to become an activist again. Noticing my reluctance to commit fully to ISB, a senior member and good friend of mine, the barrister Omar Faruk, took me to meet the Egyptian leader of the Muslim Brotherhood, Kemal Halbawi, their strategist in Afghanistan. Halbawi, I was told, was the Muslim Brotherhood's emissary to Afghanistan and had tried to bring the warring factions together. Now he was in London to try to strengthen the presence of the Muslim Brotherhood there. Halbawi was a chubby man with a gruff voice. I prayed with him that night. It was Ramadan and Muslims say extra prayers during that month. Dr

Halbawi led Omar and me in prayers, and to my amazement he was keen to pray more than the basic requirements. His extra prayers were the first I had heard in Islamist circles, and he sat holding a string of prayer beads while he recited them. Again, I was taken aback. Only Christians used prayer beads, or so we had been taught.

Halbawi and I spoke about the Hizb. I wanted to hear his refutation of them but he was more concerned about promoting his own mentor, the founder of the Muslim Brotherhood, Hasan al-Banna. The more I spoke with Halbawi, the more I realized this was not a man who was committed to an organization or a structure, but one who was really a devotee of the charismatic, assassinated martyr of the Islamist movement.

My time in ISB was a confusing period in my life, more so because the organization itself was seeking a clear path. It was during my time with ISB that I visited the Palestinian Islamist Azzam Tamimi, widely considered to be a leading member of Hamas in Britain. I also met the leader of the Tunisian Islamist movement, Rashid Ghannoushi, who sought political asylum in Britain. While attempting to sever links with Islamism, we were busy meeting leaders of world Islamism in London: Halbawi, Tamimi, Ghannoushi. What were the ISB? Were they Islamists or British Muslims, looking to lead an ordinary life? Or both? Would they support the coming caliph? Why did they – and I – find it so difficult to sever Islamist ties?

I had tried to be a Muslim and felt as though I had failed. At that time, being a young Muslim could only mean being an Islamist. All other options were considered to be a throwback to a colonized form of Islam. There was no other significant alternative, no voice. Grandpa's Islam was for elderly people from the Indian subcontinent and now, after my membership of three different Islamist organizations, I considered most of what Grandpa was doing to be *bid'ah*, newly invented matters in faith, not endorsed by orthodox Islam. I had been successfully indoctrinated: even though I was no longer a member of a group, Islam had become politicized for me. Despite my interest in Imam Hanson, I couldn't accept Islam as a spiritual pursuit.

Not content within a confused ISB, I disassociated myself from them. I saw myself as a veteran of the Islamist movement now. I had done my fair share of leafleting, speaking, recruiting, marching, rallying, leading. There was a sense of burnout; I wanted a quieter existence but was always on standby to assist whenever there was a real need. Today, across the world, I believe there are tens of thousands of people in this position. They harbour a confrontational worldview, but are not actively involved in the world of the Islamist movement. However, a cataclysmic event would bring these people, along with new recruits, back to the organizational front line. In my case, I stayed in touch with friends from the ISB, particularly Omar Faruk, occasionally had dinner with them, but concentrated all my energies elsewhere.

So now I wanted to lead a 'normal life', but had no clear idea what I wanted to do, other than to learn more about certain subjects. I had monitored the 1997 election campaign closely and, in defiance of Hizb's teachings, voted for Tony Blair. That year the Hizb had put up posters in all Muslim areas of Britain saying that it was *haram* to vote and we would burn in hell if we did. Because the Hizb ordered me, and Britain's 2 million other Muslims, not to engage with the political process, I decided to do the opposite. I voted and went further. I joined the Labour Party – an act of defiance.

Omar Bakri had left the Hizb and formed his own organization, called al-Muhajiroun, in 1996. In essence, they both wanted to Islamize the world, but the Hizb believed that the Middle East was their first priority and Omar believed that the whole world, including Britain, should have equal priority.

The 1997 election campaign was an exciting time, and I was excited too. The country was at the cusp of renewal – 'new Britain' as Tony Blair had called it. Of all the arguments he and Gordon Brown made against the Conservative government, there was one I failed to understand: economics. Having passed my history finals, I now wanted a job where I could learn more about economics and how the world of business worked. Faye too had graduated, although she was planning to return to university to complete a Postgraduate Certificate in Education, hoping eventually to teach. That summer she had taken a temporary job with HSBC bank. While at secondary school I had done two weeks' work experience with the Midland Bank and my first bank account had been opened with them at the age of eleven. All their young customers received a sports bag with a study pack inside it, which included the first dictionary I ever owned. Faye's summer experience had been positive and she recommended I apply to work with its successor, HSBC.

At the interview, I was asked why I wanted to work there. My ideas were clear: 'To learn more about banking, finance, economics, and the corporate world. My fiancée is working with you at the moment and she tells me that you have an educational training programme in place.'

The interviewer, a polite lady called Sadie Jones, then explained to me the in-house training programme that HSBC offered. There were various modules one could study, taking afternoons off as study leave, and then, within four years, secure a degree in Finance & Banking from the University of Manchester Institute of Science and Technology (UMIST) as well as become a member of the Chartered Institute of Bankers. Membership of an institute did not appeal to me, particularly not one where, I thought, English toffs drank French wine in bow ties. I wanted to study more. It was in books and study that I found myself most comfortable.

Two days after the interview Sadie called me and offered me a position at HSBC's flagship central London branch in Holborn. I was thrilled. However, there was one problem. After the interview, I had read the brochures from the Chartered Institute of Bankers and realized that the 'banking exams' I had been so keen to study for in order to improve my knowledge of economics were designed for junior managers who aspired to higher positions. By expressing an interest in studying before even getting the job I had come across as a would-be high flyer.

'You're too ambitious,' she said. 'You're a confident young man with high aspirations, and we're worried you may find the bank too repressive.'

Embarrassed, I reassured Sadie that my feet were firmly on the ground and she sent me a contract to sign.

I had graduated and got a job with a global bank working in the City of London. HSBC had done security checks and for about a week I was worried that my involvement with radical Islamism might show up. To my amazement, no such issue appeared and somehow I forgot that I had ever been an activist with Hizb ut-Tahrir. I had blanked my memory. At HSBC I adapted well. The energy and drive that I had previously deployed in Islamist activities, I now used to advance my career and improve my life. Faye and I had been together for nearly four years and I knew I wanted to be with her for the rest of my life. In order to get married, we needed to save money. I worked at Holborn branch by day and studied for my banking exams in the evenings.

I did well in my exams. I had not studied economics before, so I worked extra hard. While at Holborn I got to meet hundreds of HSBC's top customers working in offices in Fleet Street and Chancery Lane: judges, barristers, management consultants, goldsmiths, senior accountants from KPMG, and an older clientele who made use of the branch's deposit boxes.

I was able to strike up conversation easily with the judges

and senior managers who visited the branch and establish their financial needs. After all, they were talking to their banker and they had no reason to adhere to the English rule of 'not discussing money'. Behind closed doors I was amused at how un-English moneyed people became when talking about money.

The people I introduced to the wealth-management division were no mere customers but elite 'private clients'. The private client manager in Holborn Circus was a suave young operator named Maurice Diver. Soon he and I became friends.

In Tony Blair's Britain we liked to think we were now meritocratic, and that the old boy network was disappearing. Wrong. Maurice was promoted to area manager for the stock-broker belt and given a whole floor in a shining new building in Surrey, from where he would oversee twelve private client managers and expand HSBC's client base.

On Maurice's last day at Holborn, he came to my desk and said, 'How do you fancy working for me, mate?'

I was nonplussed.

'I need someone young and dynamic,' he continued. 'Someone who wants a future in the bank, to manage the office for me and look after my clients while I expand the business, recruit new managers, and liaise with my own bosses. Basically, you'll be my assistant. I need you in that role for two years. At the same time you learn the ropes and, all being well, you'll become a private client manager. I think you'll be good at it. You're good with clients – they trust you with their money. They tell you more about their plans than they do any of the others on this banking floor. I have had some great business from you. I'll have to advertise the position, of course, but I'd love you to apply for it.'

That gave me a real ego boost. Perhaps I was destined to be a high flyer after all.

Islamism was a distant memory. I was busy building my career and had no time for the underworld of mosques and marches, shouting and sabotage. Bosnia seemed irrelevant. That was then; this is now. Why shouldn't integration be possible in Britain? I did not drink, and yet I went to J. D. Wetherspoons on Chancery Lane for lunch. At the office Christmas party it didn't bother me when my colleagues got drunk and stumbled into the stationery cupboard for a quick fumble. Like a good tabloid journalist, I simply made my excuses and left. And I felt a whole lot better than they did the following morning. Besides, there were plenty of teetotallers in modern Britain. My abstinence didn't worry my colleagues or clients in the least.

Over in Surrey, Maurice was recruiting new staff for his office. I was interviewed along with several other candidates and in late 1999 I became Maurice's assistant, with joint responsibility for portfolios worth £500,000.

Within two years of joining HSBC, aged just twenty-four, I had escaped the branch network, and moved into the elite private banking arm. If I did a two-year stint in Surrey, I would be in line for a City job with my own portfolio of clients to manage. The world was my oyster. It seemed that nothing could go wrong. But it did.

My parents at last had something to be pleased about. True, we differed on religious grounds, for I still rejected their form of spiritual Islam and refused to attend the *mawlid*, or gathering in which the Prophet and God are remembered. But in worldly terms at least I was now respectable. And in just a few months' time, in August 2000, their son would be getting married.

But I was fooling myself as well as my loved ones. Really I was a sleeper Islamist, anti-American, anti-Israeli, just so busy building a career and enjoying life that I couldn't be bothered to pursue the convictions still festering in my subconscious. I did not feel the least bit guilty. As far as I was concerned, I had done my fair share. I had recruited scores of Muslims to the Islamist cause, many of whom were still active in YMO and the Hizb. I had distributed thousands of leaflets. I had no desire to return to active Islamism of any sort, whether it was the Maw-dudian YMO, the Nabhanian Hizb, or the Hamas-inspired ISB. I wanted to be alone with the ones I loved, my family.

During my time at HSBC I had networked with countless senior managers. I had met many business leaders and the one thing that struck me most was how miserable most of them were. Many had climbed to the top of the ladder by sacrificing their family life for a pension and share options. I began to question my motives. Ironically, in the Hizb we had made much fanfare about three questions that every human had to ask, and it was these that I asked myself now: *Why am I here? Where am I heading? Where did I come from?* Mortgage slavery was not my idea of living the dream any more than the darkness of a life in Islamism.

Hector Fothergill was HSBC's probate manager. As part of our complete financial services provision, when we signed up clients HSBC was often appointed executor of their estate. Of course we charged a commission for the probate service so, in effect, when a client died, the bank made money. As always, familiarity bred contempt and it was not uncommon for advisers to tell Hector cheerfully about 'an old codger who'll pop it soon'. Hector would often receive notification of a death from the coroner as if he had won the lottery. 'Yes! Excellent! I really needed it this month.' Yet within minutes he would be on the phone expressing heartfelt sympathy to the widow.

Moreover, we pushed our financial products by playing on people's fears of accident, disability, or death, or the loss of their property. Either way the bank made money. To me it all seemed rather ghoulish, hypocritical, and not entirely ethical.

I became increasingly disenchanted with the artificiality of it all. My snappy silk tie began to feel like a corporate noose. That year I didn't even bother attending the office Christmas party, though it kept the office in gossip for a week. Was this really how I intended to spend my life? I needed to take stock. Where was I heading?

During the last ten days of Ramadan the Prophet Mohammed used to retreat to his mosque in Medina for a period of spiritual growth. As a young man he had frequently gone to the mountains on the outskirts of Mecca, seeking solace in God. I decided to follow his lead and took myself off to a mosque in London, away from the clamour and hype of the new millennium. My motives were not intellectual, political, or even particularly religious. This was purely introspective; it was for *me* – for the good of my soul.

11. Metamorphosis

> Companionship with the holy makes you one of them. Though you are rock or marble, you will become a jewel when you associate with the man of heart.

> Jalal al-Din Rumi, thirteenth-century Muslim poet

Since leaving Islamism, I could no longer believe in a God who wanted us to govern in his name. In fact, I did not even think of God as 'he' any more. For me, God was beyond gender, limitation, and even conceptualization. God was a human construct, a human projection. God had been belittled by organized religion, particularly by literalist extremists of all persuasians.

The Prophet Mohammed also experienced this loss of faith in the dominant norms of society and religion of his time. That was one reason he retreated to the mountains of Mecca. The Prophet believed that the anguished cries of a man in pain were communion with the divine. Such a primordial state of Mohammedan spirituality, lost to most humans, was what drove me to rediscover the essence of Islam. Like the Prophet, who in seventh-century Arabia had found conventional religion distasteful and the clamour of Meccan business life unappealing, I found the Islam of my day unpalatable. I had, by now, tried all its forms. Organized religion had failed me.

Although I was born a Muslim, and became an Islamist, I had read widely about other religions. Being born a Muslim did not mean that I had to remain a Muslim for the rest of my life. That sort of totalitarianism I did away with when I left Hizb ut-Tahrir.

I was in search of spiritual solace, meaning for my life, and whoever offered it would win my commitment.

The Buddha, who lived approximately five hundred years before Jesus, had left little in the way of notes for future generations. I found it remarkable that he quit his luxurious surroundings in search of truth and enlightenment, but we know very little about what really happened. Hinduism proved too abstruse for me; there were far too many gods and goddesses. The earnestness of the modern Hare Krishnas in Oxford Street made me recall my own Islamist fervour. The zeal of the convert, about which Shakespeare warned, rang alarm bells in my head every time I saw a non-Indian Hindu. Judaism was really a non-starter, since I was not born to a Jewish mother. Besides, since ancient times, Jews have been considered a people, a race, rather than followers of a religion.

I gave much thought to Christianity. Since my birthday is on Christmas Day, I have always felt a certain empathy with Jesus. But in my mind, if there was a God out there, God did not have children. And certainly man did not, could not, become God. And the entire idea of the Trinity, despite my many attempts to understand it, always seemed incredible to me.

In most religious traditions there is a relative dearth of primary source material. In comparison Islam, the newest monotheistic faith, was unique in that its holy book, the Koran, was written during Mohammed's lifetime. We know more about Mohammed than we do of other prophets, and he is historically well documented. Did he commune with the divine, as did Jesus, Moses, and Buddha? For me, the answer is yes. And on those grounds, I still considered myself a Muslim, a believer in the Prophet.

On the eve of the new millennium, six days after my twenty-fifth birthday, I lay on the floor of my local mosque as the celebrations started and the others who were in retreat ran to the open roof to see the fireworks. Those days in spiritual retreat did me the world of good. Tired of materialism, disillusioned with fanaticism, I had lost my anchor in life. Still, deep down there was a spiritual craving, a yearning for something beyond the immediacy of daily existence. In this I was hardly unique. Throughout history people have sought to discover what lies beyond and have been overcome by spiritual elevation.

I thought about the Afghani prince, Ibrahim Ibn Adham, who looked up at the stars from the roof garden of his palace and wondered how he could discover the creator behind the night sky. A Muslim mystic shouted from outside the palace walls, 'You won't find God by living in opulence, O Ibrahim.' Deeply moved, Ibrahim became a founding father of Muslim mysticism. He abandoned his luxuries and became a wandering Sufi and an inspiration to many through the ages. I sought what many before me had sought: inner tranquillity. But where was I to find it?

In an odd way, my retreat was at once selfish and selfless, designed to benefit both myself and others. As it was Ramadan I was fasting during the day. In the evening Ahbab, my younger brother, would bring me home-cooked meals to break the fast. Then at night I would stand in prayer with the local Muslim community. Afterwards the small number of us in retreat would sleep for about five hours. Then we would wake and conduct prayers, followed by private recitals of the Koran.

I suddenly realized that the last time I had really concentrated on the Koran had been during my travels with Grandpa ten years earlier. For all my ostentatious commitment to Islam and Muslims, all my desires to bring about a Koranic government, I had lost touch with its holy book.

At some point during that retreat I vowed to commit genuinely to the Koran. But there was one problem, unfinished business from my Islamist days: I still did not know Arabic. I wanted to *feel* the original language of the Koran. How could I learn? The last time I had tried, the Saudis had attempted to recruit me. Then I had ended up with the Islamists from the ISB. Could I learn Arabic without becoming embroiled in politics?

I left the mosque with one wish: to learn Arabic, the language of the Prophet Mohammed and of the Koran that he articulated. Without Arabic I felt I would be dependent on handed-down Islam from Islamists, Wahhabis, or others. I prayed to Allah that he would make this dream true.

I knew very few Muslims who had learnt Arabic for themselves. The Islamists were busy with politics, the Salafis were busy talking about the correct creed of monotheism. The only Muslim I knew of who had been to the Middle East and seriously studied Arabic and traditional, pre-modern, Islam was the American convert Imam Hamza Yusuf Hanson.

As an Islamist, Islam was all there was to it. Our kind of Islam: political, domineering, and soulless. Imam Hanson had explained that we had to raise ourselves beyond Islam, while not losing its teachings and practices, and enter into a level of *iman*, faith, and then *ihsan*, perfection.

I began to listen to Imam Hanson again, and so to realize that I had been stuck at the preliminary level of Islam for over a decade, all the while confident that I was at its apex: the Islamic state. It never occurred to me that if Islamic governance was of such importance, why did not one classical Muslim text have a chapter dedicated to this? The entire notion of the 'Islamic state' is a modern phenomenon.

Imam Hanson's grasp of the Arabic language, and the deep meanings he drew from Arabic words, left me dumbfounded. I bought more of his audio lectures and started to listen to them as often as I could. He had a lot to offer. For nearly a year I listened to almost every single one of his lectures and learnt about what seemed like a completely new religion.

Looking back, like most of us at that time, Imam Hanson was affected by the radical wave of anger that was sweeping Muslim circles; Islamism was not absent in him. He had lived for ten years in the Middle East and returned home with some very anti-American, anti-Western, and confrontational attitudes. To me, a post-Islamist, those sentiments seemed merely normal, not politicized. I had been committed to active removal of the entire system, Imam Hanson merely criticized the CIA and successive American governments.

However, he, like me, was going through a period of transformation. Was he first and foremost an American or a Muslim? Could he be both, or must one prevail? The events of September 11 would answer the question for both of us.

Imam Hanson's lectures led me to material from another American, Shaikh Nuh Keller, which also helped me see Islam in a different, more spiritual light. They were not teaching Islamism, set up as an alternative to Marxism, but firm beliefs, the certainty of the Sufis. Theirs was an Islam deeply rooted in classical Muslim scholarship, introspection, and spiritual enrichment, transmitted from the hearts and mouths of men in an unbroken chain of narration, known as an *isnad*, from early times to the present. They taught Islam in its entirety, including the art of *tasawwuf*, or Sufism. In a world full of material competition, fashion, individualism, immediacy, display, youth, wealth, glamour, and concentration on all that is external, Sufism and Sufi-oriented scholars taught the opposite. We were to turn *inside* and attempt to cleanse our hearts of feelings of anger, enmity, arrogance, envy, rancour, jealousy, and other vices that distance us from the truth and put us in conflict with creation. Once God is in the heart, then the limbs respond smoothly to his worship. Without a pure heart, worship is burdensome and tiring.

I understood Imam Hanson's words completely: my lethargy towards worship, my distance from God, resulted partly because true faith had not touched my heart in a decade. I wore it on my sleeve, abused it for political ends, but I had lost the essence of Islam: spiritual surrender to serenity.

Sufi-oriented scholars helped me anchor my soul after five years of political Islamism, a shallow, anger-ridden, aggression-fuelled form of political belief, based on exploiting Islam's adherents but remote from Islam's teachings.

St Augustine said that 'the true philosopher *is* the lover of God', and the Muslim Sufis certainly knew *how* to love God. At *rihla* programmes, or spiritual retreats, I saw grown men weep with yearning for God and his apostle Mohammed. Where Jesus of Nazareth had washed the feet of his disciples, Muslim Sufis kissed the hands of their brethren, a sign of deep humility and recognition that they knew not who was most loved among them in God's sight. Now, to bow and prostrate myself in prayer had meaning for me: abject humility, total lack of vanity in following the Prophet Mohammed's motions of prayer before the unseen but all-seeing God. The Prophet had prescribed humility as an antidote to the haughtiness of the Arabs in Mecca. Refusing to bow, they rejected him. Now, in humility, I found a new energy. Suddenly there was sweetness to prayers, nourishment for the soul, when previously they had been a dull chore necessary to obtain acceptance in mosques, a mask of religiosity to attract potential recruits to the Islamist cause.

For the first time in my life I began eagerly to anticipate the next of the five daily prayers. The Prophet had taught that a servant is closest to God in prostration, when one's forehead, the bearer of intellect, is bowed in recognition of a higher knowledge, a celestial realm. In such a posture, deeply conscious that I was not following an ideology but an age-old tradition passed down from generation to generation from the Prophet, I was able to unearth inner harmony in life.

After my horrible experiences as an Islamist I remained wary. I marvelled at Sufi-oriented scholars from a distance but was not quite ready to commit myself, fearing the same trap of a personality cult that I had fallen into with Omar Bakri. In public I remained distant from these great masters of the Muslim spiritual tradition. Privately, I listened to their speeches, read their articles, and bought their books.

In August 2000 Faye and I were married and spent our honeymoon in Turkey. While exploring the Turkish cultural capital we met Sufis of the Naqshbandi order in most mosques. I asked a shopkeeper near the Blue Mosque where the real *awliya*, people of God, were in Istanbul and he took me to Charshamba, on the hilltops of Istanbul's Fatih district. There, old men with long white beards and radiant faces welcomed us to their humble community. Their daughters were hospitable to Faye, attempting to speak to her through gestures and showing her around the bazaar. Inside the main mosque in Charshamba there was a spiritual presence that I had not experienced before. In corners of the mosque men in white turbans sat in deep meditation, facing Mecca. Students of the Turkish saint popularly known as Mahmud Effendi, they practised the silent remembrance of God in the way of the Naqshbandis, based on an intensely spiritual breathing exercise in which each breath is used by the Naqshbandi aspirant to remember God.

At the entrances to the mosque were frames of photos of the tomb of the Prophet Mohammed. I felt that I was in a different world, a different time. The silence, the dimly lit interior, the rows of oak shelving holding old manuscripts of the Koran calmed my soul. But I still felt contrition. Most of the men were much older than me and they had led a lifetime of prayer and meditation. They had escaped the persecution of the extremist secularism of the post-1924 Turkish state and found inner calm among the chaos of the city. Would I be able to lead such a life? I doubted it. But I knew I wanted to.

After evening prayers the men humbly walked out of the prayer hall, untied their cotton turbans, and hid them inside their cloak pockets. The fundamentalist secularist Mustafa Kemal Ataturk had banned expressions of religion in Turkey, including the wearing of turbans and headscarves. Still the spirit of Islam whirled like a dervish in the hearts and minds of its most God-loving adherents, the Turkish Sufis.

An elderly worshipper at a mosque, noticing my intense interest in Sufism, told me a story that has never left me. Beside the Sea of Marmara, sitting at the steps of the tomb of a Sufi, the old man pointed to the boats out at sea and told me how the great sultan, Suleiman the Magnificent, a contemporary of King Henry VIII, had once sat on a boat with a Sufi.

'How I yearn to have the peaceful heart that you have. My worries are ceaseless, my kingdom troublesome,' said the sultan.

'Do you really want inner peace?' asked the Sufi.

'Yes!' replied the sultan. 'Can you offer it to me?'

'Pass me that ring on your finger,' said the Sufi.

Looking puzzled, the sultan removed his diamond ring and handed it over to the Sufi, half hoping that this was the price of inner calm. The Sufi stared the sultan in the eyes and, without warning, dropped the priceless ring into the sea.

'How dare you?' yelled the sultan in a frenzy.

The Sufi smiled, unperturbed. The sultan called upon the members of his entourage to dive overboard and recover it. The Sufi raised his hand, indicating that the sultan should hold back his courtiers. Calmly, the Sufi put his hand into the water and miraculously pulled out the ring.

'As long as this ring is of any worth to you, O Suleiman, you will not have inner peace. Inner contentment is derived from our detachment.'

Detachment from the material world was a key plank of Sufi teaching. Walking the Sufi path, I realized, was not going to be easy.

During our time in Turkey I met an American convert to Islam. Initially, he had been a Salafi, studying in Saudi Arabia. In the Prophet's Mosque in Medina he met Mahmud Effendi and left Saudi Arabia to study traditional Islam under him. Shaikh

Naeem Abdul Wali, originally Gary Edwards from Indiana, took me to Bursa to meet his shaikh.

Mahmud Effendi was a frail old man who walked with the support of his disciples, who held his hands as he slowly moved forward. In a cool mountaintop house he spent his summer with some of his disciples, away from the heat of Istanbul. My moments with him were brief, as he had to return to rest, but I felt an overawing presence in his company. He made me feel pure, clean, and gentle. His facial movements were soft, like those of a child, and his smile was innocent and sincere. He walked into the guestroom, where Faye and I had been waiting with others, and his humble majesty overcame us. Simply to look upon him reduced Faye to tears.

Such were the real men of God, able to move hearts, bring forth tears of joy, and purify the inner realms of those who visited them. My long trip to Bursa had been more than worthwhile.

I spent as much time with Shaikh Naeem as I could. I had to use my discretion – this was our honeymoon, after all – but Faye was more than gracious in appreciating what I was trying to do: understand Sufism and Islam in Turkey.

Shaikh Naeem, like his spiritual master, wore a turban and dressed in a long, flowing robe in emulation of the Prophet. Grandpa had done the same. And I couldn't help noticing other similarities between him and my first spiritual teacher. Had Grandpa been right all along? Shaikh Naeem venerated his teacher as my father honoured Grandpa. The gentle conduct of the Turkish Sufis in Charshamba, their pristine turbans, their attachment to the Prophet, all brought back buried memories of my own childhood with Grandpa.

Faye and I enjoyed our honeymoon in Istanbul, and we both returned to London with a treasure we had not previously possessed. Throughout Istanbul we came across people selling poetry and portraits of someone they called 'Mevlana', 'our master'. Who was he? Again, a man in robe, turban, and flowing white beard. During our last visit to the Blue Mosque and its immediate surroundings, I saw a young woman selling pictures of 'Mevlana' with his poetry, some of which was in English. One in particular caught my eye and I immediately bought it as a souvenir:

> Everyone is so frightened of death,
> But the true Sufis just laugh;
> Nothing overpowers their hearts.
> What strikes the oyster shell
> Does not harm the pearl.

'Mevlana' had addressed my own dread of death. I liked his parables: the oyster shell for the human body and the pearl for our soul. But what did he know about the pearl? What is our soul? I set about learning more about this poet. I discovered that his name was Jalal al-Din Rumi and he lived in the thirteenth century. Rumi today is the best known, most widely read Muslim mystical poet in the world. He is also the founder of the Mevlevi order, known to us in the West as 'whirling dervishes'. How did Rumi overcome his fear of death? Why did he rejoice? I returned to London and collected as much of Rumi's poetry as I could. For a thirteenth-century Muslim scholar, Rumi was remarkably liberal and insightful. He was not, however, without the blemishes of his time, particularly in relation to gender equality.

Now, no longer a mental prisoner of Islamism, I was able to put people in their historical context. If Shakespeare had been racist and anti-Semitic in his plays, then it was because he reflected his times. If Rumi had expressed sexist sentiments, he too had been a product of his period. I tried to avoid judging the past through contemporary lenses.

Rumi wrote much on the subject of death and the afterlife. He went so far as to admonish his followers:

Do not cry, 'Alas, you are gone!' at my graveside:
For me, this is a time for joyful meeting!
Do not bid me 'Farewell' when I am lowered into my grave:
I have passed through the curtain to eternal grace.

Rumi's firm belief, his certainty, did not have a place in my heart. That old Islamist trait, knowing *all* the answers, still lingered in the depths of my mind. To this dithering, Rumi answered:

When you put a cargo on board a ship, you make that venture on trust,
For you do not know whether you will be drowned or safely reach the other shore.
If you say, 'I will not embark till I am certain of my fate,' then you will do no trade:
The secret of these two destinies is never disclosed.
The faint-hearted merchant neither gains nor loses; nay he loses,
For he is deprived of his fortune. Only those who are zealous in their search, who faithfully seek the flame, find the light.
Since all affairs turn upon hope, surely faith is the worthiest object of hope, for thereby you win salvation.

Sufism was about *hope* and *faith*. Life itself was about hope and faith.

Rumi's poetry conveyed deep spiritual meanings. Growing up in Britain, I was not introduced to Rumi and his contemporaries, for there were many such scholars. Rather, my introductions were to Mawdudi, Qutb, Nabhani – all of whom loathed Rumi's tradition of tolerance and tranquillity. Rumi taught that 'the religion of Love transcends all other religions: for lovers, the only religion and belief is God'. To Islamists, such all-encompassing wisdom was anathema.

★

Later that year, Shaikh Naeem was invited to Britain for the first time to address students at Hounslow mosque. As I continued to learn more about Sufism and tried to walk the Sufi path with the distant aid of Rumi and living Sufi teachers such as Imam Hanson and Shaikh Nuh Keller, I began to frequent this serene west London mosque. After teaching at Hounslow for a fortnight Shaikh Naeem stayed on for a week and I was honoured to have him as a guest in our house.

My parents had noticed my increasing calmness, aversion to watching much television, and immersion in the works of Rumi and the speeches of Imam Hanson and Shaikh Keller. My father was initially sceptical that I had really renounced Islamism, but he was slowly beginning to discern a change deep within me, much deeper than anything he had previously witnessed. My mother knew this sooner than my father, and lavished me with love as though I were a newborn child. All the while Faye continued to motivate me, always eager to share my latest discoveries and insights.

When Shaikh Naeem came to stay with us that year, my father's doubt was washed away. He had expected an Islamist of sorts, a modernist political Muslim. Shaikh Naeem's appearance, based like Grandpa's on the Prophet's, put his fears to rest. He was overjoyed that his long lost son had, at last, truly *come home* again.

The Sufis taught me a great deal about the habits of the Prophet. I knew of no other Muslim group that brought him to life as the Sufis did. To them, he was al-Habib, the Beloved.

In my Islamist days I spoke about al-Habib a lot, but I really had no conception of who he was, other than a political leader. The man and his life were just abstract constructs to me. But in the company of Sufis I discovered who the most misunderstood man in history really was. I continued to meet people who internalized every single one of the Prophet's traits: happiness,

compassion, love, fairness, gentility, and an aura of inner contentment. The Prophet was alive in their hearts, and found
expression in their conduct.

I accompanied Shaikh Naeem to as many places as possible,
and tried to learn from him all I could. He was another example
of an American who had embraced Islam and was now setting
a fine example to so-called born Muslims such as myself. I went
with him to the University of Cambridge to meet the renowned
Muslim scholar Dr Tim Winter, whose articles, translations of
classical Muslim texts, and taped lectures had helped me embrace
classical, traditional Islam.

We met him in his office at the Faculty of Divinity and talked
for a long time. It was a Friday, so we went together to weekly
congregational prayers at the local mosque. I was expecting to
be addressed by an imam from the local Bangladeshi community
but, to my surprise and delight, it was Dr Winter who delivered
the sermon, in both Arabic and English, and led prayer in the
sweetest harmony I had heard from a convert to Islam.

After prayers we resumed our discussions. Dr Winter also
spoke Persian and Ottoman Turkish, and was a specialist in
European Islam as well as medieval schools of theology. He
and Shaikh Naeem discussed religion, history, current affairs,
and literature as I listened and learnt, occasionally asking for
clarification.

I discovered much that day at Cambridge, but one simple but
crucial phrase stands out: 'it depends'. This was how Dr Winter
began his answer to nearly every question we asked, before
going on to consider various alternatives. To a former Islamist
with a polarized view of the world, Dr Winter's nuanced
response was a mighty eye-opener. To this day I remain bewildered why Dr Winter, also known as Shaikh Abdal-Hakim
Murad, is not considered the scholastic authority for Islam in
Britain. He has impeccable credentials, having studied with

leading scholars in the Arab world, and is at home with main-stream British Muslims. Instead, the media turn to unqualified, shallow, robotic Islamists to explain Islam to their audiences.

By the middle of 2001 I was committed to spiritual Islam. I was determined to leave Britain and study Arabic and traditional Islam in the Middle East. I had nothing to do with Islamists, kept my distance from all forms of Muslim politicking, and simply concentrated on memorizing the Koran and observing the divine presence that is God, trying always to grow in love and veneration of the Prophet. Islamism, as far as I was concerned, was distant, buried history. But modern Britain was receding as well.

That year I left my job at HSBC and downgraded to a clerical job in local government so that I could concentrate on my Koranic studies in the absence of sales targets and overtime. As the months passed an immense spiritual energy grew within me. I was at peace with myself and the world around me; my soul was tranquil and no amount of pressure caused me stress. I would wake at dawn and revise the previous day's chapters. In the evenings I would work on new chapters. Faye and my youngest sister Rashida would listen to my readings before I went to see my Koran teacher on Saturday afternoons. I maintained this spiritual discipline for over two years and tried to emerge a better person: I felt – I *knew* – I was closer to God than I had ever been, and the spiritual void I experienced while in Islamism had been filled. I no longer categorized people as Muslims and non-Muslims, as I had done as an Islamist, but simply as people.

We were all God's creation, children of Adam. We had a common heritage, honoured by God in the Koran. My belief in humanity expanded my horizons, made me feel a more complete human being in service to God and creation.

I also became a better Briton. One day, on my way back to

London from Cambridge with a Sufi teacher, I did not stop at a red light, a hangover from my Hizb days when it was common practice to ignore the law of the land. The Sufi gently touched my arm, smiled and said, 'Our master, the Prophet, came to perfect our manners. Breaking the law, even a minor traffic violation, is bad *adab*, discourtesy.' I blushed in embarrassment. The Sufi approach was so gentle, and yet so overpowering. There was no grand explanation – just simple humility. As the Chicago-born Shaikh Nuh Keller said, 'Sufism is about you. It is about falling in love with the divine.'

Eventually I memorized almost half of the Koran. The more I learnt, the more I felt that this knowledge was a trust, a gift from God. My memory was too weak to retain 3,000 verses, and yet with God's mercy it did. I supplemented my Koranic studies with frequent visits to gatherings of spiritually inclined Muslims. I regularly attended seminars of visiting teachers from various Sufi pathways, and of Sufis who did not adhere to any particular spiritual order. They taught the secrets of travelling the spiritual path: humility, repentance, awe, kindness, hope, and yearning for visions of the Messenger of God. I tried my utmost to exhibit all those traits, but learnt also the need for constant vigilance against one's own shortcomings, errors, falls from grace, and moments of desolation, and that I must remain open to correction, guidance, and advice from my superiors in my journey towards God. 'The life not tested by criticism', Socrates once said, 'is not worth living.'

As far as I was concerned, Islamism had now been *completely* flushed out of me. I could not have been more wrong.

Whoever kills an innocent person, it is as though he has killed entire humanity.

The Koran

It was extraordinary that the Muslims of the Sufi tradition who helped me regain my sanity were *all* Americans. They may have led me to other mainstream Muslim scholars who were English, such as Dr Tim Winter, and others who were Yemeni, Syrian, or Egyptian, but the primary reintroduction to what I consider true, spiritual Islam, the essence of the faith, came to me from American Muslims who had discovered Islam through the Sufis they had met.

I now thought I was at peace with the world, had dispensed with my Islamist tendencies, and was fully focused on my Koranic studies. I met Hizb ut-Tahrir activists on the streets of London, occasionally at mosque doors distributing their propaganda of separation and disengagement from British life, but I was now beyond that. I ignored them, rejected the leaflets they pressed upon me, and saw them for what they were: misguided, deluded, and dated.

Faye, my parents, and a small circle of new, Sufi-oriented friends encouraged me to concentrate on my studies. During this insular period of my life I had no interest in interacting with people or spending much time with my friends. I was most peaceful when I was with the Koran, melodiously chanting and memorizing the words that the Prophet had pronounced more than a millennium ago. Out of joy, my father would buy me

small bottles of Arabian musk or sandalwood perfume to apply
when I sat to study. 'This will remind you of the Prophet,' he
would say. 'He loved perfume.'

While I was at Hizb ut-Tahrir, the leader, or *mushrif*, of my
weekly cell meeting would often say that 'the concepts of the
Hizb stay with you for ever. You will always carry the ideas of
the Hizb.' Not me, I thought. I was almost gleeful at having
been able not only to leave the Hizb, but to discover authentic
religion and to reject the politicization of it. I no longer shared
the Hizb's vision of a cataclysmic Islamic state which would
right all the wrongs of the Muslim world.

On the morning of 11 September 2001 I had woken up early to
stand in solace in the divine presence, memorized and revised
sections of the Koran, and then gone to work. Sometime in the
afternoon, my mobile phone's news alert from the BBC notified
me that an aeroplane had crashed into the World Trade Center
in New York. Initially, I thought nothing much of it, beyond
sadness at such a terrible accident. Then several other alerts
followed: this was no accident but part of a larger terrorist attack
on New York and the Pentagon which had left thousands dead.

From my desk, I could see London's Canary Wharf. Instinctively, I looked up to see if it was still standing. To my amazement, I noticed other colleagues doing the same thing. People
were gathering in groups to discuss what was happening.

I found it difficult to accept that an attack on the United
States was an altogether negative development. Moreover, the
bandying about of the term 'Muslim terrorists' made me feel
very uncomfortable, as though the two words were in some way
equivalent. I was quick to remind my colleagues that when
Timothy McVeigh, a Christian fundamentalist, had carried out
attacks on Oklahoma in 1995, the front page of the British
newspaper *Today* had said that he had done so 'In the Name of
Islam'. That turned out to be wrong. 'We should hold our

horses,' I counselled. 'This could be another McVeigh.' Besides, an attack on America would not only elicit approval from some Arab and Muslim quarters; Latin America and parts of Europe would applaud it too.

Despite my professed Sufi spirituality, a part of me was joyful. Worse, the spiritual Muslim in me failed to detect the remnants of the arrogant sleeper Islamist still residing within. I never asked myself why I found the term 'terrorism' objectionable. Islamists believed that the West used 'terrorist' as shorthand for Muslim resistance fighters in Palestine, Chechnya, and other conflict-ridden parts of the world. As far as they were concerned, there was no such thing as a 'Muslim terrorist', only resistance fighters with legitimate struggles. It was the duty of all Muslims to support their cause in Palestine, Kashmir, the Philippines. There was never any condemnation of their killing innocent people, of using suicide bombings to cause mass devastation. The Palestinian suicide bombings were considered by *all* Islamists of *all* persuasions as legitimate, and endorsed by their skewed and unscholarly reading of Islamic law.

Even though I had accepted Sufi Islam, and consciously tried to decontaminate my mind, there were still aspects of Islamist political strategies that I thought of as 'normal': an acceptance of terrorism, an unconscious belief that those who 'opposed Islam' were somehow less than human and thus expendable in the Islamist pursuit of political dominion over palm and pine.

I had not heard a single Muslim scholar of any repute speak out against either suicide bombings in Palestine or the hijacking of aeroplanes. In Muslim political discussion, dominated by Islamists across the globe, killing Jews in Israel was considered to be a means to an end: the annihilation of Israel.

If there were Muslim scholars and organizations who rejected terrorism, then their voices were silenced by the domination of the public sphere by Islamists. To question acts labelled by the West as 'terrorist' was a sign of betrayal of the *ummah*. Even among Western liberals there were those who 'understood' how and why suicide bombings occurred. As long as it was in Palestine and Israel, we could intellectualize the problem, philosophize about the psychology of suicide bombers. Even many non-Islamist Muslims called such crimes 'martyrdom operations'. The barbaric events of 11 September 2001 changed all that. The global political climate altered irrevocably.

I went home, washed, and immediately left for a gathering. As was my practice at the time, I had not watched any television, nor had I updated myself on developments. Any attack on the bullyboy of the world, ardent supporter of Israel, puppet-master of Arab dictators, and exporter of McDonald's-style globalization was certainly good news for the rest of us. Perhaps Americans would now ask themselves why they had been given a bloody nose.

In Sufi circles we rarely ever discussed politics. There was no distinct political culture, no clarity on the conflicts of the world, and certainly no condemnation of Islamist terrorism. There was a vague hope that somehow these crises would solve themselves and we would all return to our spiritual orbits to work for the betterment of our souls. Religion and politics were genuinely separate. This created two problems: most Sufis I knew had little or no political awareness. They somehow believed that it was not something they needed to engage with, and on one level they were right. There are millions of citizens in Britain who do not vote. However, the acuteness of the problem lies in the second issue: in the absence of traditional Muslim guidance on politics, many Sufis accepted Islamist paradigms of political engagement. Consequently a loathing of Muslim rulers, a desire to see the overthrow of regimes and their replacement with 'Islamic' governments, and enmity towards Israel, the USA, and Britain became unquestioned. The political void was not always filled with participatory, democratic politics, but the ubiquitous speechifying of Islamists at colleges, universities, and mosque entrances. Looking back, I am astounded at the depth of the psychological damage caused by Islamism.

That evening, at a Sufi gathering I asked what we were doing to celebrate.

A group of young Muslims, waiting before a shaikh arrived and we started our *dhikr* session, looked up at me.

'Celebrate what?' asked Adam, a well-connected Sufi Muslim.

'America has been hit today. Shouldn't Muslims be happy?' I replied.

'*Astaghfirullah*,' he said in Arabic. 'Seek refuge in Allah. This is not our way. The media are already suggesting that Muslims are behind this. By Allah I hope we are not, for this is terrible.'

'Why is it terrible?' said another young Muslim, seated on my left. 'The Americans kill Muslims through Israel in Palestine, have their military bases in Saudi Arabia, and support the dictators of the Arab world. If Americans are killed, we should be happy, because they kill us.'

'My brother,' said a patient, sombre Adam. 'We have the political leaders we deserve. It is not our tradition to violently remove those who occupy seats of power. The Americans are not our teachers; if they kill like barbarians, we do not respond like them. Our master, our guide, is the Prophet. Do you think our beloved Prophet would be happy to see so many innocent people massacred in cold blood? Tell me, do you? Have you forgotten his honouring of life, even animal life? I hope Muslims were not behind the carnage and killing in New York today.'

At that moment I thought the skies had landed on my head. For all my self-belief that I had left Islamism, and cleansed my mind, it dawned on me that I was a long, long way from travelling on the Sufi path. Adam was miles ahead of me. I was silent, looking down in shame at the floor.

Adam had correctly realized the spirit of the Prophet. Even in moments of calamity, the true lover of the Prophet drew lessons from his beloved. In this instance I had failed to do so.

It was time for me to turn to God, speak with the Prophet, and seek forgiveness. I remained silent for the rest of that evening, pondering the enormity of my mental crime which had found external expression in my comments. I had endorsed mass murder.

Lost in my thoughts, I barely registered a debate raging between Adam and another young Muslim, Gamal.

'The Prophet engaged in jihad! The Americans have been killing Muslims all across the world. Why shouldn't we kill them? I hope it *was* Muslims who were behind today's attack.'

Adam was steeped in classical Muslim tradition. He had taken classes from Imam Hanson and Dr Winter directly. In private, Imam Hanson had taught his students what he had not yet stated in public: suicide bombings, plane hijackings, terrorism, were *haram*, forbidden in the scriptures of Islam and against the letter and spirit of the Prophet's teachings. How I wished Imam Hanson, Dr Winter, or Shaikh Keller had put this on record before 11 September. That way, at least, I would have been able to face my contradictions sooner. But I understood their concerns: they would have been condemned by angry Islamists in the Muslim community as American stooges.

'My brother,' replied Adam. 'The Prophet took up arms after thirteen years of torture, persecution, and killing of his companions by pagans. His jihad was to bring peace. Do you think what happened today, or what so-called jihadis are doing in the world, will bring any peace? Read the *sira*, the biography of the Prophet. Have you forgotten how he redirected an entire army when he saw a bitch was giving birth to her puppies? In a valid jihad, the Prophet forbade killing priests, women, children, or non-combatants, and burning trees and livestock. As believers in the Prophet we must adhere to those rules in a jihad for peace . . .'

On television that night I watched the horror of the day's

events unfold. Filled with remorse, I turned to God for forgiveness and prayed for world peace. That night I vowed to play my part to bring it about. In the months that followed 9/11 I found myself in the uncharacteristic position of confronting fellow Muslims in support of non-Muslims. I drew inspiration from the fact that I was not alone. The Prophet's companions sided with non-Muslims against Muslims in settling civil disputes on many occasions. For me, Islam was about truth, humanity, and compassion. It was not about supporting Muslims regardless of whether they were right or wrong. The dominant outlook among Muslims in my local community, however, was that Muslims were *always* right, especially when confronting the United States.

In discussions in mosques, prayer halls, Muslim bookshops, and between Muslim colleagues at work, there was no topic of conversation more pertinent than 9/11. There was a ridiculous rumour circulating that over 2,000 Jewish people had been tipped off by the Israeli embassy not to attend work on that day.

In an attempt to atone for the damage I had done previously, I took on Muslim pessimists and deniers. All sorts of conspiracy theories were advanced by my fellow believers that 9/11 was not the work of Muslims.

'Why not?' I asked a fellow worshipper at a mosque.

'Because Muslims are not sophisticated enough to do something like this.'

'So, in principle, you're not against killing Americans en masse. You're just not convinced that Muslims were behind it.'

That type of double thinking, in denial and yet proud at the same time, was ubiquitous. On Green Street, in a large Islamist bookshop, I stood one evening and watched a Channel 4 News analysis. The elderly father of the shop owner, an acquaintance of mine from my YMO days and a figurehead in Jamat-e-Islami, told me, 'There is no such thing as al-Qaeda. What is this new thing? It is all American games.' Anyone speaking out against bin Laden, terrorism, and al-Qaeda was immediately sidelined.

In those heady days it was left to an American to rise and defend his country, and with it, our faith.

Within weeks of 9/11 Imam Hanson was on the White House lawn with leaders of other faiths condemning Islamist terrorism. Watching Shaikh Hanson on television, singing 'God Bless America' with the US President, forced many of us to question if it was Islam we were interested in or the forces of political Islam. Imam Hanson declared, 'Islam was hijacked as an innocent victim on that plane on September 11th 2001.'

In October Imam Hanson visited Britain and gave interviews to the BBC and the *Guardian* newspaper outlining the Koran's condemnation of terrorism. In unequivocal terms, and sensing a current of Muslim support for 9/11 and attacks on the West, he stated: 'If you hate the West, emigrate to a Muslim country.'* In a post-9/11 climate, that was a powerful message to Muslims in the West.

I monitored Imam Hanson's media interviews closely and went to see him at a mosque in Maida Vale, where he addressed a large Muslim crowd at a Q-News event. Personally I was delighted that President Bush had made the right choice and met a sane Muslim scholar rather than one of the closet extremists who usually represent Muslims in America, though he made a grave mistake in not heeding the advice of religious scholars and instead forcing the world into a 'with us or against us' polarization. Hitherto Imam Hanson had been phenomenally popular among British Muslims, particularly those with a Sufi orientation. However, in a post-9/11 climate, even his closest enthusiasts began to express doubts about the great imam. How could he meet Bush? Why had he sung 'God Bless America'? How did he know for sure that Muslims were behind 9/11?

Imam Hanson's personal safety was at risk. It was clear to me that he was an intelligent scholar who had realized that remaining

*Interview with Jack O'Sullivan in the *Guardian*, 8 October 2001.

silent in the face of extremism, in the name of 'Muslim unity', had deprived moderate Muslims of a voice. Nearly every Muslim representative body, mosque, and publishing house was under Islamist control. If now Imam Hanson's own students questioned him even after 9/11, what anger would his speaking out against extremism have provoked before then?

At that meeting Imam Hanson categorically condemned suicide bombings and plane hijackings to a lukewarm crowd. The murmurs of disapproval could be heard from two rows behind me. Imam Hanson had been fortunate that no one from Hizb ut-Tahrir had stood up to heckle him, but others were waiting in the wings. After Imam Hanson delivered his passionate plea for an end to extremism in Muslim discourse, and his clear condemnation of taking innocent lives, whether in New York or Tel Aviv, he sat down on stage, took out his rosary beads from his pocket, and remembered his Lord.

Then a recently returned Taliban-captive, the British journalist Yvonne Ridley, stood up and crudely contradicted a Muslim scholar of the highest repute. Herein lay the problem. She called suicide bombers 'martyrs' and seemed to encourage support for violence and terror. Scholarly maturity and erudition were being challenged by an aspiring amateur Islamist. Soon Ridley converted to what she thought was Islam, though it seems to me she accepted not the religion but the political ideology.

As an Islamist I had dismissed the expertise of scholars on Muslim affairs and taken my religion from amateurs. I was not alone; my mentors had done the same. Mawdudi, Qutb, and Nabhani all despised the *ulama*, traditional Muslim scholars. Our Friday prayers on campus, for example, were not led by *ulama*, or even by trainee *ulama*, but by young activists who had no knowledge of the basics of theology or Arabic. A town planner taught us in my *halaqah*, a charity worker trained us in my *usrah*. Almost without exception, Islamism is detached from the *ulama*. Yet Muslims believe that God's first command to the Prophet was *iqra*, or 'read'. Islam was preserved in book form, the Koran, and the Prophet valued erudition and knowledge, making it obligatory for his followers to learn as much as possible. The Prophet had taught those who accompanied him, the *sahabah*, who in turn taught others and thus the time-honoured tradition of teaching and learning survived among the *ulama* to present times. Genuine Muslim scholars see themselves as bearers of a trust that they inherited from their teachers, who took it from theirs, all the way back to the Prophet in a verifiable transmission known as *isnad*. It is this *isnad* which firmly grounds traditional scholarship, as opposed to activist Islamism, to the source of Islam: the Prophet.

In early 2002 Faye and I registered for part-time Saturday-morning Arabic classes at London University's School of Oriental and African Studies. The classes were full and the cohort was varied. September 11 had created a new curiosity about Muslims, Arabs, and Arabic.

Faye and I were in different classes. In my class, I was extremely focused and not there to make new friends. However, my cap and beard, grown in imitation of the Prophet, drew attention to the fact that I was an observant Muslim. As we introduced ourselves before the first class began, a young lady sitting at the front was the first to speak.

'Hi! My name is Kelly and this is my second term of learning Arabic.'

From her accent and self-assurance I assumed she was American. However, our teacher, an Egyptian Arab, obviously required confirmation.

'Where are you from?' he asked.

'The United States,' she said, almost blushing. And then immediately, 'No, I am not an American spy. My last teacher thought I was from the CIA! I am an ordinary American who wants to learn more about the Arabic language and culture.'

There was an open mind, a curiosity to learn behind those remarks, and a determination not to be pigeon-holed. Most of the Americans I had known had been Muslims. Kelly was to become my first non-Muslim American friend. The Arabic teacher's line of questioning annoyed me: why did he care where she came from? He did not ask that question of anyone else.

I mentioned to Faye the teacher's interrogatory questioning and the unwarranted need to justify Kelly's presence in class. The following Saturday, during the coffee break, I congratulated Kelly for her strength in standing up to him. We spoke for a while and, for the first time in many years, I was able to converse with an ordinary American without any feeling of rancour or animosity. Post-9/11, for a former Islamist, that was a miracle.

Kelly, I learned, was a business consultant and fluent in French, Italian, and Spanish. She was married to an Englishman and now lived in London permanently. Born in the outskirts of Chicago, she was studious and well-mannered. We both shared a passion for Arabic, for different reasons, and had an avid interest in current affairs.

Soon we were exchanging e-mails on history, philosophy, poetry, ethics, and, of course, religion. Kelly was an agnostic and a borderline atheist. She was also liberal in her political and social views. I knew that many of my Muslim friends would disapprove of me befriending an agnostic, liberal, non-Muslim American female. My old Islamist acquaintances would see this as entering blasphemous territory, befriending the worst of our ideological enemies. My becoming close friends with Kelly was a deliberate attempt to prove to myself that human love and friendship could be built on the basis of our common humanity, and we need not hate and desire destruction simply because of our differences, be they religious or otherwise.

For both of us our friendship was a huge personal outreach programme. Kelly had hundreds of questions to ask me about Islam and Muslims, and I had hundreds for her about modern

America. For me, Kelly was the litmus test of whether I was able to befriend an American without wishing to convert her, or impose my views on her. She questioned me on Muslim status of women, capital punishment, human rights, jihad, and all the while she maintained her liberal views. And why not?

After hours of discussion, we were amazed by how similar our worldviews were. Despite her agnosticism and rejection of her Catholic upbringing, we were able to see eye to eye on almost every controversial issue. Where we disagreed, we did so with respect and understanding for the other's position. However, underlying our differences was a common desire to see a healed human race, free from the fanaticism of secularism or religion.

Kelly never pre-judged Faye or me. Faye wore a headscarf, I a Muslim skullcap, Kelly a baseball cap. And yet we were all able to get along. Today, Kelly remains one of my closest friends.

Imam Hanson visited Britain again in late 2002. When Faye and I mentioned him to Kelly, to our astonishment she wanted to come and hear him speak. Kelly shocked Faye and me by wearing a Muslim headscarf out of respect for both the mosque and the scholar. I so wished other Muslims could see that an agnostic, liberal American from Chicago sits among us in hijab, not because she is convinced, but out of respect for her fellow human beings. Kelly gave me hope that amid the chaos of extremist, literalist Christianity in America, there were decent people who sought a better, more compassionate world.

After that meeting, for the first time in my life, I approached Imam Hamza Yusuf Hanson and shook his hands. I had been taking Islamic lessons from him via audio tapes and CDs for two years; I considered him a teacher and an inspiration. In person, he was a kind, observant scholar with a gentle handshake. I felt as though he did not look at me, but *into* me. It was a surreal experience.

'How are you?' he asked, as though he knew me.

I knew he was facing a tough time from extremist elements within the Muslim population in Britain and America, so in an attempt to encourage him to continue with his magnificent work of calling people to God, away from political Islam, I told him that he had deeply touched the lives of both myself and others I knew. I informed him about my intent to study in the Middle East and he took a genuine interest in my memorizing the Koran. I was humbled and embarrassed by the attention he gave to someone as insignificant as me. To make matters worse, he asked me to pray for him. I left the mosque that afternoon more convinced than ever that Imam Hanson was not an advocate of moderate, spiritual Islam because that was what the West, particularly the United States, wanted, but because at its essence, that's what Islam is: moderation. The Prophet Mohammed spoke several times to his companions about his way being a middle way, and in one of the most authenticated statements warned against extremism. I knew, I had experienced, what the Prophet was warning against.

Imam Hanson and his teachers were not creating a new Islam to suit the West, but manifesting the primordial persona of the Prophet Mohammed, reclaiming the Prophet's faith from the hijackers of planes, assassins of presidents, murderers of the innocent, and seekers of political power. If Imam Hanson's conduct had touched me, it was because he had taken the Prophet as his role model. The Prophet took an interest in the lives of people who surrounded him; he often asked the children of Medina about their pets. His high rank with God did not prevent him from being humble towards his friends. Once, the Prophet asked his former enemy Omar, the later caliph, to 'remember me with your Lord, O young brother'. It was this sublime character that had touched Imam Hanson's life, and in turn my own.

That was my first and last meeting with the Californian scholar who, like me, had travelled a path of conflict and anger only to realize the mistakes he had made and stand courageously to oppose hatred in all its forms, secular and religious.

13. The Road to Damascus

My religion is love's religion: where'er turn her camels, that religion
my religion is, my faith.
  Ibn Arabi, thirteenth-century Muslim theologian

After 9/11 I knew that my time of trying to live an isolated
existence, enjoying the company of the Sufis, was over. The
world's media were now discussing my religion, something I
had considered extremely precious and personal. More than
ever I needed to learn Arabic to help me understand my faith at
its core.

After months of discussion, Faye and I decided that Damascus
in Syria would best suit our needs. Imam Hanson had studied
with Bedouin tribes, pure in tongue and piety, in the deserts of
sub-Saharan Africa. Faye and I settled for a metropolis.

As we worked towards our move, I increasingly wore Arab
clothes and lived like a hermit: minimal food, no television, and
long hours of study. As I reconnected with my faith, all around
me Islamists were emerging as a strong voice. Islamist groups
organized conferences, the media gave them vast amounts of
airtime, and they began to be seen as 'mainstream' Islam. I, a
spiritually oriented, moderate, mainstream Muslim, like millions
of others, had nothing to say. We did not advocate suicide
bombings, challenge the governments of countries, threaten to
hijack – why should we make the news?

With British Muslim leadership firmly in the hands of Islamists
at the Muslim Council of Britain, and a similar Islamist takeover
of other representative bodies in the United States, I ignored

the new Islam industry. My old acquaintances, Inayat Bungla-wala most prominent among them, and other Islamists were dominating the airwaves as representatives of British Islam. Mainstream Muslims at mosques succumbed to Islamist pressure to join the MCB in the name of 'Muslim unity'. In itself, the aim was laudable. However, the public face of the MCB, as well as its many politburo-styled committees, was constantly dominated by Islamists. Mainstream British Muslims from vari-ous Sufi traditions were not considered worthy of becoming leaders of the MCB. They were mere support fodder, a con-venient statistic for MCB leaders with which to harangue government ministers and browbeat the media. The politicking of the MCB and its own extremist sympathies was to come to the fore after a terrorist attack on Britain.

My years of Islamist ranting now seemed so hollow, meaning-less, and destructive. It was God, I read in the Koran, who bestowed political leadership, *mulk*, and it was God who with-drew it. To me God was no longer a legislator but an existence that breathed life into the deepest vessels of my heart. 'God moves between a person and his heart,' I recited. In another verse: 'I am closer to you than your jugular vein.'

God was no longer beyond human reach, in need of govern-mental endorsement. God was around us, in us, for us.

Repeatedly the Koran called for reflection, meditation, and contemplation on the world. It offered parables to trigger our remembrance of God. The Koran desired *yusr*, or ease, and not hardship in adherence to faith. There was an elasticity, nuance, and plurality in the message of the Koran that Islamists had somehow overlooked, in the process reducing our noble faith to terrorism, anger, and conflict.

While Faye and I planned our studies in Syria we took Cambridge courses to qualify as teachers of English as a foreign language so we could support ourselves while we were studying.

We both resigned from our jobs in London, reassured our worried families, and prayed that all would go according to plan. In early 2003 Saddam Hussein effectively invited the US army to invade Iraq by playing cat-and-mouse games with United Nations arms inspectors. Our families and friends cautioned us to stay away from the Middle East. There was talk of US tanks rolling into Damascus after Baghdad, statues of Hafez and Bashar al-Asad to be toppled. Syria was Iraq's neighbour, and Faye and I felt as though we were heading for a war zone. Should we go, or wait until the war ended? But if the war spread to Syria, we might never get to learn Arabic at all.

With Faye's agreement, I decided to leave first, to test the waters. At Damascus airport I was met by a British friend, Peter, who offered to put me up in his student flat.

'Three of us live there because it is very close to the institute at which we study,' he explained to me as we boarded an old bus.

'How many rooms do you have?' I enquired.

'Three,' he replied.

'So how do you have a spare room? I am more than happy to book into a hotel till my wife arrives,' I suggested.

'No, no. It's quite all right. One of my flatmates, Qaleem, left this morning for jihad. His room is empty.'

I was not sure if I heard right. 'Sorry?' I said.

'Jihad. Qaleem has gone for jihad in Iraq. Several students from our institute went with him,' explained my fully composed friend. 'Isn't it on the news in Britain?'

I could not believe my ears.

'You're not seriously suggesting that fighting for Saddam Hussein is a jihad, are you? After all, this man declared a so-called jihad in 1981 against the Iranians and then killed nearly a million Muslims. He called it a jihad when he occupied Kuwait.'

'Shhhh,' said my friend. 'This is Syria. You'll get us arrested.'

I was dumbfounded that young Muslims in Syria could possibly think they were fighting a jihad in Iraq. I had come to learn

Arabic in a country where students from religious seminaries were rushing to aid a military dictator.

Deeply disturbed on my first evening in a dusty, polluted Damascus, I went with my friend to pray the *Esha*, the last prayer of the day. Unlike young people in Britain, most young Syrians prayed as their parents did. No rebellion in prayer, at least. After prayers I expressed gratitude to God for bringing me to a land where I could study the language of the Prophet, but complained that he had put me in the room of an active and misguided jihadist.

I had travelled far enough from political Islam to know that America and Britain toppling Saddam did not warrant a jihad. Besides, my friendship with Kelly had taught me much about America and Americans.

Despite my friend's requests, I had not unpacked my bags yet. I decided I would sleep on the sitting-room couch and then move out as soon as possible.

When we reached his flat we could hear the racket inside from half a street away. Muttering in disapproval, Peter opened the door and I followed him in.

'Qaleem!' he exclaimed. 'What are you doing here?'

He was addressing a skinny, smiling, loudly-spoken teenager. Other students from the seminary had heard that Qaleem had returned, and they were there to honour him rowdily. Al-Jazeera blasted at full volume from a TV in the corner.

Peter introduced me to Qaleem and we exchanged nods. He spoke no English and I no Arabic. Peter explained that Syrian border guards had sent Qaleem back to Damascus – the government did not want Syrians fighting for Saddam Hussein. I was pleased to hear the government of the land, at least, was sane.

Suddenly, Qaleem requested quiet as al-Jazeera interviewed a political analyst. Qaleem listened briefly and then punched the air, spat at the screen and yelled, '*Jasoos! Jasoos!*'

'It means "spy",' translated Peter.

'Why is the speaker on television a spy?' I asked.

'Because he supports the removal of Saddam. Anybody who argues for democracy in Iraq these days is condemned by most Arabs. In Iraq, a *jasoos* will be killed.'

That sent shudders through me. Was I a *jasoos*? Here I was with Saddam enthusiasts where I believed in a free and democratic Iraq. Something deep within me warned me to be silent and learn from the passions of powerless people.

In the hours to come Iraq's notorious Minister of Information, Saeed al-Sahhaf, rallied the Arab world by promising victory over the Americans and denying that Americans could possibly enter Baghdad. To Sahhaf's hollow rhetoric, Qaleem and others cheered.

CNN and the BBC were broadcasting pictures of American troops approaching Baghdad, but the young people surrounding me refused to believe their eyes. There was an inherent distrust of Western news organizations, an inclination to reject them as biased reporters of events, supporters of Israel and enemies of the Arabs. Any call against the West, even from a dictatorial murderer like Saddam under the banner of a false jihad, easily won acceptance because of this underlying hatred of the West, based on British and French conduct during the middle of the twentieth century. Unless the wrongs of history are corrected, particularly in relation to Palestine, that mindset of hatred will persist.

I observed Arab anger but vowed to remain silent until I had learnt Arabic myself.

Soon, with Peter's help, I found a small flat in Salihiyyeh, midway up the historical Mount Qassioun. Faye arrived and we distanced ourselves from the student jihadis and slowly drew closer to Sufi Muslims from the West studying Arabic and Shariah in Damascus. We enrolled at the Languages Institute of the University of Damascus and studied Arabic full time while Faye taught English part time at the British Council, and I did the same, first at the university and then with her at the Council. My application to work at the university resulted in a stressful time for me: the head of faculty, Dr Waddah al-Khateeb, insisted that he would have to obtain security clearance. The Syrian intelligence services contacted their British counterparts and I worried that perhaps my Islamist past would show up. Would I be expelled from Syria? I was relieved when I was cleared, but what if I had been an unreconstructed Hizb member, or an extremist from another group? My worries about lax security were soon to prove well founded.

Our days were tough, challenging, and physically draining, but every day we were bestowed with a renewed drive and passion to persevere. Those days were also memorable for the many new friends and acquaintances we made. We studied with Germans, Russians, Italians, Japanese, Iranians, Turks, French, Spaniards, and, of course, Americans. Often the classes became forums for inter-faith dialogue. Where better to bridge the gaps between Islam and Christianity than in Damascus – the city on the road to which St Paul saw the light?

Most of the students in several of our classes were Muslims. And yet, when discussing controversial topics or simpler things in life such as attitudes to humour, Faye and I found ourselves forming alliances with Americans, Canadians, and Australians. Away from Britain, something was happening to us: we had more in common with other English speakers, Caucasians, than we dared admit.

My teachers were respectful and committed individuals. Many were Muslims, some were not. But they all refused to call me by my first name: Mohamed. This was an honoured name and reserved for the Prophet, not to be used in vain. My middle name, Mahbub, means beloved in Arabic and that caused embarrassment among both my female teachers and my own peers. It was then that I decided on Ed, the last syllable from the Prophet's and my own name, as a suitable compromise. Veneration and love for the Prophet Mohammed ran deep in Syria; they were hallmarks of a true Sufi. Street beggars forced passers-by to dig deep into their pockets by whispering, '*Ala Hubb al-Nabiyy*': for the love of the Prophet. The muezzins, after their calls to prayer, sang songs of love.

On the advice of my father I searched for a Sufi master. During my search I spent much time at a serene mosque above the tomb of Ibn Arabi. Ibn Arabi was born in Spain in 1165 and travelled widely before settling in Damascus, where he died in 1240. Patron saint of Damascus, he was a prolific writer and provocative thinker. Where Rumi taught that the way to reach God was through intense, divine love, Ibn Arabi's method combined virtue, knowledge, and experience.

Every visit was calming and cleansed the soul. I came away feeling closer to God, wanting to engage in worship, and trying to be considerate of those who surrounded me, regardless of faith, race, or gender. After morning and dusk prayers at Ibn Arabi's mosque, an elderly teacher of the Koran, Shaikh Sukkar, would sit and listen to adults reciting the Koran. Those sights reminded me of my childhood days with Grandpa. Ibn Arabi's mosque attracted Sufis from all over the world: I saw Turks, Iranians, Africans, and Asians pay their respects to this master of esoteric knowledge.

I do not claim to *be* a Sufi: it is an exalted rank not deserved by one who sleeps full nights, away from the pre-dawn prayer mat. Those who know me are all too aware of my failings. I succumb to the whispers of the *nafs*, the lower ego, far too often. In Arabic, the word for human is *insan*, derived from *nisyan*, which means forgetfulness. As a human, or *insan*, one who forgets, I am given to frequent amnesia, lapses in conduct, and distraction from God. But my hope in the eternal and infinite mercy of God, the benevolence of His Messenger, and the warm calls of the *awliya*, the people of God, keep me going. Rumi's invitations keep me running back:

Come, come, whoever you are,
Wanderer, worshipper, lover of leaving.
This is not a caravan of despair.
It doesn't matter that you've broken
your vow a thousand times, still
come, and yet again, come.

All the while, I regularly called my parents at least twice a week. They would assure me that I was in their prayers and encouraged me to study well. 'Give our greetings to the saints of Damascus,' my father would say. He would mention St John the Baptist's tomb and those of other saints. Damascus was a city filled with tombs of saints and companions of the Prophet. Following my father's advice, I visited these islands of peace and conveyed his greetings to the sleepers in the mausoleums. Faye and I went to the mosques of Syria with our non-Muslim friends, something we could not have done in Britain. All across the Old City there were ancient mosques and churches surrounding the awe-inspiring, eighth-century Omayyad mosque. Mixed groups of women and men freely walked in this house of God, visiting the tomb of John the Baptist, known to Muslims as Yahya. I derived most tranquillity walking between the room in which the great medieval Imam Ghazali studied and the area in which he prayed in the Omayyad mosque during his ten-year spiritual retreat.

Visiting the tombs of the pious instils tranquillity in the soul. The Prophet Mohammed instructed us to visit graves, for it helps to remember the afterlife. An added benefit of memorials to the spiritually blessed is that something of their blessing touches the visitor. I have experienced this at mausoleums across Syria, Jordan, Lebanon, and Turkey. Alexander the Great, when visiting Achilles' tomb, is said to have lamented, 'O fortunate youth, to have found Homer as the herald of your glory'.

To be able to walk freely in the mosques of Syria with Faye and her female friends was no small privilege. Under ultra-strict literalist interpretations of Islam, influenced by cultural factors, most mosques in Britain would not have welcomed Faye. Syria enabled us to be together.

Soon my mother and later my brother and sisters visited us in Damascus. Together we enjoyed the many historical sights of the city, visiting mausoleums of saints my mother held so dear. We brought to life the childhood stories she told us of the Prophet's grandson Husain by visiting his tomb and by standing in the prayer niche of Husain's son, Zain al-Abedeen. At last my religion had converged with that of my parents in the sacred sites of Damascus.

Among young Islamists references to non-Muslims were almost always to the *kuffar* (while many of the same Islamists took offence at being described as 'Pakis'). The term *kafir* is used in the Koran in the context of the brutal persecution of early Muslims at the hands of pagan idolaters. To reinvent that terminology and use it to refer to a population that is mainly Christian, or at least theistic, is an abject failure to understand the Koran. Worse, it indicates a serious sense of superiority, arrogance, and separation. In Syria, the Muslims referred to Christians and others not as *kuffar* but as *masihiyyeen*: people of the Messiah. Where did we go wrong in Britain? Why had we opted for such harsh language?

The word *kafir* has gained a deeply destructive meaning in the contemporary European Muslim mindset, connoting eternal damnation and enmity. In the Koranic archetypal sense the word is a simple derivation of the verb *kafara*, 'to cover'. The assonance is telling. Cover what? To cover the blessings of God, to deny God. Christians and Jews in the Koran, believers in God, are not referred to as *kafir* but as 'people of the book' and thus deserving of reverence. The Koranic condemnation of *kafir* refers to the Arab pagans who violently rejected the Prophet Mohammed and his message of Abrahamic submission to one God back in the seventh century.

This vital linguistic nuance was lost on me. It was not until I learnt Arabic for myself that I reached the kernel of the hatred of the *kuffar* that had been planted in me through language. But it is not only about language. The spirit of the Prophet's teachings has been lost among Muslims in the West. Away from constant talk of Koranic 'references' and 'evidence' in Muslim circles in Britain, I was able to assess the magnanimity of the teachings of the Prophet. Those familiar with the life of the Prophet will know that he was persecuted, attacked, humiliated, and forced to leave Mecca because of a campaign led by a pagan named Abu Jahl. Among the Prophet's companions, Abu Jahl was the epitome of evil. And yet when Abu Jahl's son, the warrior Ikrimah, embraced the Prophet and became Muslim, the Prophet gently explained to his companions that Abu Jahl should no longer be condemned. Harsh words uttered by those who had been persecuted by Abu Jahl might have hurt Ikrimah's feelings. This inner condition of the Prophet, replete with compassion and good will, is lacking among Islamist-influenced Muslims.

As I learned more Arabic and grasped better the spirit of the Prophet, my appreciation of other faiths increased. I had always regarded Christianity as a Western religion and Islam as an Arabic, Eastern faith. But long before Christianity arrived in England the religion developed by Jesus' disciples had been an established part of people's lives in Syria.

My time in Damascus changed my perception of the Christian faith for ever. Arab Christians of all denominations freely and with no qualms used the word Allah for God. At first this was extremely difficult for me to digest. Allah, I thought, was the preserve of the Muslims. Granted, I knew that it was a translation of God, but did not realize that 'Allah' was an intimate part of the lives of millions of Arab Christians. Everywhere in Damascus, Muslims and Christians used phrases that I thought only Muslims used: *inshallah* (God willing), *mashallah* (as God willed it), *alhamdulillah* (praise be to God). There was no sense of religious zealotry or grandstanding in the name of God. The mutual recognition and respect between Christians and Muslims in Damascus had a lot to teach Muslims and Christians in Britain. Even Britain's Rudyard Kipling expressed 'thanks to Allah, who gave me two, separate sides to my head'. Muslims did not have a copyright on the term.

Inside the tomb of a Christian saint in Sednaya, on the outskirts of Damascus, I saw Muslim women in meditation. Beside them sat Christian nuns. Only the colour of their headscarves differentiated them.

The people of Malula spoke Aramaic, the language of Jesus. I stood beside people in the markets and churches and listened to the words that Jesus spoke. Jesus was revealed to me anew on that day as an oriental, not the blue-eyed Caucasian I had become accustomed to. Christianity, like Islam, was a religion from the Middle East.

The Christian women who were visiting Malula, as well as the many Muslim women, all wore the hijab. Almost without exception, images of the Virgin Mary show her in hijab. In Protestant England the hijab or wimple had become the preserve of Catholic nuns and immigrant Muslims. Here, in Syria, were the historical roots of hijab, a Byzantine practice prescribed by the Prophet as a mark of dignity and modesty for his female followers in seventh-century Arabia. Hijab was not new to Muslim women. At best it was an expression of Eastern ideas of modesty.

As time went by Faye and I felt increasingly at home in Damascus. To our relief, the war in Iraq did not spill into Syria and my jihadi acquaintances from my first evening in Damascus were spared further calls to arms.

At university Muslims from the US, Britain, France, and Germany had full beards and wore Arab-style robes. The women wore full hijab and *jilbabs*, or flowing coats. In contrast, on campus there was not a single bushy-bearded Syrian student. They mostly wore trendy goatees and the women were much better dressed. To my astonishment, leading imams at many mosques were clean shaven or had neatly trimmed beards. How could that be? We wore Arab clothes and liked to appear as Arabs in Britain and yet the Arabs I thought I dressed like did not exist! I had confused modesty with ethnicity. One did not have to wear ethnic clothing to appear modest – Syrian imams in Western-style shirts and trousers were living proof of that.

Hizb ut-Tahrir and other Islamists wore Western clothes, yet they despised the West. I had turned to traditional Muslim clothing to reject Islamism from within and without. Now I discovered that the best of traditional Muslims, Syrian Muslim scholars, had accepted Western dress codes, and yet remained modest and loyal to their faith. And, interestingly, orthodox Christians in Bab al-Tuma, the old Christian quarter of Damascus, wore long robes, grew flowing beards, and donned skull-caps. What I, along with thousands of Muslims in Britain, considered 'Islamic' clothing is essentially the outfit of Arab Christians.

Syrians, unlike most Muslims from Britain, did not wear their Islam on their sleeves. They did not need to. In a Muslim country they did not have to show they were Muslims. Interestingly, the minority Christian community did not need to illustrate their faith in public either. Faye and I began to rediscover our Western wardrobes.

Looking back, Islamist ideas of gender relations reveal much about their attitude to life. Mawdudi advocated that Islamist women ought to wear the face cover and maintain strict segregation from men. In Britain, among observant Muslims of most persuasions there was a culture of not shaking hands with the opposite gender. In Syria, observant women readily offered their hands to me. Much of Muslim social sensitivity is about understanding different social contexts. What is considered sexual in the East is not so in the West.

In late 2004 I saw two members of Hizb ut-Tahrir from Britain register for Arabic courses at the university. I knew them from a meeting I had attended in Bayswater: they were Arabs and had studied at Imperial College. Immediately I wondered why they were really there. The Arabic language administrator at the university was a good friend of mine. I alerted him to the Hizb's presence on campus.

'But they are here to learn Arabic,' he protested.

'They *are* Arabs!' I protested. 'They do not need Arabic classes. They're using the classes as a pretext to stay in Syria and recruit for their group.'

At the time, I was also teaching at the university, so my concerns about extremists on campus were not easily dismissed. Soon, Syrian intelligence interviewed me. They thought that I had sounded the alarm not because I cared for Syria, but because I was worried about Britain. I mentioned that Britain's first suicide bomber, Asif Hanif, had passed through Damascus en route to Tel Aviv.

It turned out I was right. For the first time in many years, several Hizb ut-Tahrir cells were functioning in Damascus. Police raids led to arrests and the seizure of Hizb material. London, it was clear, was still sending Hizb ut-Tahrir members to the Middle East with the protection of a British passport and the consular assistance of Her Majesty's Diplomatic Service.

One of the most painful aspects of my stay in Syria was the inability of Syrians to accept me as one of them. As an Islamist I had yelled about the global *ummah*, the 'One Nation' of the global Muslim community. Almost every day in Syria, whenever

I interacted with new people, they asked me where I was from. Worse, when I replied that I was from Britain, they always responded, 'No, where are you *really* from?' My brown skin could not belong to Britain; it had to come from elsewhere.

Such questions of 'origin' infuriated me. I would argue that the millions of Syrians from the coastal regions crossing into Lebanon could not possibly claim to be 'Arab'. They were a conquered people. If they could become 'Arab' by virtue of speaking Arabic, rejecting their Phoenician heritage, and accepting Islam, then I was British by virtue of birth, upbringing, and acceptance of British values of tolerance, freedom, and the English language. Such debates were frequent. Just as the Syrians did not take well to being told that they were not 'originally Arab', I did not take well to their rejection of my Britishness.

The longer I was away from Britain, the more British I became. Syria forced me to ask myself who I was. Sharing a religion was not sufficient to bond me with Syrians, much as I adored my Arab friends.

Faye and I found ourselves keeping company with fellow Brits from the British Council. Within a year I had more white non-Muslim friends in Syria than I had ever had in Britain. We gathered for dinner and tea parties at various homes and discussed questions of religion, identity, acceptance, and expatriate life. A theory that had been floating round my mind became crystallized: human beings could form groupings and associations based on factors other than religion. I shared with my non-Muslim friends a common language, country, culture, and belief in the broad values of plurality, fairness, and acceptance of the other.

At home in Britain these values had seemed trite; living in the Arab world among people who were not born into freedom, they were priceless. In countless discussions with Arab friends I was free to express sentiments that they dared not even think about, let alone utter. I had become a stronger, confident Brit, bold enough to challenge ideas that I perceived as wrong. The timidity of my first night in Damascus was no more.

Much of my strength came from my TEFL work at the British Council, still considered as the cultural arm of the British embassy by most Syrians. Almost without exception the Syrians I taught were extremely polite and courteous. Many were genuinely shocked that a Muslim from Britain would choose Syria in which to study, and then teach them English. Often my classes became a debating forum for politics and current affairs.

I decided to form a debating society at the British Council in which Syrian students of English could interact with British and American students studying Arabic. Despite some initial reservations owing to the lack of freedom of speech in Syria, the society flourished and has become part of the institutional fabric of the Council. Today it continues to be a focal point for lively discussion and debate in Damascus.

As an Islamist I had been 'passing concepts' to undermine Britain and the West. Now I made it my business to take more seriously than most other teachers the British Council's commitment to promoting modern British culture. I ensured that every single student left my classes with a better understanding of modern, diverse, vibrant Britain. Citing universal values of human rights, freedom for women, rights of oppressed minorities of all categories, and conflict resolution through non-violent means, I initiated discussions of social and political issues in Syria ranging from domestic violence, religious tolerance, the Arab–Israeli conflict, to the hopes of young people. The optimism of most young Syrians was always uplifting, although there were moments of despair when Hitler was considered to be a hero and the Holocaust was denied.

Again and again, students expressed the view that Britain was a colonial power, an enemy of Islam that was plotting against the Arab world, that 9/11 was not perpetrated by Arabs, that they were only learning English to 'get to know the enemy'.

'Was I their enemy?' I asked. British Muslims worked in the civil service, the media, in parliament, the professions, were millionaires, and practised their religion freely – how could Britain be an enemy of Islam?

I hope Faye and I changed the perceptions of Britain among the hundreds of Syrians we came into contact with. We were fierce and, I believe, convincing in our arguments and defence of Britain. However, there was one argument I could not win.

Many of my students asked why, if Britain was not an enemy of the Arabs and Muslims, did it give shelter to the Arab religious fanatics who wanted to kill and replace political leaders of the Arab world. Why was Britain home to Abu Hamza, Abu Qatada, and Omar Bakri, rejects of the Middle East?

Keen to avoid my own Islamist past, I tried to explain the British traditions of allowing freedom of expression and giving refuge to the persecuted. Britain had a long history of taking in dissenters, including Karl Marx. I failed to convince either them or myself. Islamists bore no comparison to Karl Marx. One student even warned me that these fanatics would cause problems for Britain, as they had caused problems in Syria in the 1980s. 'Watch out,' he said. 'They will turn on Britain.' That warning, given in 2004, would soon prove all too prophetic.

With trusted friends I discussed the most private topics that Syrians do not comment on in public. As an Islamist I had repeatedly called for the forceful removal of all Arab leaders, puppets of the West, and their replacement by an all-embracing caliph. My Syrian friends, speaking to me in their mother tongue and at complete ease, pointed out to me that Syrians had united with Egypt in 1958 to form the United Arab Republic. The experiment was a total disaster.

Without my prompting, they spoke in disparaging terms about the 400-year 'Turkish occupation' of Syria. Nabhani preferred to call this a 'unified Islamic state'. The reality on the Arab streets, as I experienced it in countless discussions, was far removed from the aspirations of Islamists operating in Britain. To my surprise, in private meetings in Syrian homes, young people of all religions expressed support and admiration for their president, Dr Bashar al-Asad. Where was the passion for a new president? Regime change, an idea advocated by neo-cons in Washington and Islamists in London, was not the priority of ordinary Syrians. Most Syrians criticized government ministers and hated government bureaucracy, but supported their president.

In Syria, Omar Bakri's homeland, there was no public support for the ideas he had implanted in our minds. Syrians desired economic betterment, political transparency, and infrastructural development, but they were in no mood for an expansionist Islamic state in their country. Nor were they keen to import Western democracy, not after the debacle in Iraq. The toppling of Saddam Hussein had prompted whispers in Damascus of regime change, but soon, particularly after the Abu Ghraib prison scandal and the complete breakdown of law and order in Baghdad, most Syrians I met opted for the security of the regime they knew, rather than the insecurity of the American promise of freedom. Stories of the commandeering of Iraqi houses by American soldiers spread amongst the chattering classes. Iraqis I met in Damascus, fleeing the chaos of Baghdad, told me that American troops had initially commanded respect as they picked up cigarette stubs from the streets and tried to keep Baghdad clean. But soon, as the attacks against them increased, they had begun to use the same tactics as the old Saddam regime. Iraqis from Mosul told me about incidents of poor soldiers from the Deep South in America stealing gold and money from wealthy Iraqis' homes.

After two years in Syria I was ready to come back home to London. Although I grew to love Syria, particularly Damascus, I knew it would never be home for me. Syria taught me much. However, as with every country, it had its faults: a macho culture, widespread sexism, latent racism, homophobia, anti-Semitism, and a highly corrupt bureaucracy. Britain might not be perfect, but it was better than this. Though sad at the prospect of leaving many of our new Arab friends, Faye and I discussed returning to London.

During my early months in Damascus, while teaching at the university, young Syrian women would often tell me about the changes that were taking place in their society. Syrians generally, and women in particular, are genteel and gracious. At the end of one course I was confounded by the large, elaborate bouquet of flowers the students presented to me. I was also given CDs of Fairouz, a Lebanese musical legend, and Arabic books to help with my own learning. Such generous gifts were all the more poignant because I knew that poverty levels in Syria were high. Better-paid medical doctors and civil servants earned under 8,000 lire a month (less than £100), and students at the university paid their fees with money borrowed from their parents.

In view of such economic difficulties, large numbers of Syrians, in common with other Arabs, had flocked to the Gulf countries, particularly Saudi Arabia, returning during the summer months. These included many of my students. During my stay in Syria I discovered that there were significant cultural, social, and physical differences between the Arabs from the Levant and those of the Gulf states. Even in matters of religion there was an unbridgeable gap. The notion that Arabs are a homogeneous, monolithic people is a potent myth of our times.

The Arabs of the Levant are radically different in culture, customs, taste, and outlook to their counterparts in the Gulf. Damascene Syrians would often tell me that Saudi influences were corrupting Islam in Syria. Students in my classrooms reported incidents of their own family members who had undergone a personality change while working in Saudi Arabia, becoming stricter in their behaviour and claiming purity of religion. They refused to listen to music, meet female relatives, or pray at most mosques in Damascus, claiming that the imams there were 'deviant' and constantly proselytizing about the 'one God', or *tawheed*. Hearing this reminded me of my days at Tower Hamlets College and the Wahhabis.

Despite the widespread dislike of Saudis in Syria, there was one factor that endeared the Kingdom of Saudi Arabia to the hearts and minds of not only Syrians, but a billion Muslims spanning the globe: the sacred cities of Mecca and Medina. Muslims often accept the abuse and mistreatment they receive at the hands of Saudis out of deference for Islam's holiest places.

In Muslim homes throughout Syria, Turkey, Jordan, Lebanon and Britain will always be found a picture of the Ka'bah in Mecca or the sepulchre of the Prophet in Medina. Observant Muslims pray facing Mecca several times a day; it is the city in which, according to Muslim tradition, Abraham, Hagar, and their son Ishmael lived for a period. The Prophet Mohammed was born in Mecca and persevered through relentless persecution at the hands of Meccan pagans for a decade before migrating to Medina, where he passed away. Early Muslim history revolves around Mecca and Medina, the Koran focuses on events in these two cities, and the life of the Prophet is set in these ancient Arabian metropolises.

Throughout history, women and men have found solace, contentment, and transcendence in the shade of the Ka'bah in Mecca, or beside the Prophet's tomb in Medina. Faye and I wanted to do the same. So, rather than going straight home, we applied for and were offered jobs at the British Council in Jeddah, Saudi Arabia's 'most liberal city'.

Two years in Syria, away from Islamism in Britain and in the company of amiable believers of many religions in Damascus, had, I knew, decontaminated my mind. Now, more than ever, I felt free. I saw British Muslims arrive in Damascus and struggle with an Islam that was comparatively liberal, discomfited at the sight of unveiled women, clean-shaven men and celebrations of the Prophet's birthday, and bemoaning the absence of Islamist organizations. Many asked, 'Where is Islam?' I wanted that question to be asked back in Britain, for what they expected to see in Syria was a projection of their own literalist brand of British Islam.

Two weeks before we left Syria, Faye and I decided to shed our spectacles. We underwent laser surgery on our eyes and saw the world anew. Syria had both corrected my vision and removed the Islamist blinkers for ever.

14. Saudi Arabia: Where is Islam?

Islam is written in books and the Muslims are in their graves.
  Hasan al-Basri, Muslim scholar-saint, d. 728

As we stood at Jeddah airport, I hoped that the security officers would not search our bags. I had taken the precaution of sending all my books on politics, history, Rumi's poetry, Sufism, and comparative religion back to Britain, but deep in my suitcase, I had buried a book of daily litanies recited by the Prophet and beautiful Arabic poetry in praise of him written by the famed sage of Arabia, Imam al-Haddad (d. 1720). As the guard began to root through my belongings I clasped my hands and prayed he would not discover it. Thankfully, he didn't.

Wahhabis are a deeply literalist sect. Metaphors, allegories, love, and transcendence have no meaning for them. They are exceptionally harsh towards Muslims expressing love and dedication to the Prophet. To Wahhabis, that borders on worship and is therefore idolatrous.

My own experience of life inside Islamist organizations was that they were *all* at one with the Wahhabis in creed. It is a fact that Wahhabis do not pray in Sufi mosques, considering the majority of the world's Muslims to be polytheists, or *mushriks*, because of our aversion to literalism in understanding God's attributes. In Britain and in Syria Wahhabis avoided praying at ordinary mainstream mosques and would attend only mosques managed by themselves or the Muslim Brotherhood.

In addition to Wahhabi and Islamist literalist ideas of God, both sects believe that the Prophet ought not to be venerated, that Sufis are too close to the Prophet, that celebrating his birthday is an imitation of *kuffar* Christian practices, and that visiting the tombs of saints is tantamount to idolatry. Sufism and other Muslim traditions are deviations from the 'true faith'. To Wahhabis, selective Muslim sources are to be accepted as literal Truth, and emphasis must be on the oneness of God, *tawheed*. On theological grounds, Wahhabis may disagree with older, more established traditions of Muslim thought, but the difficulty arose when they started to slaughter Sufis, Shias, and other Muslims. By killing those they disagreed with and later having oil wealth, Wahhabis ensured their dominance of modern Muslim thought, in tandem with Islamism, and the commitment to an Islamic political state. The problem we call 'al-Qaeda' is a bastard child of modernist Islamism and reactionary Wahhabism.

How did Wahhabism start? The Wahhabi mindset emerged from the central Arabian wastelands of Najd, among the followers of Ibn Abd al-Wahhab bin Sulaiman al-Tamimi, commonly known as Ibn Abd al-Wahhab, a puritanical eighteenth-century Muslim leader. Adopting the discarded writings of the medieval theologian Ibn Taymiya, Abd al-Wahhab rejected the established practices of the local Najdi population (in what is now the central region of Saudi Arabia), including respect for Muslim saints and preservation of historical tombs. Ibn Abd al-Wahhab could not fathom such things: to him, worship, understood in the narrowest way possible, meant obedience to a great God in the skies. There was no need for intermediaries, devotion, training, scholarly guidance, or adherence to time-honoured practice. All this could, and would, be done away with.

In 1744–5 Ibn Abd al-Wahhab negotiated a deal with the then nomadic tribe of Saud, forebears of the current Saudi royal family: in exchange for support in their quest for local political domination, the Saudis would back Ibn Abd al-Wahhab's mission to impose his literalist interpretation of Islam at a local level in Najd. Detractors referred to Ibn Abd al-Wahhab's cult as

Wahhabism (*Wahhabiyyah* in Arabic) and tried to oppose the spread of the sect's ideas. However, under the political patronage of the Saud tribe, Wahhabism went from strength to strength.

Between 1745 and 1818 the Saudi–Wahhabi alliance rode roughshod over local traditional forms of Islam: they subdued other clans, destroyed Muslim shrines, slaughtered thousands of Muslims in neighbouring Hijaz, and expanded as far as Karbala in Iraq in 1801, where they killed thousands more and destroyed Islamic holy sites, claiming such activities would purify Islam from 'idolatrous' influences. They not only killed Muslims of Sufi and Shia persuasions, but deliberately sought to annihilate those who had a bloodline that went back to the Prophet Mohammed, locally known as the *sayyids* or the *ashraf*.

In response to the rise of the Wahhabis, in 1818 the Ottomans sent armies from Egypt to quell the extremists. Yet by 1912, with the Ottoman Empire in its death throes, the group had re-emerged. Ibn Saud, now leader of the Saud tribe, gained prominence and strength with British support, as did his bed-fellows the Wahhabis. Locally they were known as the Ikhwan, precursors of the current Mutawwa'een (*mutawwa'een* is the colloquial plural form of *mutawwa'a* – literally, 'those who enforce obedience'; more commonly, 'the religion police'. Officially known in Saudi Arabia as the Committee for the Promotion of Virtue and Suppression of Evil, the Mutawwa'een is a government-funded organization which watches over the nation's morality.

In 1934, with the establishment of the Kingdom of Saudi Arabia, the Saud tribe continued to honour their 1744–5 agreement with the family of Ibn Abd al-Wahhab, now increasingly known as Aal-Shaikh, meaning the 'family of the shaikh'. Had it not been for the discovery of oil in Saudi Arabia, and the unique association of the country in Muslim minds with the site of Mecca and Medina, then Wahhabism would have been nothing more than a renegade, deviant sect within Islam. But the missionary zeal of Wahhabism was enhanced manifold by geography and the financial advantages of black gold.

To this day every Saudi embassy has a missionary arm, staffed by Wahhabis, to monitor Muslim activity in the host country and help support Wahhabism financially. When I had sought to learn Arabic at the Muslim World League, the attempt to recruit me to a Saudi university had been backed by the Saudi embassy.

Today the majority of the world's Muslims still adhere to moderate Islam: deeply personal, highly spiritual, and Sufi influenced. However, this cannot be taken for granted. Saudi Arabia remains committed to training clerics in the Wahhabi mould, and tens of thousands of them have been sent to all corners of the globe to propagate this simple, desert form of Islam. Britain and the West are particular targets for Wahhabi literalism.

Despite Islamist protests that the Saudi monarchy is not sufficiently Islamic, the Kingdom of Saudi Arabia is as close to the type of country Islamists wish to create as exists. In Saudi Arabia my Islamist days came flashing back to me as reminders of what I had tried to bring about. While I was there, I kept a detailed diary. At first the luxury of living in a modern city with a developed infrastructure cocooned me from the frightful reality of life in Saudi Arabia. During our first two months, Faye and I relished our new and luxurious lifestyle: a shiny jeep, two swimming pools, domestic help, and a much higher, tax-free salary than we had received in Syria. After our comparatively frugal existence in Damascus, this was paradise.

We both knew that Westerners were confined within compounds in Saudi Arabia, and more so following recent Wahhabi attacks on Western interests. The world's media, under Saudi guidance, referred to this as 'al-Qaeda terrorism' inside Saudi Arabia. But then al-Qaeda itself is a hybrid beast, a marriage of convenience between Islamism and Wahhabism whose offspring is terrorism. The terrorist attacks on the American embassy in Jeddah in early 2005, as well as several attacks in Riyadh and other cities, were conducted by Wahhabis and their followers who abhorred the Saudi monarchy: chief among them was Osama bin Laden.

In Jeddah we lived in a compound owned by the Bin Laden company, next door to the company's head office. Within weeks, I discerned that compound life was a microcosm of the expatriate lifestyle in Saudi Arabia. It represented the social structure that Saudis imposed on their foreign workforce and had the following pecking order: Americans were at the top, followed by Brits, then other Europeans, then Lebanese, Syrians, Egyptians, Yemenis, and other Arabs, followed by the Sudanese. Asians (Filipinos, Indians, Pakistanis, Bangladeshis) were at the bottom of the pile, above only poor black Africans from Chad, mainly staying beyond their pilgrimage visas.

Throughout my stay in Saudi Arabia I never divulged my Asian ethnicity. My goatee beard and good Arabic ensured that I could pass for an Arab. Besides, I had family members in Saudi Arabia on my mother's side and, technically speaking, an 'Arab' is anyone who speaks Arabic. When the perennial question of why a brown person was teaching English at the British Council came up, I simply explained I was in Saudi Arabia to discover the land of my ancestors. I was now considered to be 'originally Saudi'. My decision to withhold my full background from the Saudis enabled me to learn things that I would not have known otherwise. After Syria, I refused to be pigeon-holed by Arab racism, to be seen as an inferior *hindi*, or Indian. In the racist Arab psyche, *hindi* is as pejorative as *kuffar*. In countless gatherings I silently sat and listened to racist caricatures of a billion people by Saudi bigots.

In the pecking order, then, I was on a par with the Saudis. In fact, in many cases I was considered 'superior' because I was also British. The British–Saudi combination both impressed and gained the trust of my many Saudi acquaintances, appararent from small but significant acts such as the Saudi security guards waving our car through security checkpoints, to young Saudis confessing their deepest fears and anxieties to me, talking freely about Osama bin Laden as 'one of us'.

With my mother's Saudi family members I was at ease, exhibiting the mannerisms, etiquette, and behaviour that confirmed I belonged. I rode in our new jeep dressed in flowing white tunic and sporting a trimmed goatee. Faye wore her *abaya*, the long black garment worn by all Muslim women in public in Saudi Arabia.

But looking like a young Saudi was not enough: I had to act Saudi, *be* Saudi. And here I failed.

My first clash with Saudi culture came when, being driven around in a bullet-proof jeep, I saw African women in black *abayas* tending to the rubbish bins outside restaurants, residences, and other busy places.

'Why are there so many black cleaners on the streets?' I asked the driver. 'And why do they carry all that cardboard around with them?'

The driver laughed. 'They're not cleaners. They are scavengers; women who collect cardboard from all across Jeddah and then sell it. They also collect bottles, drink cans, bags . . .'

'Don't we recycle these things here?'

'No. Too much trouble. The women do a good job, generally.'

'You mean you don't find it objectionable that poor immigrant women from Africa work in such undignified and unhygienic conditions on the streets?'

'Believe me, there are worse jobs women can do.'

Though it grieves me to admit it, the driver was right. In Saudi Arabia women indeed did do worse jobs. Many of the African women lived in an area of Jeddah known as Karantina, a slum full of poverty, prostitution, and disease. Living in a plush compound for Westerners and rubbing shoulders with Saudi bankers, journalists, educators, businessmen, clerics, and the like had blinded me to the real Saudi Arabia. Disregarding British Council advice, I headed out to Karantina, the most unsecure and dangerous quarter of Jeddah.

I wanted to see for myself how black immigrants lived in Saudi Arabia. The hallmark of a civilization is, I believe, how it treats its minorities. My day in Karantina, a perversion of the term 'quarantine', was one of the worst of my life. Thousands of people who had been living in Saudi Arabia for decades, but without passports, had been deemed 'illegal' by the government and, quite literally, abandoned under a flyover.

A non-Saudi black student I had met at the British Council accompanied me. 'Last week a woman gave birth here,' he said, pointing to a ramshackle cardboard shanty. Disturbed, I now realized that the materials I had seen those women carrying were not always for sale, but for shelter. While rich Saudis zoomed over the flyover in their fast cars, others rotted in the sun below them.

Now my assumed Saudi identity brought shame to me: how could I walk around Karantina? My companion asked if I was still keen to do so; there had been recent murders and even the Saudi police were afraid to enter the place. I was aghast. I had never expected to see such naked poverty in Saudi Arabia.

As we returned to our car an elderly Saudi man turned up with clothes and food for the refugees. It was such occasional gestures of humanity that helped maintain my faith in human goodness.

In the distance, I noticed a woman praying. She stood immediately outside her cardboard shack and bowed, now rising, now prostrating. Her shelter was too small for her to pray in private.

At that moment it dawned on me that Britain, my home, had given refuge to thousands of black Africans from Somalia and Sudan: I had seen them in their droves in Whitechapel. They prayed, had their own mosques, were free, and were given government housing. How could it be that Saudi Arabia had condemned African Muslims to misery and squalor? It was a harrowing experience. As far as I was concerned, Muslims enjoyed a better lifestyle in non-Muslim Britain than they did in Muslim Saudi Arabia. At that moment, I longed to be home again.

All my talk of *ummah* seemed so juvenile now. It was only in the comfort of Britain that Islamists could come out with such radical, utopian slogans as one government, one ever-expanding country, for one Muslim nation. The racist reality of the Arab psyche would *never* accept black and white people as equal.

Standing in Karantina that day I reminisced and marvelled over what I previously considered as wrong: mixed-race, mixed-religion marriages. A Friday or Saturday night in one of Britain's town centres, where people of all ethnicities mixed freely, seemed like an illusion. The students to whom I described life in modern multi-ethnic Britain simply could not comprehend that such a world of freedom, away from 'normal' Saudi racism, could exist.

Saudi racism was not limited to Karantina. It was an integral part of Saudi society, accepted by most. My students often used the word 'nigger' to describe black people. Even dark-skinned Arabs were considered inferior to their lighter-skinned cousins. I was living in the world's most avowedly Muslim country, yet I found it anything but. And alongside the racism and intolerance I was appalled by the imposition of Wahhabism in the public realm, something I had implicitly sought as an Islamist.

Since the founding of the Kingdom of Saudi Arabia, two Wahhabi-educated generations have been busy imposing 'Islam' on their society. But if it truly had been Islam, then any Muslim would be delighted to live there. In fact the mainly Muslim 7-million strong immigrant workforce loathed life in Saudi Arabia and, given the chance, would prefer to live almost anywhere but there.

At the British Council I helped people prepare for British immigration examinations – professionals who had spent their entire working lives in Saudi Arabia and now wanted to leave. There were Egyptians, Syrians, and Indians; bankers, account- ants, engineers, and business managers. I asked many why they wanted to leave. Invariably their reply was that they did not want their children to suffer the same miserable lives that they had.

These people had built Saudi Arabia from the desert that it once was. Yet, despite years living in and working for the good of Saudi Arabia, creating the country's infrastructure, they had no hope of ever gaining Saudi citizenship; they were foreigners and always would be.

Again, memories of the West came back to me: millions of people had been naturalized as British citizens, millions more in the United States and Canada. Western countries had shared their history and identity with others. Why was Wahhabi Saudi Arabia so different? What was so special about being 'Saudi' that it could not be conferred upon others?

Had I not reached Saudi Arabia utterly convinced of my own faith and identity, then I might well have lost both. Wahhabism and its rigidity could easily have repelled me from Islam. It was only my experiences with Sufism and its broadness, its culture of tolerance, humanity, and love, that kept me within the Prophet Mohammed's fold.

Working for the British Council in Saudi Arabia was a radically different experience from my time in Syria. Students in Syria were intellectually engaged with current affairs and progress in science and technology, brought up subjects for discussion in class, and enjoyed comparing Western culture with Arab tra- ditions. Moreover, British Council managers in Syria fully understood and helped realize the *raison d'être* of the Council: to promote modern Britain in all its diversity. Thus gay and Asian teachers, for example, were welcomed and supported. In Saudi Arabia I felt as though I were working for a Saudi organization, not a British one. Nepotism, corruption, sexism, and racism were tolerated because we could not be seen to offend 'local culture'. Why is the British Council in Syria more boisterous than its counterpart in Saudi, when we consider Syria to be part of the 'axis of evil', and Saudi Arabia an 'ally' in the fight against terrorism?

Despite fitting in perfectly, on the outside at least, and living in a country that had segregated every public institution and banned women from driving on the grounds that it would give rise to licentiousness, I was repeatedly astounded at the stares Faye got from Saudi men and I from Saudi women.

Faye was not immodest in her dress. Out of respect for local custom, she wore the long black *abaya* and covered her hair in a black scarf. In all the years I had known my wife, never had I seen her appear so dull. Yet on two occasions she was accosted by passing Saudi youths from their cars. On another occasion a man pulled up beside our car and offered her his phone number. In supermarkets I only had to be away from Faye for five minutes and Saudi men would hiss or whisper obscenities as they walked past. When Faye discussed her experiences with local women at the British Council they said, 'Welcome to Saudi Arabia.'

After a month in Jeddah, I was becoming seriously worried for Faye's well-being. I heard from an Asian taxi driver about a Filipino worker who had brought his new bride to live with him in Jeddah. After visiting the prominent Balad shopping district, the couple caught a taxi home. Some way through their journey, the Saudi driver complained that the car was not working properly and perhaps the man could help push it. The passenger obliged. Within seconds the Saudi driver had sped off with the man's wife in his car and, months later, there was still no clue as to her whereabouts.

We had heard stories of the abduction of women from taxis

by sex-deprived Saudi youths. At a Saudi friend's wedding at a luxurious hotel in Jeddah, women dared not step out of their hotel rooms and walk to the banqueting hall for fear of abduction by the bodyguards of a Saudi prince who also happened to be staying there.

Why had the veil and segregation not prevented such behaviour? My Saudi acquaintances, many of them university graduates, argued strongly that, on the contrary, it was the veil and other social norms that were responsible for such widespread sexual frustration among Saudi youth.

At work, the British Council introduced free internet access for educational purposes. Within days the students had downloaded the most obscene pornography from sites banned in Saudi Arabia, but easily accessed via the British Council's satellite connection. Of course we appealed to the students not to abuse the facilities, but to no avail. In Syria, where unrestricted internet access was also available, not once did I encounter such difficulties.

Segregation of the sexes, made worse by the veil, had spawned a culture of pent-up sexual frustration which expressed itself in the unhealthiest ways. Millions of young Saudis were not allowed to let their sexuality blossom naturally and, as a result, they could see the opposite gender only as sex objects.

Using Bluetooth technology on mobile phones, strangers sent pornographic clips to one another. Many of the clips were recordings of homosexual acts between Saudis, and many featured young Saudis in orgies in Lebanon and Egypt. The obsession with sex in Saudi Arabia had reached worrying levels: rape and abuse of both sexes occurred frequently, some cases even reaching the usually censored national press.

Saudi newspapers editorialized about these worrying trends, though with reference to Saudi women's invention of temporary marriage contracts known as *misyaf* – 'a summer marriage'. These allowed women to escape Saudi Arabia with a male partner, usually to a European capital. After the 'summer', the marriage was annulled. Such arrangements were traditionally the preserve of wealthy Saudi men, but now women were finding ways of overcoming the tyranny of the monstrous *mutawwa'een*.

My students told me about the day in March 2002 when the Mutawwa'een had forbidden fire fighters in Mecca from entering a blazing school building because the girls inside were not wearing veils. Consequently, fifteen young women burned to death, but Wahhabism held its head high, claiming that God's law had been maintained by segregating the sexes. What sort of God was this?

As a young Islamist I organized events at college and in the local community that were strictly segregated, and I believed in it. Living in Saudi Arabia, I could see the logical outcome of such segregation. In Syria, and in Asian families in Britain, families were relaxed about the free mixing of the sexes. As an Islamist I had been harsh, demanding segregation at social events. Syria had opened my eyes. Our sexuality is a gift from God and we must let people make open choices, not impose an unnatural, hypocritical separation.

Still, I struggled to understand why, among some early Muslim communities, the veil was an accepted code of dress. The Prophet Mohammed had honoured women by banning female infanticide, an ancient Spartan practice adopted by pre-Islamic Arabs. He also gave women inheritance rights, and elevated their status to equal men's. No longer could a man bequeath to his son a herd of horses, a flock of camels, and a harem full of women. The pagans of Mecca complained that before long the Prophet would say that horses were human too, and had rights. Such was their incomprehension of the Prophet's emancipation of women.

Islamist Muslims are not, of course, the world's only misogynists. It is, it seems, a universal male trait, with few exceptions in tribal African communities, where the reverse is true. If Arab men expressed sexist attitudes in the medieval period, they were hardly alone. Even in more recent times Nietzsche lampooned women as cats, birds, and at best cows. He advised that we should think of women as property. In stark contrast, the Prophet Mohammed was a founding father of female emancipation.

Countless generations of Muslim men have failed to grasp the Prophet's spirit of progress, social change, and respect for humanity. Rather than continue in the Prophetic vein, and award women more rights, many Muslims stopped where the Prophet stopped in his seventh-century context. This ossification of the past continues to haunt Muslim women around the globe. And Saudi Arabia is a prime example.

In a world in which women were spoils of war, passed on from father to son as objects of pleasure, their containment in the private realm was perhaps understandable. A beautiful face could indeed launch a thousand ships. Covering it with a veil was a sensible precaution. However, in today's world, where is the need for such ancient customs?

It is interesting to note that the earliest congregational prayers for Muslims were not segregated. Even today, in the annual Haj, men and women are not segregated and it remains forbidden by Islamic law for women to wear the veil. Are there lessons here for modern Muslim scholars?

Our experiences in Saudi Arabia scotched the myth, widely held among Muslims, that Muslim countries are somehow morally superior to the decadent West. After hearing personal stories from my students about incidents of paedophilia, rape, and abuse in their families I was convinced that the West is no more decadent than the East. The difference is that in the West we are open about these issues and try to handle them as and when they arise. In comparison, in the Muslim world, such matters are swept under the carpet in an attempt to pretend that all is well.

In my Islamist days we relished stating that AIDS and other

sexually transmitted diseases were the result of the moral degeneracy of the West. And I recalled large numbers of Islamists in Britain who hounded prostitutes in Brick Lane and flippantly quoted divorce and abortion rates in Britain. The implication was that Muslim morality was superior. Now, more than ever, I was convinced that that too was Islamist propaganda, designed to undermine the West and inject false confidence in Muslim minds.

At one point during my stay in Saudi Arabia I seriously worried whether my observations were idiosyncratic, the musings of a wandering mind. I needed to discuss my troubles with other British Muslims. There were several working at the British Council and I spoke with them all. Jamal, who was of a Wahhabi bent, fully agreed with what I observed and went further. 'Ed, my wife wore the veil back home in Britain and even there she did not get as many stares as she gets when we go out here. The Saudis can tell the beauty of a woman by her eyes!' When little else was visible, I suppose they had to make do. Another British Muslim had gone as far as tinting his car windows black in order to prevent young Saudis gaping at his wife.

The problems of Saudi Arabia were not limited to racism and sexual frustration. Underscoring these deep problems was the literalist Wahhabi approach to religion that had sapped the life from the ordinary people of Saudi Arabia and attracted a small number of Europeans and Americans who came to learn what they thought was 'Islam'. They would arrive eager to be exposed to the fiery Friday sermons and then return home to ape them in European capitals. In contemporary Wahhabism there are two broad factions. One is publicly supportive of the House of Saud, and will endorse any policy decision reached by the Saudi government and provide scriptural justification for it. The second believes that the House of Saud should be forcibly removed and the Wahhabi clerics should take charge. Osama bin Laden and al-Qaeda are from the second school.

In Mecca, Medina, and Jeddah I met young men with angry faces from Europe, students at various Wahhabi seminaries. They reminded me of my own extremist days and the attempt by the Muslim World League to enlist me for a Saudi education. In Jeddah I arranged to meet two students, one from Brixton and another from Dublin. We met at the Aroma Café on Jeddah's Corniche. Their long beards, extremely short robes, and fixed gazes rendered them oddities in the upmarket surroundings. I did not divulge my own background to them, or my Sufi sympathies, and must have appeared an ignorant Muslim, heavily influenced by Western culture.

The importance of short robes comes from the life of the Prophet. It was pagan Arab custom to wear long, flowing robes to display wealth and status. To remove feelings of superiority, haughtiness, and one-upmanship in new Muslim hearts, the Prophet requested that his followers wear shortened robes. But when he saw his humble friend Abu Bakr in such a garment he said, 'Not you, Abu Bakr. For arrogance is not within you.' Wahhabis fail to understand this context of the Prophet's teachings, and adhere to his sayings literally. Worse, by shortening their robes in false imitation of the Prophet's teachings, while most Muslims do not, many harbour the very feelings of religious arrogance the Prophet sought to heal.

Still, we spoke about life in Britain, how they were coping in Saudi Arabia, and what they would do when they returned home. They were exceptionally candid in discussing their frustrations with Saudi Arabia. The country was not sufficiently Islamic; it had strayed from the teachings of Wahhabism. They were firmly on the side of the monarchy and the clerics who supported it. Soon they were to return to the West, well versed in Arabic, fully indoctrinated by Wahhabism, to become imams in British mosques. Saudi Arabia exports more than oil.

During the seven months I spent in Jeddah I prayed at mosques all across the city. All the mosques had state-funded preachers, Wahhabi men with long, unkempt beards who wore the red and white chequered Saudi Bedouin headscarf from Najd. Almost without exception, Friday sermons were highly politicized and radical. The imams prayed for jihad in Iraq and Palestine to continue, and called on God to destroy the Jews and the Americans. This mantra of destruction would have elicited an amen from me a decade earlier. Now I sat mute, not even raising my hands as is Muslim custom, but looking around bewildered. How could we? Why did we not learn from the fact that, despite Islamist prayers for destruction over five decades, Israel was still in place and America reigned supreme? Was God not telling us something in rejecting Islamist-Wahhabi prayers of cataclysm?

When I put these thoughts to a Saudi he responded by saying that early Muslims made similar prayers. I spent much time trying to convince him that early Muslims were a religious minority, struggling against the powerful Byzantines and Persians; now Muslims were a billion-strong global community – why the prayers for destruction?

Muslims, mostly Arab Muslims, have not accommodated themselves to the new post-colonial world in which they are no longer dominant as a political force. The focus of Arab anger should not be directed at the West or Israel, but at bringing about a better society with strong economic infrastructures and educational facilities, underpinned by political plurality, in their own countries. Without this focus they express themselves in the way they know best: in terms of religion. Islam, one of the world's greatest religions, has been hijacked by Arab anger expressed in Islamist political terms. Indeed, the attacks on America on September 11 were a manifestation of this very Islamist-Wahhabi rage.

The relationship between Islamists and Wahhabis is a complex one. Their historical trajectories are different, and yet they converged in the 1960s. King Faisal of Saudi Arabia, keen to subvert the Egyptian prime minister Gamal Abdel Nasser's Arab nationalist appeal and anti-monarchy rhetoric, funded Egyptian Islamists of the Muslim Brotherhood. When Nasser clamped down on Islamism, Faisal gave thousands of them sanctuary in Saudi Arabia. In 1966 Syed Qutb was hanged by Nasser, despite demands from King Faisal to spare the former's life. Soon Syed's brother, Mohamed Qutb, found shelter in Saudi Arabia as a university lecturer. As long as Saudi money and shelter were available, Islamists were happy to align themselves with the kingdom. And deeper ties were being formed: Islamists, already averse to Sufism, readily accepted Wahhabi theology. In Egypt Saudi money bolstered Islamist publishing houses. In the West Muslim communities with Islamist leadership, such as the East London mosque and many others, received Saudi funding for their projects. At Saudi universities Islamists taught essential parts of the national curriculum, thus forming ties with a younger generation of Saudis.

My Saudi students gave me some of their core texts from university classes. They complained that, regardless of their subject of study, they were compelled to study 'Thaqafah Islamiyyah' (Islamic Culture), and often to memorize such books. The Islamic Culture series includes books about Arabic literature, jurisprudence, *hadeeth* (study of the Prophet Mohammed's sayings, actions, and edicts), *tafseer* (exegesis or study of the commentary on the Koran), and other works on Islamic culture for university-level students. These books were published in 2003 (after the Saudi promise in a post-9/11 world to alter their textbooks) and were used in classrooms across the country in 2005.

I read these texts very closely: entire pages were devoted to explaining to undergraduates that all forms of Islam except Wahhabism were deviation. There were prolonged denunciations of nationalism, communism, the West, free mixing of the sexes, observing birthdays, even Mother's Day. (In Syria,

Mother's Day was observed by most people, and there was never an objection on religious grounds.) In simple terms, these were all denounced as evil.

Readers were warned about the evil effects of plurality and political parties, democracy, and a parliamentary system. Worse, several pages were devoted to blaming Jews for the world's ills.

The evidence cited for this racist and criminal worldview was the *Protocols of the Learned Elders of Zion*, a fraudulent document used by the German chancellor Adolf Hitler and other European and American leaders★ to validate their virulent anti-Semitism, which eventually led to the Holocaust.

The book, now unavailable in most countries but widely available throughout the Arab world, continues to be *the* source of evidence for a Jewish plan to dominate the Arab and wider world. I bought my own copy from a secular left-wing bookshop in Damascus. Egypt, recipient of vast amounts of US and EU aid, even produced a 41-part TV series based on the *Protocols*, and broadcast it to the Arab world as recently as 2002.

Islamist apologists point out that they are not against Jews, but Zionists. Reading these vile, hateful texts leaves me in no doubt that this was only a play on words, a shallow trick to pre-empt accusations of anti-Semitism. To them, Jew and Zionist are synonyms, selectively used to win over a given audience.

An author of the Islamic Culture series is Mohamed Qutb, teacher to Osama bin Laden and brother of the founder of Islamism, Syed Qutb. Osama bin Laden, though a civil engineering undergraduate at Jeddah's King Abd al-Aziz University, studied the compulsory Islamic Studies units under none other than Mohamed Qutb. Bin Laden attended Qutb's lectures out of interest and support, not because he had been assigned to Qutb's study group. Is it any wonder that bin Laden aspires to

★ In the United States, Henry Ford's newspaper *Dearborn Independent* often cited the *Protocols* as evidence of a world Jewish threat.

a world in which infidels either accept Islam or live under Islamist domination? Bin Laden's idiosyncratic jihad includes the violent overthrow of Arab governments, an idea first expressed by Syed Qutb from his prison cell in Cairo. Were bin Laden's beliefs and actions, in large part, influenced by his Saudi education? His early exposure to Qutb?

The Islamic Culture series catalogues Muslim history and the recent decline in Arab imperial glory by doing what most Islamists do: blaming others. Islamists of various shades (including Wahhabis and jihadis) are masters at blaming the Zionists, the Jews, the British, French, and Italian imperialists, the Turks and the Freemasons, but never themselves. Osama bin Laden's videos speak of the US as the cause of Muslim decline. This university literature was an exact replica of that mindset: it blamed others. It put forward a panacea in the form of the radical, firebrand Islam of Ibn Abd al-Wahhab. Little wonder, then, that bin Laden allied himself with fellow Wahhabis in Egypt, particularly Ayman al-Zawahiri.

It has no mention of the criticism and indeed the isolation of Ibn Abd al-Wahhab by leading Muslim scholars of his time. His own brother, Shaikh Sulaiman Ibn Abd al-Wahhab, no less a scholar, was even the first to write an extended refutation of Wahhabism.

What happened to the Muslims? I lamented. Once producers of great thinkers, grammarians, theologians, scientists, innovators, poets, jurists, and architects, today's Muslim schools and universities are producing government-fearing sycophants or extremist zealots. Where are the free-thinking intellectuals?

What I was taught in clandestinely Islamist mosques and cell meetings in Britain was being taught openly at universities in Saudi Arabia. Islamist extremism was nowhere near subsiding.

During my early trips to Mecca I often prayed alone, away from the crowds, in deep remembrance of a loving and merciful God.

I relished walking around the vast courtyard of the mosque there, slowly circulating the Ka'bah at the centre and reminiscing about the moments when the Prophet Mohammed, and before him Abraham, walked the same earth. What were their thoughts? How did they feel in what was then barren soil, with this simple structure before them? Why was their communing with the divine so powerful? All the while I would walk past humble servants of God in prayer and recitation, and Sufis in meditation. Millions across the globe craved to be in the sanctuary in Mecca – I was grateful to be able to visit it so often.

As I grew more familiar with the layout of the sanctuary, I began to discern that there was an underlying control imposed on the thousands of worshippers in Mecca. We were allowed to worship, but not to gather together for study of religion. As I walked around, whispering salutations to the Prophet, I noticed large groups of Saudi men, mostly in red headscarves, gathering round large chairs in different areas of the huge courtyard. There were at least six such gatherings, headed by Wahhabi clerics. Judging from one teacher, most of the lecture, or commentary, was on a certain book about prayer rituals. As usual they wore their red and white royal-family-imitating chequered headscarves, sometimes a plain white one, with long white robes down to their shins. Jesus once scolded the Pharisees, comparing them to bright white tombs that looked beautiful from the outside but contained only corruption and corrosion. The Wahhabi clerics today, in their pristine white robes, are no different.

For hundreds of years this courtyard was a centre of learning and erudition. Muslim scholars from all schools of thought taught here for decades at a time. Ibn Jubayr, a twelfth-century Spanish Muslim, wrote in his memoirs that several schools of thought, including the Shia school of Zaydis, were teaching in the courtyard in 1183. Today, that is no longer the case. Singular, monolithic, austere, and rigid religiosity from Najd is the order of the day.

Once, in a gathering among his companions, the Prophet Mohammed prayed, 'O Lord, bless us in our Shaam* and our Yemen.' Several people in the gathering requested, 'Bless us in our Najd, O Messenger of God.' The Prophet repeated his prayers for Syria and Yemen. They made the request for Najd again, and the Prophet prayed for Syria and Yemen. Upon their third request, he prophesied, 'There, in Najd, will be earthquakes and troubles. The horn of evil will appear from Najd.' They fell silent.

At another time, the Prophet gestured towards the east from Medina, in the direction of the Najd region, and warned three times, 'Trouble will be from there.'

Commentators on the pronouncements of the Prophet, the *muhaddithun*, have frequently pointed to these and other comments of the Messenger of God to illustrate the evil of the Wahhabi movement.

While trying to follow in the footsteps of the Prophet, I realized that there was precious little left of his heritage in Saudi Arabia. In Mecca, all historical remnants of the Prophet's life were destroyed with dynamite for fear of polytheism and in accordance with the Wahhabi mantra of 'worshipping one God'. To visit the Prophet's house in Mecca, or to view with awe the houses of his close companions, was now considered *shirk* or polytheism.

In place of history and heritage, hotel complexes have been built across Mecca. Entire mountains have been blasted away to make room for the booming hotel business. In essence, this is destruction not only of Muslim history but of Islam itself. I had grown up in a city where history was valued. In Mecca, the Prophet was no more.

Racism, anti-Christianity, destruction of Muslim heritage,

---

*Shaam, or Bilad al-Shaam, consisted of Syria, Jordan, Lebanon, and Palestine.

hatred of Jews, anti-Americanism, subjugation of women, banning of music were all inculcated in most of the Saudi youths I came across. How could these attitudes be so widespread and so deeply ingrained? Why was Wahhabism so successful?

Throughout history, whenever governments have claimed to rule in the name of religion, by divine authority, the result has been tyranny and injustice. The Umayyads, in the name of Islam, slaughtered thousands who opposed them in the seventh century, including the Prophet Mohammed's own grandchildren. Religions are not for governments or states, they are for individuals. The state can assist individuals' religious responsibilities, but governments cannot, should not, profess faith. Repeatedly in the Koran, God calls upon individual humans to better their condition, to be kind to the wayfarer, to give alms, honour their parents, believe in an afterlife, pray with spiritual presence, prepare for accountability of our worldly actions – these are not state functions.

If the Muslim Brotherhood were to seize power in Egypt – a situation not wholly inconceivable – then Hizb ut-Tahrir would condemn the 'Islamic state' for not being sufficiently Islamic, as they do today with Iran and Saudi Arabia. The perfect Islamic state is a cherished myth, sold to naive Muslims by conniving Islamists. In reality, no government would be 'Islamic' to a degree sufficient to satisfy every Islamist group. In the name of religion, these groups seek political power for their own organizational and ideological purposes.

By the summer of 2005 Faye and I had only eight weeks left in Saudi Arabia before we would return home to London. Thursday 7 July was the beginning of the Saudi weekend. Faye and I were due to lunch with Sultan, a Saudi banker who was financial adviser to four government ministers. I wanted to gauge what he and his wife, Faye's student, thought about life inside the land of their birth. Fresh from my study of Saudi school textbooks, I had many questions to ask him. Under pressure from the US government, direct references to jihad had been removed from the books, but from what I had read they still contained abundant material that could incite hatred and encourage zealots and bigots.

On television that morning we watched the developing story of a power cut on the London underground. As the cameras focused on King's Cross, Edgware Road, Aldgate, and Russell Square, I looked on with a mixture of interest and homesickness. Soon, the power-cut story turned into shell-shocked reportage of a series of terrorist bombings. My initial suspicion was that the perpetrators were Saudis. My experience of them, their virulence towards my non-Muslim friends, their hate-filled textbooks, made me think that bin Laden's Saudi soldiers had now targeted my home town. It never crossed my mind that the rhetoric of jihad introduced to Britain by Hizb ut-Tahrir could have anything to do with such horror.

My sister avoided the suicide attack on Aldgate station by four minutes.

On the previous day London had won the 2012 Olympic bid. At the British Council we had celebrated along with the nation that was now in mourning.

The G8 summit in Scotland had also been derailed by events further south. The summit, thanks largely to the combined efforts of Tony Blair and Sir Bob Geldof, had been set to tackle poverty in Africa. Now it was forced to address Islamist terrorism; Arab grievances had hijacked the agenda again. The fact that hundreds of children die in Africa every day would be of no relevance to a committed Islamist. In the extremist mind, the plight of the tiny Palestinian nation is more important than the deaths of millions of black Africans. Who in the Arab world cares that some 6,000 people die each day in Africa from AIDS? Let them die, they're not Muslims, would be the unspoken line of argument. As an Islamist, it was only the suffering of Muslims that had moved me, provoked a reaction. Now, *human* suffering mattered to me, regardless of religion.

Faye and I were glued to the television for hours. Watching fellow Londoners come out of tube stations, injured and mortified but facing the world's media with a defiant sense of dignity, made me feel proud to be British.

We met Sultan and his wife at an Indian restaurant near the British Council. Sultan was in his early thirties and his wife in her late twenties. They had travelled widely and seemed much more liberal than most Saudis I had met. Behind a makeshift partition, the restaurant surroundings were considered private and his wife, to my amazement, removed her veil to facilitate a four-way discussion between us. We discussed our travels, our time in Saudi Arabia, and the impressions we had formed.

Sultan spoke fondly of his time in London, particularly his placement at Coutts & Co. as a trainee banker. We then moved on to the subject uppermost in my mind, the terrorist attacks on London. My host did not really seem to care. He expressed no real sympathy or shock, despite speaking so warmly of his time in London. 'I suppose they will say bin Laden was behind the attacks. They blamed us for 9/11,' he said.

Keen to take him up on his comment, I asked him, 'Based on your education in Saudi Arabian schools, do you think there is a connection between the form of Islâm children are taught here and the action of fifteen Saudi men on September 11th?'

Without thinking, his immediate response was, 'No. No, because Saudis were not behind 9/11. The plane hijackers were not Saudi men. One thousand two hundred and forty-six Jews were absent from work on that day, and there is the proof that they, the Jews, were behind the killings. Not Saudis.'

It was the first time I heard so precise a number of Jewish absentees. I sat there pondering on the pan-Arab denial of the truth, a refusal to accept that the Wahhabi jihadi terrorism festering in their midst had inflicted calamities on the entire world.

At this point his wife interjected and reminded him that the number was not 1,246 but higher. She also reminded him of a film that predicted 9/11.

'Yes,' he continued. 'The Americans produced a film depicting the destruction of the twin towers by Jews before 9/11. They knew it was going to happen, so they released a film. And now they blame us!'

'And what is the name of that film?' I asked, intrigued.

Sultan pulled out his mobile phone, rang several of his friends to get me the name but they could not remember. He promised to e-mail me with its title. 'Did you read the newspapers two days ago?' he went on.

'Why?' I asked.

'The Americans anticipated a meteorite coming towards the earth so they blasted it from the heavens. Ed, they can see meteorites coming, they claim their satellite spy dishes can pick up details of cigarette packets in the desert, but they couldn't spot three huge aeroplanes? They didn't know that they would be hijacked? I can't believe that. Besides, Saudis are not competent enough to co-ordinate such an attack on New York.'

I had heard similar arguments in London and several Middle Eastern capitals that hijacking passenger planes and flying them into civic buildings, slaughtering thousands of innocent lives in the process, was somehow intelligent and Saudis and Arabs were not capable of such brilliance. I didn't even bother trying to point out the illogicality of their arguments. They were convinced they were right and nothing was going to change that. Not to mention that making such accusations to a well-connected banker in a Jeddah restaurant could quickly have landed me in a dark prison cell.

Sultan soon noticed that I had become somewhat reticent. 'We all like Osama; we just don't like the bother he has created for us,' Sultan said. He pointed to his wife and said her best friend was Osama's niece.

'Really?' I asked.

'We know the bin Laden family. It is a large family and they are very humble people. They have billions of riyals but they drive ordinary cars; they don't show off like the newly rich Saudi families and people respect them for that. Look at Osama – he is one of the wealthiest men in the world and he has given up everything. Most bin Ladens are like that.'

Sultan's wife emphasized that her friend was self-deprecating, too. They had attended the same secondary school and the bin Ladens had always despised ostentation.

I asked how they felt about the school curriculum in Saudi Arabia being changed.

'We don't like it,' said Sultan. 'They are doing this because the Americans are forcing our government to take out references to jihad from our textbooks. Most Saudis are very angry about this.'

Sultan's wife, directing her words towards Faye, then said, 'Osama wants Arabs to be great again, as we were in the past. And he wants us to do this through jihad. I will teach my children jihad and the true Islam that we are taught in our schools. The Americans will not change our faith. It is only in Saudi Arabia that we have a true form of Islam and we will not change this. All other countries have a faulty understanding of Islam.'

'What do you mean?' I asked, recalling the books of Mawdudi that had also spoken about a 'True Islam'.

'Take Egypt, for example,' replied Sultan. 'Women wear headscarves in Egypt but they do everything that is forbidden. That is because the Islam taught in their schools is wrong . . .' As Sultan explained himself I wondered to myself why it is that, among Arab men, Islam is always judged by the conduct of women. Saudi Islam was true Islam because their women were in black and Egyptian or Turkish Islam was deviant because their women wore coloured scarves. Was that the best argument for their brand of Islam the Saudis could come up with?

★

In my class the following Sunday, the beginning of the Saudi working week, were nearly sixty Saudis. Only one mentioned the London bombings.

'Was your family harmed?' he asked.

'My sister missed an explosion by four minutes but otherwise they're all fine, thank you.'

The student, before a full class, sighed and said, 'There are no benefits in terrorism. Why do people kill innocents?'

Two others quickly gave him his answer in Arabic: 'There are benefits. They will feel how we feel.'

I was livid. 'Excuse me?' I said. 'Who will know how it feels?

'We don't mean you, Teacher,' said one. 'We are talking about people in England. You are here. They need to know how Iraqis and Palestinians feel.'

'The British people have been bombed by the IRA for years,' I retorted. 'Londoners were bombed by Hitler during the Blitz. The largest demonstrations against the war in Iraq were in London. People in Britain don't need to be taught what it feels like to be bombed.'

Several students nodded in agreement. The argumentative ones became quiet. Were they convinced by what I had said? It was difficult to tell.

Two weeks after the terrorist attacks in London Zafir, a young Saudi student, raised his hand and asked, 'Teacher, how can I go to London?'

'Much depends on your reason for going to Britain. Do you want to study, or just be a tourist?'

'Teacher, I want to go London next month. I want bomb, big bomb in London, again. I want make jihad!'

'What?' I exclaimed. Another student raised both hands and shouted, 'Me too! Me too!'

Other students applauded those who had just articulated what many of them were thinking. I was incandescent. In protest, I walked out of the classroom to a chorus of jeering and catcalls.

At the end of term a group of Saudi and Yemeni students asked me if I would miss Jeddah when I left the following week.

'No,' I said frankly, 'I am afraid I won't.'

A young student of about sixteen replied, 'Yes, Teacher. You will not miss Jeddah or Saudi Arabia. We don't have enough Islam here. We need more Islam.'

What on earth is he babbling about? I thought.

'In Saudi Arabia we only have 70 per cent Islam. In Afghanistan, under the Taliban, they had 100 per cent Islam. Very good, Teacher. Very good. No problems in Afghanistan with Taliban. We need more Islam.'

Where he found such statistics on levels of extremism I know not, but one thing was clear: the fanatics had taught him that there was not 'enough Islam' in Saudi Arabia, despite all the loss, mayhem, perversion and hypocrisy that '70 per cent' had created there.

At this point another student announced proudly to me, 'My friend went to Iraq for jihad, Teacher. He went to Baghdad.' Miming an embrace, he continued, 'My friend held an American car and he died a *shaheed*, a martyr. We need more martyrs for more Islam.'

They had been brainwashed so effectively by the Saudi religious authorities that they now saw themselves as friends of martyrs, not murderers. They were keen to continue the tradition.

The first student piped up again: 'Teacher, in Iraq we have two cities where we have 100 per cent Islam. Life is perfect!'

'Really?'

'Yes, Haditha and Qaimah,' he said with pride. 'There, there are no American soldiers. One day, all of Iraq will be like this when your country and America leave Iraq.'

Yes, Iraq was a mess and horrifying blunders had been made during its invasion, but the way to solve the country's problems was not by bombing innocent Shia people and police recruits.

That was Wahhabi thinking: the Shia Muslims were infidels who thus deserved to die as much as the occupying troops did.

The Saudi continued calmly, 'If the British don't leave Iraq, then more people will die in London. There will be more bombs.' Here was a teenager studying at the British Council, endorsing the murder of innocent people with complete equanimity. To him, as to many young Saudis, this was normal. I felt profound sadness at how nothing had changed in Saudi Arabia, home to most of the perpetrators of 9/11.

The British media, caught unawares by the new threat of home-grown terror in Britain, recalled Britain's first suicide bomber, Asif Hanif. Asif blew himself up in a bar in Tel Aviv in April 2003. At the time, I was in Damascus and the *Sun* had sent its reporters to Damascus University, assuming that Asif became a suicide bomber during his time in the city. The *Sun* had got it wrong: Asif was radicalized not in Damascus but in London. Omar Bakri confirmed that he had met Asif and his accomplice before they left for Syria.

Although we were both in Damascus at the same time, I never saw Asif there. But I knew him – I had met him in Hounslow mosque – and I remember him as a kind man. One Sunday afternoon in 2002, tired from an intensive study pro-gramme at the mosque with the Syrian scholar and spiritual guide Shaikh Mohammed al-Ya'qubi, I had gone to the cafeteria in search of a cup of tea. Asif was busy doing the unglamorous job of clearing the mess left behind by 200 lunching students. He was working voluntarily.

'What can I do for you, brother?' he asked.

'A cup of tea please, if you wouldn't mind?'

'Oh no, brother, of course I don't mind. You're our guest. It's our duty to serve.'

As we spoke I recognized him. I recalled that I had eaten *iftar*, a light meal to end a day of fasting during Ramadan, at his family home the previous year when a mutual American friend had been visiting Britain. He had given me a lift to the station, speaking fondly during the journey of traditional Muslim scholars in Syria.

Asif was a teddy bear of a character: generous, kind, selfless and committed. He, like me, went to Damascus to study Arabic and the Koran. Regrettably, his good nature was exploited by Islamist militants from Hamas. The qualities that made Asif a great Muslim host – selflessness and commitment – were the same traits that, when corrupted, transformed him into a suicide bomber.

Asif was only twenty-one when he died. Young and vulnerable, he came under the influences of an older, more developed Islamist from Derby by the name of Omar Sharif Khan. Both men had explosives attached to them that day in Tel Aviv, but Omar's failed to detonate. Sharif did not simply wake up one morning, see Israeli aggression against Palestinians, and decide to kill himself and as many Israelis as possible in Tel Aviv. He had travelled a path of rejection, confrontation, and ultimately violence.

Sharif was a mathematics undergraduate at King's College London. During his first year he started to attend meetings organized by Hizb ut-Tahrir on campus. He became close to a Hizb member, Reza Pankhurst (released in 2006 after serving a four-year prison sentence with my old friend, Majid Nawaz). Soon Sharif became close to Omar Bakri and followed him when he left the Hizb to form al-Muhajiroun.

Whether Sharif can be 'proven' to be a member of the Hizb is immaterial. What is beyond doubt is that he was introduced to radical ideas by the Hizb as an undergraduate and later developed those ideas to the point where he planned to die for Hamas. Asif's recruitment to suicide bombing came about against a backdrop of increasingly radicalized young Muslims in communities across Britain. Interestingly, neither Asif Hanif nor

Omar Sharif Khan came from an unemployed, disenchanted inner-city Muslim community; both had middle-class backgrounds.

After Asif's death his shocked English neighbours and former schoolteachers spoke highly of him. The Asif I knew did not believe in killing innocent civilians in Britain or any other country, but Islamist rhetoric had convinced him that Israelis, without exception, were not innocent but occupiers of the Palestinian homeland. Israel was a war zone, most Israelis had undergone military training and all were, therefore, legitimate targets.

Even in Syria many seemingly Westernized students of mine made that point very clear to me: killing Jews in Israel is acceptable. These were not Hizbullah or Hamas supporters, just ordinary Syrians expressing a commonly held viewpoint.

As an Islamist, I too believed that the taking of Jewish and non-Muslim lives was perfectly acceptable if it would facilitate Islamist domination. Islamism, with its heavy emphasis on religious identity, dehumanized others. Only Muslims were worthy of our attention; and then only those Muslims who would listen to us. The trigger for my enlightenment was when I saw at first hand the destructive power of Islamist ideas in emboldening British Muslim teenagers to confront others in the name of religion, a confrontation that ended with a young man lying dead in a pool of blood outside Newham College.

The suicide bombing campaign in Israel has brought only misery, destruction and poverty to the Palestinian people. Leaving aside the Koran's proscription of suicide, even as a political strategy suicide bombing has backfired disastrously, provoking far worse Israeli reprisals and the strengthening and extension of the Israeli West Bank barrier wall which physically separates the two communities.

Killing innocent people is wrong, regardless of where it occurs. Neither is there an excuse for state terrorism: the governments of Britain, the US and Israel are as guilty as any 9/11 hijacker. We must not stoop to the level of the terrorists, kill and torture innocent people, and hide behind cries of 'collateral damage', 'rogue elements'. The scandalous abuse of prisoners at Abu Ghraib boosted al-Qaeda's recruitment drive and today no serious democrat can proudly hold up Western democracy as an example in the Middle East.

But, just as voters can decide at the ballot box who should lead them, Muslims can make their own choices. If the taking of innocent lives, Israeli or otherwise, continues to be 'acceptable', if Islamist thought continues to influence Muslim minds, then what happened in London on 7/7 will be as nothing in comparison with what is yet to come. For when the political pretexts of Palestine and Iraq have been dealt with, Wahhabi-inspired militants will turn to other social grievances: drinking alcohol, 'impropriety', gambling, cohabitation, inappropriate dress – these and a host of miscellaneous others will become excuses for jihad, for martyrdom, feeding the tumour of Islamist domination which grows in the Wahhabi and Islamist mind. Why else was Bali bombed, Egyptian tourist resorts attacked, and plans made to bomb nightclubs in London?

I fear the unleashing of a firestorm of violence by home-grown Wahhabi jihadists, inflamed by Islamist rhetoric, on the major cities of America and Britain.

Jihad originated in chivalry on the battlefield, not cowardly suicide attacks on innocent people. The Prophet's teachings were not abstract. He reprimanded even his bravest fighters for killing unarmed soldiers. When he returned victorious from Medina to his home city of Mecca he declared a general amnesty to those who only a decade previously had tortured his nascent community of believers in the most violent way. Meccan pagans killed Sayyidah Sumayyah, Islam's first martyr and one of the Prophet's first followers, by piercing her vagina with spears, and still the Prophet Mohammed remained merciful, forgiving.

While the Vikings were preparing to unleash two centuries of mayhem on Europe, in the small Arabian city of Medina the Prophet Mohammed was creating holistic humans. The people and the faith he bequeathed to the world created civilizations from Spain in the west to China in the east.

Even in battle, the Prophet's spirit of fair play shone through. During the Crusades, Saladin famously threw a sword to Richard the Lionheart so that he might defend himself fairly rather than be at a disadvantage.

The Prophet preferred treaties, peace, conciliation but, when all these failed, he was not afraid to fight. Muslims are not pacifists. As one of my teachers once said, we take up the sword to take the sword out of madmen's hands. Today, the sword is once again in the hands of the madmen.

My time in Saudi Arabia bolstered my conviction that an austere form of Islam (Wahhabism) married to a politicized Islam (Islamism) is wreaking havoc in the world: Baghdad, Tel Aviv, Haifa, Cairo, Istanbul, New York, Madrid, London . . . the list of cities that have suffered Islamist wrath goes on. This anger-ridden ideology, an ideology I once advocated, is not only a threat to Islam and Muslims, but to the entire civilized world.

I vowed, in my own limited way, to fight those who had hijacked my faith, defamed my Prophet, and killed thousands of my own people: the human race. I was encouraged when Tony Blair announced on 5 August 2005 plans to proscribe an array of Islamist organizations that operated in Britain, foremost among them Hizb ut-Tahrir. At the time I was impressed by Blair's resolve. The Hizb should have been outlawed a decade ago, and so spared many of us so much misery. Sadly, the legislation was shelved in 2006 amid fears that a ban would only add to the group's attraction, so it remains both legal and active today. But it is not too late. Will the British government deliver?

★

Throughout our seven-month stay in Saudi Arabia Faye and I maintained our equilibrium by visiting the sepulchre of the Arabian Apostle of God as often as possible. Medina never disappointed; the presence of the Prophet could be felt and we always returned to Jeddah as calmer people. The Prophet Mohammed frequently used to pray to God, '*Allahumma antha al-Salam, wa minka al-salam*', 'My Lord, you are Peace and from you is peace'. In his city, that peace is palpable.

Medina was not free of the discord and dissension of Wahhabism. Wahhabi religious police, zealous and harsh, patrolled the Prophet's mosque to ensure that nobody worshipped him there. Arrogant guards looked down with contempt at the visitors – to them we are *mushrikeen*, polytheists, like the 'misguided Christians' who deify Jesus. The Wahhabis cannot comprehend the difference between love and worship. Never in the history of Islam has the Prophet been worshipped or deified. Islamic theology is sufficiently sound to prevent Islam from St Paul's type of Christology. And yet the Wahhabis rant on about polytheism among Muslims.

They broke up gatherings of Shia Muslims and forcefully moved on spiritual Muslims who wished to recite poetry at the tomb of the Prophet. On many instances I found myself standing in the intense heat outside the mosque beside lovers of the Prophet from central Asia, Turkey, and Pakistan. They wept out of yearning for him and I wondered why they had been expelled. Why could Wahhabism not allow the Prophet's followers to be close to the one they loved? This Wahhabi mindset, this inability to tolerate difference, forcibly removing any who exhibited non-Wahhabi behaviour, was symbolic of Wahhabi confrontation with the wider world. Al-Qaeda is only one manifestation of Wahhabism.

Non-Muslims do not have access to Mecca and Medina. They do not know about the daily battles of pilgrims with strict Wahhabism, the demolition of our heritage, and the imposition of extremist literalism in worship on Muslim pilgrims. Every year Wahhabi authorities control the Haj and actively discourage expressions of love and attachment to the Prophet. The inclination towards literalism and extremism, and the removal of love and joy from religion, stem from an attack on the traditional Muslim veneration of the Prophet. What started in the eighteenth century in Najd as opposition to mainstream Islam and its practices has now reached the capitals of the West. Whether attacking Muslims or non-Muslims, the underlying principles are the same: scriptural rigidity, bigotry, intolerance, and violence.

Two days before we left Saudi Arabia we went to the Prophet one last time. I approached his tomb and said my goodbyes. In 1183 the Spanish traveller Ibn Jubayr wrote that he knelt beside the sepulchre and 'kissed the earth on its sacred sites'. Today's Muslims risk being kicked in the face by the Wahhabi guards if we so much as bow our heads.

As I walked away from his serene presence, the magnificent Green Dome more distant with my every step, my dry eyes began to water. The pirates that control access to this sea of love may not allow my humble boat to return, but I have been taught that the spiritual presence of the Prophet can be invoked from afar by those who love him and I comfort myself with this knowledge. The extraordinary fragrance of rose musk, much loved by the Prophet, which I had smelt in the alleyways and mountain paths of Medina, is no longer confined to this ancient city.

15. Return to England

I am slowly discovering England, which is the most wonderful foreign land I have ever been in.
  Rudyard Kipling

When I was in the Middle East, I often missed many aspects of life in Britain and yearned to be home. Now I'm in Britain, I miss the warmth of Arabs, the joys of ubiquitous Arabic, and the landscape of minarets and mountains of ancient cities. Just as my Britishness had come to the fore while living in the Muslim world, my Muslimness now seeks expression. I feel as though I belong to both the East and the West, and sometimes find it difficult to reconcile the two sides of my personality. Then I remind myself that, before I am anything, I am human, and in this I am at one with the world.

Still, I belong to two communities: Muslim and British. In some cases my twin identities merge neatly and sometimes they are at odds. I am a follower of the second largest religion in the United Kingdom, and the behaviour of my co-religionists is of great significance to both me and my country.

For me, being a Muslim is not a political identity – Islam does not teach us a monolithic approach to life. The Prophet did not create new systems of government, but adopted existing paradigms from seventh-century Arabia. His was not a radical break with the past. When the Muslims of Indonesia, India, China, Persia, and Africa embraced Islam they did not disavow their own native cultures; their architecture and customs testify to that fact. In Mecca I met Muslims who were unalike in their background and culture but united in their belief. For me that is the true *ummah* – a spiritual community, not a political bloc.

Upon returning to England I enrolled at the University of London for postgraduate studies. Visiting different campuses and libraries reminded me of my days with Hizb ut-Tahrir. I thought that, after the suicide bombings of 7 July 2005, and the intense media scrutiny of extremism in Britain, the Hizb might have withdrawn from activities at universities, and Islamists at least be displaying some signs of contrition.

Outside the university's Senate House library I met my old friend from college, Majid Nawaz, recently returned from serving a four-year prison sentence in Egypt for plotting to overthrow the Mubarak government. It was a memorable if hasty reunion. Several years ago, on the very same spot, I had blown Majid's cover to one of his potential recruits, Ali from Iraq. Majid had been busy buying Ali lunch, discussing politics and indirectly introducing Ali to 'the concepts'. At the time, I had recently left the Hizb and had some harsh words to say about Majid. We parted on a sour note.

Now here we were again. Majid was in a hurry because a local student Islamic society had invited him to deliver the Friday sermon and he was running late. We exchanged numbers and agreed to meet. The old bitterness, it seemed, had passed away. Still, meeting Majid reminded me of our days at Newham College, where we watched the Hizb's ideas transform from thought to action. The murder of an innocent student, a direct consequence of the Hizb's ideas, I took as a personal warning and changed my own life. But Majid remained with the Hizb and now sits on the national executive committee of Hizb ut-Tahrir in Britain.

We soon met again and went for lunch at the Institute of Education cafeteria. We spoke for hours, always returning to the subject of Hizb ut-Tahrir. I told Majid that I was writing this book and listed my criticisms of the Hizb. To his credit, he agreed that much was wrong with the organization: its arrogance, extremism, superiority complex, confrontational style, cultism, rejection of Britishness or any national identity, and serious lack of spirituality.

'How could it be, Majid,' I asked, 'that when I was in the Hizb we broke up meetings and caused chaos when Amnesty International visited a mosque in East Ham, on the grounds that they opposed capital punishment and were thus anti-Islamic, but when you were interviewed by Sarah Montague on BBC's *Hardtalk* recently, you were happy to quote Amnesty's campaign for your release? Does that not seem hypocritical?'

I put it to him that when the Egyptian government arrested and jailed Majid and others from the Hizb they claimed that, as British citizens, they were entitled to preferential treatment, a fair trial, and British government intervention. Yet while in Britain, these same individuals rejected their British identity, saying they were 'Muslims living in Britain' and harshly condemning anyone calling themselves a *British* Muslim. And on these grounds of Muslim separatism, as late as 2005, the Hizb actively discouraged Muslims from participating in the British general election, arguing it was sinful, *haram*, for Muslims to engage in democracy.

Again, Majid emphasized that the Hizb had changed. He conceded that it had come under the influence of Omar Bakri, and strayed from 'the ideology'. 'But how could a party that prides itself on its intellectual purity and depth allow an individual to derail it? Don't you think poor Bakri is being forced to carry the can?' I asked. And so we kept going round in circles, Majid defending the Hizb and me, his old comrade, condemning it.

One particular point Majid made stayed with me, however. In an attempt to remedy the Hizb's detachment from God and spirituality, Hizb members were now compelled, under orders from the Arab leadership in the Middle East, to study the writings of Imam Nawawi, a thirteenth-century scholar-saint whose popular tomb in the village of Nawa I had visited in Syria. The Hizb was hoping that study would instil spirituality, yet that is the work of living spiritual masters. But the Hizb was not sufficiently humble to learn from these living masters, for that would mean sitting at the feet of Muslim scholar-saints who approve of, and in many cases are linked to, the very governments that the Hizb wishes to overthrow.

Still, I was pleased that the Hizb had at least now moved beyond Nabhani, a twentieth-century Islamist ideologue, and studied the works of genuine Muslim luminaries. I registered the 'new Hizb' in my mind and went about my studies and family life. I stayed in touch with Majid. Despite fundamental disagreements and dogged discussions, on a personal level we remain friends.

Had the Hizb really changed? Was there any substance to the new claims that the Hizb was a 'non-violent' organization? How could an organization committed to the creation of a violent state seriously brand itself as 'non-violent'? Majid and I have had long discussions on the Hizb and my conclusion is that there are now at least two strands within it. The first is desperately trying to ensure survival in Britain by adopting a more moderate tone and appearance in an attempt to gain acceptance among the constituency that matters most to them: the Muslim community, now increasingly under government pressure to sideline extremists. Britain remains vital to the Hizb, for it gives the group access to the global media and provides a fertile recruiting ground at mosques and universities. The second strand is more radical and committed to the writings of Nabhani and less concerned about engagement.

Most members of the Hizb's national executive belong to the former, while most rank and file members, it seems, incline towards the latter. Nevertheless, I am not convinced that as an organization they have disavowed their commitment to an all-powerful Islamist state, dedicated to military confrontation with Britain, France, the United States and Israel.★ The foreign policy of this state rests on propagating the Islamist ideology, destroying Israel, annexing neighbouring countries, and killing whoever stands in their way, Muslims and non-Muslims alike. As one Hizb activist recently admitted to me after my showing him Nabhani's writings, 'Sometimes force must be used to implement and expand ideology.'

The writings of Nabhani, to which the Hizb remains committed, clearly outlines such a vision for a violent state, dedicated to jihadism.

Soon after my return I attended a public debate entitled 'The Future of Islam' at the London School of Economics, the same venue where I had heard Omar Bakri declare that, in warfare, Muslims were allowed to eat their enemies and thus did not require aid, but weapons to win the battles for global domination. More than a decade later, did Bakri's influence remain?

New faces had appeared on the Muslim lecture circuit. The two speakers, Professor Tariq Ramadan from Switzerland, grandson of the founder of the Muslim Brotherhood, and the British–Pakistani author Ziauddin Sardar, locked horns over their conflicting visions of 'the future'. Despite their disagreements, they were both united in their call for a rereading of the Koran, and a fundamental reinterpretation of the meaning of the sources of Islamic law. Such a discourse, they believed, was tantamount to rejecting the literalism of extremists, and a rejection of capital punishment among other things.

There were jeers and boos from certain members of the audience, some more confident about their knowledge of Islam than the speakers. After the event the same individuals were arguing loudly with other members of the audience in order to attract attention, and distributing leaflets about the 'War on Islam', Islamist parlance for the War on Terror.

★See Article 184 of Hizb ut-Tahrir's draft constitution for the Islamist state.

Memories of my Hizb days came rushing back to me. As I observed the young men from a distance, I recognized two of them. They were Hizb ut-Tahrir activists. What were they talking about? I approached a gathering of people and the Hizb activist saw me and extended his hand to greet me.

'Wow! Where have you been, man? Haven't seen you for years!' I briefly explained that I had been abroad and asked after his older brother, whom I also knew. He answered my questions quickly and then turned to asking about me again. His line of questioning was designed to establish if I was still an Islamist or if I'd sold out. I regretted saying hello to him. As I turned away, he shouted, 'You faggot!'

I attended congregational Friday prayer at a University of London college. The preacher, a stocky Arab student from the Palestinian Territories, rose to castigate the recent election results of the Palestinian Authority. As in the 1990s, religious sermons are still being delivered by political activists in British universities. Hamas had won, but the sermonizer's argument was that they should not have participated in the first place. The only way to regain Palestine was by all-out war, or jihad. His mantra, 'Democracy is hypocrisy', rang a few old bells in my head. He attacked the Palestinian Fatah movement and the American occupation of Iraq before turning his vitriol against 'the latest attack of the West against the Muslim *ummah*'. References to Hamas, Fatah, and Iraq were only a prelude to his main grievance: derogatory cartoons of the Prophet Mohammed that had recently been published in a Danish newspaper.

I did not recall seeing the speaker in Hizb ut-Tahrir circles during my time. But his inflammatory rhetoric and considerable skill in rousing Muslim sentiment made me suspect him to be a Hizb activist. I recognized the training. He ended his sermon by calling on God to destroy the *kuffar*.

I looked around me; the prayer hall was tense, but in the name of 'Muslim unity' the Hizb had ensured that opposition to such rhetoric would always be deemed a betrayal. Nobody opposed the speaker. The radicalization of yet another generation of young Muslims continues unabated.

After hearing him attack the USA at another meeting, and calling for the killing of future Muslim leaders who opposed the Hizb's coming caliph, I learnt that the preacher was indeed a leading member of Hizb ut-Tahrir, responsible for dealing with the Arabic media.

Soon afterwards a plethora of events was organized by student union societies with names such as the 'Open Mind' or 'Thought Society' on various London campuses. These were, of course, front organizations, and from Muslim friends I learnt that other equally innocuous cover names were deployed at other British universities. I attended several such events where prominent members of the Hizb had been smuggled in under names assumed for the occasion. They were sometimes introduced as media figures from Channel 4, Sky News or the BBC, but never as members of the Hizb. The Hizb game of charades continues.

In one meeting, filled with anti-American statements, a prominent Hizb member stated that 'some people in Britain should be bombing Washington DC'. To his mind, that was the 'logical conclusion of unilateral action' conducted by the US to attack al-Qaeda in various countries. Could I believe Majid's claims of a reformed Hizb when their speakers, while publicly condemning terrorism in media interviews, privately sow the seeds of it?

As we left the prayer hall a young undergraduate distributed leaflets about a protest outside the Danish embassy that afternoon. There was no mention of who had organized the protest. His zeal reminded me of my leafleting days. The sermon had raised the temperature; the leaflet guided us to action. Was the Hizb still active on British university campuses? Apparently, yes. Had the Hizb really changed? Apparently, no.

On TV that evening images from that demonstration were broadcast all around the world. Radical Islamists, their faces covered by Saudi and Palestinian scarves, yelled, 'Democracy, hypocrisy. Democracy go to hell. Denmark go to hell. Freedom go to hell. Behead the *kafir*. Bomb, bomb Denmark. Bomb, bomb USA.'

The demonstration had been organized by the Hizb's more candid offshoot, al-Muhajiroun, but the rhetoric and ideology were the same. The following Friday the Hizb organized its own demonstration to which an activist from Bedford turned up dressed as a suicide bomber.

Listening to the fierce rage of the Friday preacher, watching the burning of the Danish flag on television, hearing the charge of Islamophobia brought against Western governments from less extreme Islamists, I wondered how the personality at the centre of the row, the Prophet Mohammed, would have dealt with this. During his own lifetime he was subjected to the worst forms of abuse. Islamists I spoke to claimed that the *Jyllands-Posten* newspaper had violated the sacred by depicting the Prophet as it had. But the sacred was also violated during the time of the Prophet, before his eyes, on several occasions.

In a famous incident an Arab man from the desert came into Medina, entered the most sacred of places, the Prophet's mosque, and urinated within the holy grounds. What did the Prophet do? He cleaned the mosque with his own hands and forgave the ignorance of the Bedouin. Why does the ignorance or racism of a Danish newspaper provoke so much rage among modern Muslims? Where are those Prophetic traits of forgiveness and compassion? For if the cartoonist did not know the merciful Prophet, Muslims should.

Other demonstrations followed in Trafalgar Square. Islamists masterfully manipulated Muslim sensitivities and successfully linked political issues to the Danish cartoons. My non-Muslim friends, a Danish journalist among them, were dumbfounded by the irrationality of attacking embassies, boycotting Danish dairy products, and calling for bombings and beheadings.

Increasingly it became apparent to me that Islamists could still be successful at mobilizing Muslims, in Britain and elsewhere, partly because there exists heartfelt reaction against genuine imbalances in the world, from Palestine and Iraq to Darfur and Afghanistan. The Friday preacher knew full well that the cartoons on their own were not sufficient to provoke an uprising, so in true Hizb fashion he linked them to other issues: the American occupation of Iraq, the War on Terror, and the Arab–Israeli conflict. Why else would the calls for bombings at the demonstrations include the USA? The ideological confrontation was highlighted by attacks on democracy and freedom. Just as Omar Bakri had trained us in the 1990s, issues had been linked to capture the popular imagination.

Bakri was expelled from the Hizb not because he called for the assassination of Prime Minister John Major in 1991, at which time he was leader of the group, but because he disagreed with the Hizb's Middle East leadership in 1995. Bakri wanted greater concentration on Britain while the leadership wanted greater focus on the Middle East, the launch pad of the Islamist state. The terrorist attacks on London were conducted by suicide bombers from Beeston, Leeds, home to three of the four bombers. Omar Bakri had preached in Beeston. He emphasized to the media that he was not responsible for the suicide bombings, but he desperately wished that he had been. It was, in Bakri's eyes, a praiseworthy act.

The events of 7/7 did not occur in a vacuum. The suicide bombers were not trained in isolation, away from Britain, in Afghanistan and Pakistan. Long before the overthrow of Saddam Hussein in Iraq, in Britain's Muslim communities the ideas of a global jihad, an *ummah* transcending Britain, and preparation for the all-powerful Islamist state were, and still are, accepted as normal and legitimate.

Siddique Khan, the lead 7/7 suicide bomber, spoke of 'my people' as those in Iraq. He declared that he was 'at war' with Britain, and in this war he was 'a soldier'. Khan did not see fellow Brits as human brothers and sisters. I too once expressed such sentiments. The 7/7 suicide bombers were symptomatic of a deeper problem: unbridled Islamist ideology gaining a stronger hold in Britain's Muslim communities. That ideology and its prescriptions are becoming the acceptable norm for expressing political disenchantment against 'the West' – a mythical conception just as much as 'the *ummah*'.

Regardless of Islamist myths of a glorious, unified Muslim history spanning fourteen centuries, most Muslims know that Shia Islam broke away from what became mainstream Sunni Islam because of the bloody civil wars within our religion. The details of this history are a subject in their own right, but we would be ill served were we to forget that the so-called Islamic state of the Umayyads killed the noble grandson of the Prophet Mohammed, Imam Husain, and other members of the Prophet's family. Islamists, masters at misreading history, see a lesson in this: opposition to the so-called Islamic state warrants the killing of Muslims, even the Prophet's own family. They will exploit such 'evidence' to annihilate mainstream Muslims who oppose the expansionism and so-called jihad of the Islamic state.

I believe the duty to combat extremist rhetoric, the preamble to terrorism, does not lie with the government alone. Muslims have a responsibility to stand up and reclaim our faith. It is Muslims who are able to recognize Islamist extremists most easily. Before extremists are on the radar of the intelligence community, we see the changes in modes of prayer, selective mosque-attendance patterns, modification of behaviour and of dress, an increasing harshness in attitude, and condemnatory rhetoric.

My warnings to university authorities and student union officials where I saw the Hizb and other groups recruiting in

Britain on my return were repeatedly met with arguments defending the right to freedom of speech. If an organization is not illegal, how can it be barred? I understand why most British Muslims simply refuse to confront extremism. My time outside Britain has perhaps instilled in me an urgency that is lacking in British Muslim circles, a reflection of the wider British willingness to turn a blind eye, avoid a fuss, and hope that somehow it will work out in the end.

If British policy makers and elected officials are content to tolerate intolerance, and give a platform to those who are committed to destroying democracy and advocate religion-based separatism, why should a minority Muslim population turn on its own? While I was in Syria, the British and American governments exerted unprecedented pressure to expel from Syria Western Muslim students who were studying privately and not enrolled at universities. Syria was deemed a training ground for terrorists, as was Pakistan. Demands were made that Syria expel Hamas members from Damascus, and Pakistan close several of its madrassas. But when the British government is content to allow a sophisticated extremist organization to operate and recruit in Britain, why should Syria or Pakistan do their job for them?

Unsettled by the prominence of the Hizb in London, despite Tony Blair's unfulfilled threat to proscribe the organization, I wondered how my teenage hangout, the East London mosque, had fared. In late 2006 I visited the mosque to meet an old friend and see if the management had moved away from Islamism. After all, many of the leaders of the East London mosque are now influential in the Muslim Council of Britain, with access to ministers and large sections of the media. Sadly, I was disappointed.

Despite two High Court injunctions in 1990 in response to violence at the mosque, and its role as a platform for various Islamists (later to include jihadis such as Abdullah el-Faisal, now serving a prison sentence for soliciting murder and inciting racial hatred in Britain), the British government subsidized and facilitated the expansion of the East London mosque into Europe's largest Islamist hub, the London Muslim Centre (LMC). Prince Charles was scheduled to officially open the centre.

The Saudi-trained imam of the mega-mosque continues to lead a faction against modernizing elements and, like Saudi clerics, prohibits gatherings of 'dissenting' Muslims: opponents of Islamism or Wahhabism.

The chairman of the mosque, the mild-mannered Dr Abdul Bari, a lifelong admirer of Mawdudi and public host of several leaders of Jamat-e-Islami from Bangladesh and Pakistan during my involvement with the mosque, now heads the Muslim Council of Britain.*

At the mosque bookshop I bought an updated copy of Qutb's *Milestones*, published not in Riyadh but in Birmingham, England, in early 2006. It contains lengthy articles in the appendices from leading Wahhabis, chapter headings such as 'The Virtues of Killing a Non-Believer', and ideas such as 'Attacking the non-believers in their territories is a collective and individual duty.' Just as I had done as a sixteen-year-old, hundreds of young Muslims are buying these books from Islamist mosques in Britain and imbibing the idea that killing non-believers is not only acceptable, but the duty of a good Muslim. I showed the passages to a Muslim friend that evening and we shook our heads in disgust. From such messages are suicide bombers born.

This literature was on sale five minutes' walk from the Muslim Council of Britain's new offices. And there was more. Mawdudi's books, the very same ones that I had read, were still on

---

*Since as early as 1991 Dr Bari has played host to leaders of Jamat-e-Islami in East London mosque and other public venues. I witnessed his promotion of Matiur Rahman Nizami, Abdul Qader Mollah, Delwar Hussein Sayedi, Khurshid Ahmed, and later the then leader of Jamat-e-Islami in Bangladesh, Professor Gulam Azam.

sale and prominently displayed. In my day, we only spoke about the bravery of 'our brothers' in Jamat-e-Islami and saw black-and-white pictures of 'martyrs' in monthly bulletins from the subcontinent. Nowadays Islamist activists can buy full-colour videos of Jamat-e-Islami cadres engaged in pitched battles with fellow Muslims in Dhaka, leftists from the Awami League. The Qutbian belief that killing non-Islamist Muslims of a secular persuasion is permissible is being acted upon in the Muslim world and disseminated in Britain's Islamist mosques.

The Islamism of Mawdudi's school is not principled, but politically pragmatic. In Bangladesh Jamat-e-Islami activists are literally engaged in street battles against leftists, but in Britain Islamists from Jamat's British front organizations are active members of George Galloway's far-left Respect party. Front movements of the Arab Muslim Brotherhood are leading members of Respect too. Galloway was given a hero's welcome at the London Muslim Centre after he ousted Oona King in a highly controversial election campaign in 2005.

During the British local council elections of 2006 I supported my local Labour councillor's successful campaign for re-election. While canvassing I learnt much about how Respect employed race and religion to help them win votes. Respect party Islamists exploited the nationalist identities of the Pakistani and Bangladeshi communities in east London, referring to the war in Iraq and persuading them to vote according to colour, religion, and language, as if these are political beliefs in their own right. In some cases these tactics yielded results. Islamists I knew from my own past were elected as Respect councillors. At the same time the Christian People's Alliance campaigned similarly among the Afro-Caribbean community, playing on their religious sensitivities. All the while Labour councillors I campaigned with shied away from confronting these issues. Foreign languages in campaign literature and canvassing were honoured with the title 'community languages'. What's wrong with English?

The multiculturalism fostered by the Labour government had created mono-cultural outposts in which the politics of race and religion were now being played out before my eyes. A Respect activist outside a polling station asked me why I was campaigning for white Christian candidates. Was I? Since when had politics been reduced to this? Do all 'white Christians' think the same way? Besides, one of the two councillors in my ward was an atheist.

I raised my concerns with a Muslim friend who arranged for me to have lunch with the president of a leading Islamist organization in Britain, a man known for his public condemnation of terrorism. Unaware that I was no longer an Islamist sympathizer, never mind an activist, he let slip that he considered that he saw nothing wrong in the destruction of the *kuffar*, or prayers that call for that destruction. I asked him how this could be when the Koran repeatedly acknowledges that the majority of the world's people will not be Muslims, and pointed out that God has rejected extremist prayers for destruction for over forty years. 'God will answer those prayers in good time,' he replied.

For how much longer, I ask, will we tolerate the hypocrisy of such people enjoying British life while calling for its destruction? When will Islamists halt this doublespeak?

I returned to Britain because I believe it is my home. I want my children to grow up here. I do not want them to consider Islamism as an option, as I once did. So I worry when I see young girls, many below the age of eight, wearing hijab to primary schools. If hijab is a mechanism for modesty and an indication of sexual propriety, however debatable, then it belongs firmly in the wardrobe of adulthood. When Muslim parents send their young children to school thus attired it tells me that the hijab is losing its spiritual significance and is instead becoming a marker of separatist identity politics. I see young boys changing out of their school shirts and trousers into Saudi-style white flowing robes before heading off to the mosque in the evenings. Why is Gulf clothing, designed to ease life in the hot Arabian desert, being imposed on British children as a symbol of religion? What is wrong with Western clothes?

Other, more insidious, Saudi influences are permeating British Islam. Wahhabism in Britain comes in many forms, as does Islamism. Today's jihadis are Wahhabis who have taken up arms against the Saudi rulers and their backers, Western governments included. Many imams in our mosques are Saudi-trained. They appear as important guests at some of the largest Muslim events. Others visit from Saudi Arabia. Salman al-Audah, a firebrand cleric once jailed by the Saudi government and known for issuing fatwas for a jihad against Britain and America in Iraq in 2004, addressed a crowd of over 20,000 in London's Docklands in late 2006. When al-Audah's son, acting on his father's fatwah, followed the thousands of young Saudis who rushed to Baghdad, his son was conveniently captured by border guards and returned home, out of danger. The hypocrisy of Wahhabism made head-lines across the Arab world. Why are such people granted a platform in Britain?

The ideology, however disparate, that led to the successful suicide bombings of 7 July 2005 and many similar though thwarted attempts since then is still alive and firmly rooted among Britain's young Muslims.

I returned to Britain to discover a sophisticated, entrenched form of Islamism and Wahhabism on the rise, but extremism is not limited to Muslims. The far right, much like Hizb ut-Tahrir, is rebranding itself and gaining new ground. I had not expected to be called a 'f—— Paki' by West Ham fans during a football match within weeks of coming home. What the white majority in Britain take for granted, their sense of belonging, is not so easy for ethnic minorities.

Since my return I have observed British Muslims being brow-beaten by certain sections of the media and government, de-manding 'integration' and an end to 'parallel lives'. The implied accusation, of course, is that Muslims are guilty of terrorism and that an undefined 'integration' will put a stop to it.

In mosques, after prayers, many of my Muslim friends rightly ask what we are supposed to integrate into. 'Big Brother' lifestyle? Ladette culture? Binge drinking? Gambling? Most Muslims are already upright Britons, contributing to their country as much as any other British citizen.

When Faye and I return home from a night out and walk past heaps of rowdy, drunken teenagers vomiting on the streets we despair as much as anyone else. Anti-social behaviour in our cities, high rates of abortion, alcohol abuse, and drug addiction are abhorrent to all right-thinking people, not just Muslims. The neglect of the elderly, shunting them off to 'care homes', does not sit comfortably with most Muslims. When the centre of social life in modern Britain is the local pub, where do Muslims and others fit in? Can an orange juice ever be enough?

Still, amid the clamour of lifestyle choices, political demands, social confusion, and religious extremisms, many British Muslims are quietly developing a rich, vibrant Muslim sub-culture in Britain, incorporating the best aspects of their multi-faceted heritage: ethnic ancestry, British upbringing, Islamic roots. This harmony is borne out by the silent majority of law-abiding and loyal Muslims who work hard in business and the professions across Britain, not seeking to turn religion into politics. Such people help maintain the National Health Service, our schools, transport system, and other core areas of national life. They, not the jihadis, are the true heroes of British Islam.

And all is not lost, for there are signs of a resurgence of interest in spiritual rather than political Islam. Large numbers of young British Muslims are rediscovering the traditional Islam of their parents. Descendants of one particular bloodline of the Prophet, represented by the much-loved Habaib from the Hadramaut valley in Yemen, have been touring Britain, re-injecting Muslims with love, compassion, and attachment to the Prophet.

It was the Habaib who introduced moderate Islam to entire nations – Indonesia, for example.

In gatherings remembering the Prophet's birthday, or *mawlid*, replete with metaphysical meanings, they lead lovers of the Prophet in song and emulate the Beloved's exemplary conduct. *Mawlid* gatherings are a highlight of the Muslim cultural calendar across the Muslim world, but are of no significance to Islamists. No one from the Muslim Council of Britain leadership ever attends. Yet these people, so distinctly out of line with mainstream Muslim practice, are effectively the voice of British Muslims.

Disturbingly, that voice is often listened to by those who should know better. Iqbal Sacranie, a leader of the MCB, supported the fatwah against Salman Rushdie in 1989. His knighthood in 2005 illustrates that holding such opinions is no bar to official recognition in British society, regardless of what message this conveys to younger Muslims.* Conversely, a well-trained Muslim scholar, the late Dr Zaki Badawi, offered his home as sanctuary to the beleaguered author. Similarly, while some British Muslim women refuse to remove their face veils in public, or shake hands with the Metropolitan Police commissioner, the rector of Al-Azhar University in Egypt, arguably the highest authority on Muslim scripture, freely offers his hand to female visitors from the West. Such differences in attitude are rooted in the ability, or lack of it, to conceive the spirit of the Prophet's teachings.

Love and attachment to the Prophet is at the heart of a *mawlid* gathering, not the scriptural rigidity and mental paralysis of literalism. For me, the underlying scholarly methodology that

---

*In television documentaries, including the BBC's *Panorama*, and public meetings organized by the London-based City Circle organization in late 2006, Sir Iqbal refused to retract his infamous statement that 'Death is perhaps too easy' for Rushdie.

endorses the celebration of the Prophet's birthday signifies a more tolerant, inclusive, flexible approach both to scripture and to life.

Without doubt, a British Islam is emerging. It remains to be seen whether it will be in harmony with the world in which it finds itself, or if it rejects and repels it. The direction we take at this critical juncture will determine the type of Islam we bequeath to future generations. The future of Islam is being shaped now.

Afterword: What About America?

The bosom of America is open to receive not only the Opulent and Respected stranger, but the oppressed and persecuted of all Nations and Religions; whom we shall welcome to a participation of all our rights and privileges.

George Washington, 1783

If they are good workmen, they may be of Asia, Africa, or Europe; they may be Mahometans, Jews or Christians of any sect, or they may be Atheists.

George Washington, in a letter to Tench Telghman, 1784

It was my first visit to the United States. I was expecting to be stopped at the airport, harassed, interrogated and perhaps detained. Since 9/11, Muslim communities across the globe are filled with horror stories of encounters at American airports. My friend from college days, Majid Nawaz, who had spent four years as a political prisoner in Egypt, was with me. Together we had attended countless anti-American rallies in Britain, and witnessed many US flag-burning rituals. Now, in our thirties, and after a decade in the wilderness, we had changed. But would America understand us? Would we understand America?

Like good Brits, we patiently stood waiting in the long queue at Washington Dulles Airport. Suddenly, Majid's name was called from the loudspeaker, telling him to go to the front of the line. Then mine. Were we in trouble? Majid had visited the United States recently, appearing as an expert witness for the Congressional Homeland Security Committee chaired by Senator Joe

Lieberman. Majid had been one of Hizb ut-Tahrir's most intelligent, vociferous, and articulate leaders, travelling to Pakistan, Denmark, and Egypt advocating the group's ideas and setting up secret cells. The Hizb, in essence, was identical to al-Qaeda, differing only in terms of the tactics it chose to achieve the desired result: political power. Majid has been banned in several countries and is wanted by Pakistan's ISI, their intelligence agency. But he had recently rejected extremism and, after years of study and reflection in prison, had become a public advocate for liberal democracy, using scriptural evidence to support peaceful Muslims – who represent the vast majority – in their struggle against religious extremism. His rejection of Hizb ut-Tahrir made headlines in the British press, and the British prime minister quoted Majid in parliament. But now we were in America, and during Majid's recent trip, federal escorts had accompanied him everywhere, fearful that he might violate US security regulations and not quite sure what to make of him. Would he, would we, face the same fate again?

An immigration officer at Washington Dulles Airport, accompanied by several colleagues, took us to one side, registered our passport details and asked the desk officer to clear us for entrance. Senior officials at the US Department of Homeland Security were expecting our arrival and wanted minimum kerfuffle. The polite, courteous conduct of the officers touched us both. But my mind was on the thousands of American Muslims who had been subjected to raids and arrests. Could we forget their plight?

Outside the airport, I stood with Majid and was stupefied by the number of US flags I saw everywhere. Flying at full mast at several junctures in the car park, and then above the airport, and on cars and coaches, the stars and stripes were ubiquitous. Unlike Britain, America was proudly patriotic and unreservedly expressive of national pride.

'Their flag is almost sacred to them, isn't it?' I said to Majid.

'And extremists burn it all the time. Why did we do that, Ed?

Why?' he asked, trying to come to terms with how we had been sucked into extremism.

'Why didn't anybody stop us?' I asked in response. 'We watched this happen in London, not Baghdad – what possessed us?'

Majid and I recalled how several of our fellow activists became suicide bombers, were imprisoned, or created entire organisations that linked themselves to al-Qaeda. What started off as mere talk, as rhetoric, found expression in mass murder in several European capitals, including London and Madrid. The murder we had witnessed on our college campus a decade before the attacks on London's subway on 7 July, 2005 was an unspeakable testament to the power of words. The talk of jihad, hatred, and anger never remains abstract, limited to 'freedom of speech.' It yields results.

More than anything else, what worried Majid and me was the lack of awareness in the wider society of the root causes of extremism and of the lifestyle that fosters recruitment into extremist movements. Society's demonstrated failure to grasp the urgency of the situation was also troubling, because that comprehension might precipitate policies and actions that could prevent young Muslims from becoming fanatical ideologues committed to creating a world dominated by Islamism, not Islam. To help fill this void, Majid and I started the Quilliam Foundation, the world's first think tank committed to explaining and countering Islamist thought.

We were in America to speak at Harvard and Princeton, at an array of Washington think tanks, and to meet Muslims on both the East and West coasts. We spoke with leading personnel at several government departments, US ambassadors, academic leaders, and students. And everywhere we went, we were asked a similar series of critical questions. Can America create home-grown terrorists? Will American Muslims, like British Muslims, attack their own homeland in the name of a false Islam? Britain is home to over 3,000 extremists: Can America be harbouring enemies without knowing it? The 9/11 hijackers hatched their plot in Europe: Are American-born Islamists capable of a similar monstrosity?

My answers to these questions, after meeting quite a few American Muslims and consulting with American experts on these issues, are both yes and no.

I say no because America is not Europe. The United States is, in several ways, in a much stronger position to prevent its Muslim population from becoming a sanctuary for hate-harbouring extremists. As a country, the United States accepts and even encourages public displays of religiosity, and an overwhelming majority of the population believes in one God known to Arab Christians, Jews, and Muslims as Allah. Contrary to a popular opinion influenced by right-wing polemicists, Muslims and followers of the other Abrahamic faiths do not believe in different Gods. This affirmation of religion in the public arena, which runs contrary to French and British privatisation of religion, allows for Muslims to fit in with the society, to be at home in America.

Tony Blair had to wait until he left office to publicly acknowledge his previously held Catholic convictions. To have done so while he was in office would have cast him as a religious man of sorts, someone not entirely mentally composed. His chief of public relations, Alistair Campbell, had warned him that, 'we don't do God,' and that journalists would poke fun at any notion of George Bush and Tony Blair 'praying together.' In the United States, George Bush regularly used scripture in his speeches and public comments and shamelessly exploited the religious right.

Another important factor is that compared to most European countries, the socio-economic situation of most American Muslims is notably better. Muslim immigration to America largely consists of highly educated Arabs and Asians, the crème de la crème of the Muslim world. The average American Muslim, for example, earns more than the average white American and is likely to be a doctor, banker, or professor. Muslim immigration to European countries, however, is dominated by a sense of revenge – the former subjects of European colonial powers seeking reparation. In

Britain, first generation immigrants predominately arrive from poor, rural areas of India and Pakistan. A similar profile of immigration can be seen in France, with Muslims arriving from the former French colonies of Morocco and Algeria. Their dependence on the welfare state, reluctance to integrate and hostility towards the government and its agencies create a breeding ground for Islamist radicals. In 2008, a report carried out by the Fabian Society, under the auspices of British Muslim parliamentarian Sadiq Khan, suggested that only around a quarter of British Muslims are currently 'economically active.' According to the British government's 2001 census, the proportion of Muslims who 'have never worked or are long-term unemployed' is five times higher than the national average. Alarmingly, 78 per cent of Bangladeshi and 73 per cent of Pakistani women in Britain are unemployed. As a nation, we seemingly refuse to address these issues lest we offend ethnic minorities. But unless we do, we risk amplifying these festering problems into national crises in years to come.

European imperial hangover, combined with class snobbery, soft racism, and white ethnic superiority, makes it almost impossible for black and Asian children of immigrants to feel that we truly belong, that we are Europeans. We are not. Entire countries, Denmark or Sweden for example, still consider themselves 'host nations' for their 'immigrant communities,' despite three generations of Muslims and other immigrants who have settled there permanently. The Danish cartoon controversy, for example, was partly driven by the failure of Muslims to integrate into Danish society and subsequently to solve problems domestically. Instead, Denmark's Muslim leaders boarded planes to marshal support against their country from Hamas, Hizbullah, and Saudi Arabia. On the streets of Copenhagen, I saw Majid threatened by Islamist thugs for advocating democracy to second generation Danish Muslims, whose default policy is to reject Denmark because it, in their opinion, has rejected them. They linger in the ghettoes of Copenhagen and other cities, economically inactive and socially excluded, hanging on to the fringes of Hizb ut-Tahrir radicalism, rejecting any notion of national identity and inching towards jihadism.

America, in stark contrast to Europe, is a society built on the notion of meritocracy, which offers hope to newcomers in the form of the American Dream, a guarantee of certain rights that, if taken advantage of, can lead to upward mobility within one or two generations. Many young American Muslims feel both fiercely American and fiercely Muslim, without contradiction. The strength of the American Muslim identity has resulted in the emergence of several leading religious authorities in the United States, some of whom serve as advisors and role models to Muslim communities in Europe. American Muslim scholars such as Dr Umar Abdullah and Hamza Yusuf Hanson have shaped debate among younger Muslim communities in a constructive manner, particularly in the troubling times after 9/11. It is fair to say that the American Muslim leadership is in a strong position to pioneer Western Islam, to facilitate an understanding of Islam that can find a comfortable home in the West.

Despite what seem like positive trends, however, there are dark forces simmering beneath the surface that, unless confronted, will prove to be a disaster for American national security. The crucial task at hand is to determine how and where they are operating.

Terrorism is almost always preceded by political and religious extremism, which is itself preceded by a narrow, literalist interpretation of scripture. The Wahhabite sect of Saudi Arabian Islam is the most rigid, literalist interpretation of Islam with a significant foothold. Despite what the savvy public relations campaigns devised by Bell Pottinger and financed by the Kingdom of Saudi Arabia assert, it is a nefarious, intolerant form of Islam, and has gained widespread influence on American Muslim discourse, in part because it has created new guises for itself.

Saudi universities are responsible for the export of extremist Wahhabite ideas to the United States because their graduates often end up teaching in American mosques. Calling upon their own education and training, these schools maintain curricula that lead to the emergence of narrow, bigoted individuals, many of whom are in turn assuming public roles in Muslim communities across America. When this limited intellectual focus is combined with the most basic political literacy, these graduates espouse hatred and ignorance of medieval proportions during their Friday sermons. While I was in Saudi Arabia, I spoke with Western students who readily confirmed that there were many students, from several Western countries, with extremist political leanings in their midst, students whose political views were left unchallenged while they studied Saudi theology. Saudi universities are hotbeds of religious extremism, literalism, and anti-Western sentiment, evidence of which is ample during Friday sermons in the Kingdom's mosques and in the hate-filled textbooks used in mandatory courses on religion.

In the United States, a Saudi trained cleric named Ali Timimi is currently in prison for urging his followers to wage war against the United States, and for specifically encouraging them to use firearms in violation of federal law. I remember Ali Timimi for the fiery speeches he delivered when he visited London throughout the 1990s, wearing Saudi attire and serving as an inspiration for an entire generation of extremist Wahhabites.

The two men convicted as the infamous 'Paintball' terrorists in 2004 were students of Timimi's in northern Virginia. The attention that case brought on him only enhanced his credibility among young, influential American Muslims, and his students and former students continue to issue unapologetic, hostile, anti-Western statements that sow the seeds of animosity in young minds. One such student is Yasir Qadhi, who currently manages what is called the al-Maghrib Institute, which holds classes across America, Canada, and Britain to prepare future imams and Muslim leaders. Qadhi openly campaigns on behalf of his mentor, and recently asserted that Timimi is 'one of the more sophisticated voices of reason representing orthodox Islam in the Western world.' Rather

than condemn an extremist figure like Timimi, influential preachers such as Qadhi support him.

Qadhi, too, has a certain following among young American Muslims. He is a regular speaker at the largest annual American Muslim
convention held at the Islamic Society of North America (ISNA)
and actively engages in missionary work to spread his brand of intolerant, rigid religion in Europe and America. Here, for example,
is Qadhi discussing the Holocaust at a conference in 2001:

Hitler never intended to mass-destroy the Jews. There are a number of
books out on this written by Christians, you should read them. *The
Hoax of the Holocaust*, I advise you to read this book and write this
down, *The Hoax of the Holocaust*, a very good book. All of this is false
propaganda and I know it sounds so far-fetched, but read it. The evi-
dences are [*sic*] very strong. And they're talking about newspaper articles, clippings, everything, and look up yourself what Hitler really
wanted to do. We're not defending Hitler, by the way, but the Jews, the
way that they portray him, also is not correct.

Not only is there demonstrated support for advocates of terror,
there is a failure to grasp the larger historical picture and a troubling tendency to believe in facile conspiracy theories that makes
sermonizers such as Qadhi dangerously influential to young minds,
setting them on a path to destruction. This virulent strain of extreme, historically inaccurate, Wahhabite Islam is spreading in the
United States, and thus far the American Muslim leadership, in the
name of Muslim unity, has failed to expose and oppose this trend.

This same leadership, when in communication with various
departments of the US government, has become infamous for the
anti-Israel rants that they tend to unleash before taking any other
matter seriously. I met with several of these same departments, and
high ranking officials repeatedly told me about Hamas sympathis-
ers or leaders at CAIR and similar bodies who spent the first ten
minutes of every meeting attacking Israel, regardless of the meet-

ing's agenda. The Islamism-influenced American Muslim leaders, of course, realise that Israel is here stay, and that no amount of intimidation or subversive politicking will lead to the destruction of Israel, but they persist in these counterproductive tirades.

By focusing excessively on Israel, and by failing to distance themselves from Islamist-Wahhabism, American Muslims have become oblivious to an important strain of radical, rebellious Islam that is popular among many African American converts. A descendant of the Nation of Islam, and influenced by the teachings of Malcolm X before he travelled to the Middle East, this nascent strain is decidedly anti-establishment and operates on a grassroots, street corner level, producing its own rebellious subculture. These sentiments are supported by the missionary activities of Muslim extremists in American prisons, who often present fellow inmates with a salvationist form of Islam. They preach belief in the simple promises of paradise, damnation in hell and, most importantly, forgiveness for all sins and crimes upon accepting a rigid interpretation of Islam that incorporates unfailing animosity towards the West. Richard Reid, who boarded a transatlantic flight with a 'shoe bomb,' was a convert to this type of Wahhabist Islam, and there is no doubt that similarly impressionable individuals are being preached to in US prisons every day. These converts end up harbouring a deep sense of vengeance and hatred for free societies. This anger, the prisoners' violent tendencies, and the new promises of paradise for martyrdom combine to create a lethal cocktail. For these reasons, prison conversion and radicalisation is anathema to security services across the world, particularly for the British, American, and French governments.

In addition to the above trends, there is a new issue that has thus far gone unnoticed by American policy makers and security officials. The new wave of immigrants into the United States, particularly from Muslim countries, is not like the successful, educated intelligentsia it previously welcomed. In New York I saw strong indications that what we saw in Britain – a relatively poor first generation, keen to retain its ethnic identity by conglomerating into monocultural ghettos, and which prevents its children from integrating – may well be occurring in major American cities.

In its attempt to support and recognise all cultures as equal, multiculturalism fails to empower minorities. How can the children of immigrants secure jobs in the workplace and advance economically and socially when they aren't even expected to learn English? Everything is translated for them, and this is for all immigrants, whether they are Hispanic or Muslim. A nation bonds through its language and shared culture; separate these two things and you have the vital precursors to self destruction.

It is, in many cases, the children of blue-collar workers that proved to be vulnerable to extremist groups in England, and it was in so-called multicultural communities that Islamist groups set up base and festered. Majid and I spoke with several New Yorkers from Pakistan and Bangladesh, and many of them told us that they had brought their spouses with them when they immigrated, and were now living and having children in predominantly Muslim areas, away from mainstream American culture. When they talked about their families' lives, we saw that their children's problems are similar to those that were prevalent in Britain's ghettoes in the 1980s, which contributed to the spread of radicalism of the 1990s.

Terrorism does not emerge overnight, it takes root over time. Immigrant cab drivers in New York, isolated Arab communities in Michigan, and converts in Miami live physically in America but psychologically in their native countries, and this causes their children to develop confused identities. When this happens, religious bigots are happy to step in an offer a strong identity, and they usually find eager followers. Further complicating the struggle against the spread of extremist views is the fact that religious leaders and politicians in these communities tend to turn a blind eye to the activities of the Islamists who gain power and influence, if only to maintain a sense of Muslim unity. If they've considered the long-term implications of allowing their younger community members to flirt with Islamism, then they have chosen to ignore them. These unspoken policies have even reached the highest levels of government. My country, Britain, helped support the Wahhabite movement and create Saudi Arabia – a ploy to undermine the Ottomans at the time. And your country, the United States, helped the Mujahedeen, precursors of the Taliban, fight against a rival superpower, the Soviet Union. These were short term solutions that have left us with complex problems that we will grapple with for an entire generation.

Today America faces threats from three sources. Firstly, there are already cases of home-grown terrorism in the United States, from Timothy McVeigh in Oklahoma to attacks on abortion clinics. Religious extremism is a manifest problem. With a black president, far-right terrorist activity is on the increase too.

Among small sections of the American Muslim community, there are active cells of terrorists who would strike America at first opportunity. In 2006, seven young men were arrested in Miami for planning to attack Chicago's Sears Tower, although they lacked the capability to do so. In addition to the Miami cell, the authorities have also arrested the Lackawana Six (New York), the Portland Seven (Oregon), and a group in northern Virginia, headed by Ali Timimi (mentioned earlier). Fortunately they were stopped in the planning stages, but that terrorist mindset, if left unchecked, could prove to be contagious, especially considering the efforts of Adam Gadahn – Bin Laden's white American publicist – and the ongoing war on terror as background.

Everyone arrested was a Muslim under the influence of Islamist ideas, but it's worth noting that many were male African American converts to literalist interpretations of Islam, and prison radicalisation will only cause this phenomenon to spread. With Arab and Asian Muslims providing encouragement, leadership, notions of martyrdom, and a social support network for terrorists, the United States faces a dramatic increase in radicalisation. Condemnation of terrorism is not enough for Muslim organisations; at the minimum they need to undermine the theological arguments on which Islamists rely, and thus far they've failed to do this at all.

In addition to the home-grown threats described above, America is also vulnerable from Islamist extremists from Europe and, sadly, Canada. From my meetings with State Department personnel, it is clear that American officials are trying to unravel Europe and the Islamist underworld in which extremists fester. Hizb ut-Tahrir and other Islamist groups have produced Jihadists as a result of their rhetoric, mindset, and plans of global domination. They are experts at injecting potent ideas into young, vulnerable minds, but when these same young adults realize that their intellectual approach is failing to establish the mythical caliphate, they often turn to direct action, to terrorism. From Egypt to Pakistan, wherever there are radical Islamist movements, Jihadist groups have arisen. And this now includes Canada, a country that is proudly multicultural and officially refuses to address religious radicalisation for fear of upsetting minorities. There are cells of Hizb ut-Tahrir operating in Toronto, and unless they are closely monitored, the United States could see a crisis emerge very close to home.

With the election of Barack Obama as president, the United States is at an important juncture in history, and Americans have turned a new page. Across the world, people are prepared to lend the United States an ear once more. The duties of the leader of the free world are varied and immense, but reaching out to ordinary, peaceful Muslims in order to build coalitions against extremism and tyranny is among the most vital. Islam is the antidote to extremism, to Islamism. It's important to remember that ordinary Muslims have been the greatest victims of Islamist terror, and that their desire to put an end to the threat is perhaps greater than ours. We must recapture Islam from Islamists, neutralise radical theologies, and empower pluralist Muslims. This is our first line of defence against terrorism.

Acknowledgements

The production of a book involves much more than one's own writing. I am eternally grateful to my parents for encouraging me constantly and reminding me of moments that I had conveniently forgotten. Their ongoing love, protection, and prayers remain a source of inspiration for me.

My beloved wife Faye has endured my insularity during thought and recollection. Without her practical, literary, emotional, and financial support this book, and indeed many developments in my life, would have been impossible. To her I owe much.

I am thankful to my sister Shahida for reading the first draft and providing valuable commentary, despite the demands of my new nephew, Zaki.

The Caroline Davidson Literary Agency has been unfailingly professional in handling the manuscript from its earliest stages. Caroline masterfully extracted what I had committed to the beginnings of an earlier concept, and has been generous with her time and much-needed advice. At CDLA, I am also grateful to Victoria Kwee and Harry Miskin.

I have been most fortunate to have worked with Helen Conford, senior commissioning editor at Penguin Press. Throughout, she has been an accommodating yet forthright editor, tactfully pointing out shortfalls and ensuring that *The Islamist* found a welcoming home at Penguin.

I am also indebted to a trusted and valued circle of friends who have supported my work by reading various sections of the manuscript, often at very short notice, providing critical feedback, and/or critically responding to some of my initial thoughts. They include Kelly Grant, Alex Whiting, Sidi Abu'l Fadl, Fr Damian Howard SJ, Joel Santaro, and the good people on Deenport.com.

I should also like to thank Maleiha Malik, Omar Faruk, and Majid Nawaz for sharing their thoughts with me.

Finally, I am grateful to several generous individuals for their comments, opinions, and time. You know who you are.